Regional Best
2011

Edited By William Roetzheim

Level 4 Press, Inc.
San Diego, CA

This book is printed on acid-free paper.

Published by
Level 4 Press, Inc.
13518 Jamul Drive
Jamul, CA 91935
www.level4press.com

ISBN:978-1-933769-50-9
Printed in USA

Preface

I had the pleasure of sitting on a panel during a theater festival in New York (Planet Connections, I believe) and one of my fellow panelists was theater critic and editor of *The Clyde Fitch Report*, Leonard Jacobs. While we were waiting for things to get started, I explained to Leonard that I was planning a new annual anthology of plays and I was exploring different themes or approaches. He suggested an anthology focused on regional plays. Over the next couple of weeks I thought about this, talked it over with regional theater artistic directors that I knew—and the more I investigated it the more the idea made sense. Even with successful productions and rave reviews, the substantial number of great plays that delight regional theatre audiences do not always receive the national exposure they deserve. I became convinced that the best of that work deserves a platform for even greater exposure. It's my hope that *Regional Best* will serve as that platform.

Questions naturally arise about my selection of the plays for inclusion in the anthology. The entry criteria into the process was that the play had premiered on stage at a regional theater, but that it did not yet have significant exposure in New York City. I then personally read all of the submissions, and selected the plays that I liked. What I was looking for was three things:

- As a playwright, do I feel like the play was well written and closely related, did I enjoy reading it;

- As a producer, would I like to produce this play if I had the opportunity; and

- As a theater-goer, would I like to see this play if it was on-stage?

A play that did well in all three dimensions was accepted. A play that failed in any dimension was rejected. I did not restrict the plays to any specific length, and in fact, ended up accepting everything from ten minute plays all the way up to full-length plays. The final selections were (with approximate running times shown):

- The Pie Dialogues by Joseph Lauinger (129 minutes)

- Alien Hand Syndrome by Michael Erickson (33 minutes)

- Besides, you lose your soul or the History of Western Civilisation by Julia Lee Barclay (90 minutes including improvisations)

- Laying Off by James McLindon (15 minutes)

- Safe by James McLindon (13 minutes)

- Boston Forty-Nine Flamingo by K Biadaszkiewicz (78 minutes)

- Causa Morts by Jacob Appel (107 minutes)

- Small Things by Cary Pepper (42 minutes)

- The Sweet Abyss by Jon Tuttle (128 minutes)

Finally, I should emphasize that the authors (or their agents) retain performance rights to the plays. Instructions for obtaining performance rights is included at the start of each play, and you must obtain the appropriate rights if you are interested in bringing any of these plays to the stage. But I do encourage you to do this, as a play is not truly alive except when it's on stage.

William Roetzheim, Editor
william@aitheater.org

Contents

The Pie Dialogues

By Joseph Lauinger

Joe Lauinger's plays have been performed throughout the United States and in Canada, England, Australia, and India. *Mother's Day* (2000) was a finalist at the Humana Festival and was produced at Gallery Players in Brooklyn, NY, and at the Stamford Center for the Arts in Connecticut in 2001. His one-acts have appeared at many festivals including the Samuel French Love Creek Festival (NYC), the Attic Theatre (L.A.), the Nantucket Theater (MA), and the TANYS Festival of 2000 where "What A Moon!", directed by Joe, won Best Short Play. "The Green Cheese Mystery" won the John V. Gurry Competition for Best Short Play in 2001, awarded by *Confrontation*. "Rich on Skins" won Best Play at the Shortened Attention Span Festival at the Players Theatre in Greenwich Village in 2007, and "The Chamberpot" won the Golden Curtain Award (Best of Festival) at the New Voice Play Festival 2008 at the Old Opera House in Charles Town, WV. *The Pie Dialogues* was developed under the title of *Dawn and Sean* in the 2006 Gallery Players Reading Series and won Best Play as a staged reading at the Dayton Playhouse FutureFest 2007 in Dayton, Ohio. It was produced at the Main Street Theater in Houston, TX, during February and March 2009. Joe teaches dramatic literature at Sarah Lawrence College in New York and is a member of the Dramatists Guild.

The Pie Dialogues was premiered at the Main Street Theater in Houston TX, on February 26, 2009, Rebecca Udden, Artistic Director. It was directed by Andrew Ruthven and featured Gwendolyn McLarty as Dawn and Josh Morrison as Sean.

Performing rights may be obtained from Joe Lauinger, c/o Sarah Lawrence College, Bronxville, NY 10708, now jlauinger@sarahlawrence.edu or josephlauinger@verizon.net, 914-762-0839.

Characters:
Dawn, the mother.
Sean, the father.

Setting: The play takes place in eight dialogues. Contemporary U.S. The action starts when Dawn and Sean's daughter (called Pie) is a toddler and proceeds until she is in her late twenties.

1. "What does she know?": a living room in a small apartment.
2. "Her favorite color": waiting room in a private school.
3. "The mercy rule": behind the bench of a girls' softball game.
4. "Grandma's sweater blue": a coffee shop.
5. "Perjury at the prom": a living room in a big house.
6. "Malmsey": a college-dormitory room.
7. "The whistling groundhog": table at a restaurant.
8. "Class": an airport sitting area.

SCENE ONE: "What does she know?"

> A spare and darkened living room: cheap sofa, armchair with a marble notebook on it, TV, with its dim blue glow. DAWN sits on the sofa, dozing in bathrobe and slippers, a yellow legal pad and some paperwork on her lap. SEAN enters in an undershirt, unbuckled pants, and socks. He yawns and falls into the armchair in front of the TV.

SEAN: Singing in her sleep.

DAWN: [*Eyes still closed.*] Hmm?

SEAN: She was singing in her sleep.

DAWN: Bed for me. I've had it. [*She sits up sleepily, yawning.*] What was she singing?

SEAN: Some song. I sort of recognized it.

DAWN: Something from Sesame Street.

SEAN: Don't think so.

DAWN: Well, I've got to be up early tomorrow—

SEAN: "It's Later Than You Think."

DAWN: Yeah. I just drifted off there. How long was I asleep?

SEAN: No, it's the song she was singing. "It's Later Than You Think."

DAWN: Never heard of it. You coming?

SEAN: Might try to write down a few notes.

DAWN: While you're watching TV?

SEAN turns off the TV and picks up the marble notebook. He tries to shake himself awake.

SEAN: You don't have to stay up.

DAWN: I should get through this one brief at least. [*She yawns and picks up her papers. He writes a word or two in the notebook. They both are very tired.*] Who's it by?

SEAN: What?

DAWN: "It's Later Than You Think."

SEAN: Nobody. It's like from the Twenties or something. Rudy Vallee. It's a classic. [*Singing in a monotone:*] "Oh, it's later than you think . . . dah-dah dum dee dum dee dah."

DAWN: Like that helps.

SEAN: So I'm not Rudy Vallee. She sure picks up weird things sometimes.

DAWN: Whoever wrote the song was weird, not her.

SEAN: I didn't say she was weird, I said she picks up weird things.

DAWN: All kids are weird sometimes.

SEAN: Kids are weird, period.

DAWN: Well, you're the one who wanted one.

SEAN: Whoa.

DAWN: You just have to admit sometimes . . . [*Yawning over her work.*] This shit is so boring.

SEAN: At least it's somebody else's shit you're dealing with. You're not looking at the shit you wrote yesterday and now it makes you want to throw up.

DAWN: You're too hard on yourself. Want me to make some coffee?

SEAN: You want some?

DAWN: I don't want to stay up too long. I'll make some for you if you want.

SEAN: No, thanks. What do I have to admit?

DAWN: What?

SEAN: You said I had to admit something. What?

DAWN: I don't know. Just that it's tough sometimes.

SEAN: It's called raising a child. It's reality.

DAWN: Reality is what I dealt with at Legal Aid. This is Romance. [*He looks at her.*] What? I'm glad we had her! I love her. She's my little Pie.

SEAN: We're both tired. [*Beat.*]

DAWN: Why is it always my fault?

SEAN: Come on, you promised me you'd stop that. Nobody's blaming anybody for anything. Go to bed. I'll be there in a minute. It's late.

DAWN: Later than we think?

SEAN: You wonder where kids get this stuff from.

DAWN: She must have got this one from me. Despair is in my genes.

SEAN: Don't go into a downward spiral now. Nothing's happening.

DAWN: I was joking about the genes.

SEAN: Sorry.

DAWN: You don't laugh at my jokes any more. I'm not always depressed. I admit a little post partum . . .

SEAN: A little.

DAWN: Some women get it a lot worse than I did, you know.

SEAN: They do indeed.

DAWN: Don't patronize me, okay?

SEAN: I'm not! It's a named syndrome. Things have to get pretty bad to become a named syndrome. Syndromes don't grow on trees.

DAWN: Some women actually have to get treated for it. Anti-depressants. Therapy. Trips to Europe.

SEAN: Well, I'm very grateful. You saved us money.

DAWN: Not very big on the old empathy, are you.

SEAN: What do you want me to say, Dawn? You experienced some post partum depression. Time passed. You're all right now. I'm happy for you. I'm happy for us. [*Beat.*] I can't think. I'm going to bed.

DAWN: Okay! I regret that you constantly have to deal with my anxieties which are such bullshit to you. They are to me too. Would you like a divorce? Or how about we save even more money and I just kill myself.

SEAN: Jesus. Please don't talk like that. Okay? Even in jest. That is sick talk. C'mon, let's go to bed. We're both beat.

DAWN: I have to get through this brief. McCarthy's going to ask me for an update tomorrow.

SEAN: Fuck McCarthy.

DAWN: This is my job, okay? I don't need your advice about how to do my job. [*She picks up her papers and works on them.*] Go to bed. I'll be there soon.

SEAN: All the work you do for that firm, they should have made you partner like yesterday.

DAWN: Law firms don't just hand out partnerships to women with children.

SEAN: You could always go back to Legal Aid. Go back to Reality.

DAWN: I kind of enjoy not feeling powerless all the time. Anyway, I've paid my dues.

SEAN: Well, you'll make it soon. I'm confident.

DAWN: Don't bet on it.

SEAN: Not a betting man.

DAWN: You bet on me when you married me.

SEAN: That wasn't a bet. That was love. C'mon. Let's dance.

DAWN: No music.

SEAN: [*He stands, offering his arms and singing.*] "Oh, it's later than you think dah dee dum dee dah dah dah . . . "

DAWN: You sound like a seal who's swallowed a bad herring.

SEAN: [*Barking like a seal.*] Ark. Ark.

DAWN: You'll wake Pie.

SEAN: She's out for the count. Dance with me!

DAWN: I've got to get this done—

SEAN: Well, if you won't dance with me, I'll dance by myself. [*He dances around the room, singing. DAWN laughs and joins him. They dance and sing, "It's later than you think."*]

DAWN: That's all the words? "It's later than you think" over and over again?

SEAN: That's all she sang.

DAWN: Maybe she got it from cartoons. They were showing some old Betty Boop—

SEAN: Did you know that Betty Boop had a thing for Rudy Vallee? Which they couldn't consummate. Because he was from Yale and she was only a drawing.

DAWN: Who is this Rudy Vallee anyway?

SEAN: Twenties guy. Singer. Blazer. Straw hat. Used to sing through a megaphone. [*Sings nasally "through a megaphone":*] "Oh, it's later than you think." [*His own voice:*] Sex throb of his time. Betty Boop would listen to Rudy Vallee sing and get so excited her little clitoris would quiver and her ink run out of the frame.

DAWN: You seriously need help.

SEAN: Rudy Vallee did that to all the cartoon girls. Minnie Mouse had a whole collection of Rudy Vallee 78's. She'd sit in her trailer on the studio lot listening to them between takes, drinking sangria and touching herself. Mickey used to peek through the blinds and touch himself.

DAWN: Why didn't they just touch each other?

SEAN: Couldn't reach through the frame. That's the tragedy of being a cartoon. And then there was the time Olive Oyl shouted "Rudy!" in the middle of sexual congress with Popeye—

DAWN: Shouldn't you be writing this stuff down so you can sell it?

SEAN: I could never sell these private moments. They belong to Betty and Minnie and Olive and all the lonely cartoon girls whose loins ever throbbed for Rudy Vallee in the inky night.

DAWN: You're wacked, but I love you. [*They dance a while, then stop and kiss.*]

SEAN: Thank you for the dance, miss. I think you're the prettiest girl here.

DAWN: Thank you, sir. I think you're the cutest boy here.

SEAN: Would you like to go to bed?

DAWN: But sir, we've hardly met!

SEAN: I've got a secret to show you.

DAWN: What is it, what is it?

SEAN: Can't show you here. It's a secret. A big secret.

DAWN: Do I bore you in bed?

SEAN: Does it look like I'm bored? And we're not even there yet!

DAWN: Seriously.

SEAN: Seriously? Yes.

DAWN: I knew it.

SEAN: And to relieve my boredom I'm having an affair with a Russian tennis player who wears little white socks.

DAWN: You wish.

SEAN: Yes!

DAWN: Well, I wish I were having an affair with somebody nice too.

SEAN: My Russian tennis player isn't nice. She's ferocious.

DAWN: In little white socks?

SEAN: Yes!

DAWN: Would you like it if I were more ferocious in bed?

SEAN: You're not Russian.

DAWN: I could try to be more ferocious. I could even wear little white socks. They're not very expensive.

SEAN: I could try to be somebody nice.

DAWN: You are nice. When you're not being wacked.

SEAN: Back where we started. Well, we'll just have to make do, I guess. You want to go and get bored with me? I like really want to go and get bored with you. In fact if I don't get bored in the next ten minutes, I'm going to find a picture of Minnie Mouse in the nude and —

DAWN: I'll see what I've got in my sock drawer!

SEAN: Excellent!

DAWN: Just give me one second. I should put this shit in a folder at least, so it looks like I did something. [*She does so, getting a little involved in her organizing, while SEAN waits.*]

SEAN: She was dancing too.

DAWN: She was out of bed?

SEAN: No, in bed. She was wiggling. [*Singing and wiggling:*] "Oh, it's later than you think dah-dah dum dee dum dee dah."

DAWN: Oh my God. That means her REM sleep could be disturbed. I read where symptoms like that could be a sign of psychological trauma. And she's been waking up a lot lately—

SEAN: Crap.

DAWN: No, Sean. It could totally be a symptom. I never sang and danced in my sleep when I was a kid.

SEAN: How do you know?

DAWN: My parents would have done something. You can't just ignore a thing like that.

SEAN: Call 911! Send a helicopter! Send a SWAT team! Our daughter is singing in her sleep! Somebody, help!

DAWN: It's not funny.

SEAN: Can't we just say we've got a weird kid and sleep on it?

DAWN: She's only three. You're not weird when you're three. You're three.

SEAN: Maybe she knows something we don't know.

DAWN: At three?

SEAN: Hey, you know all kinds of shit when you're three. Shit you forget later.

DAWN: Like what?

SEAN: I forget. But I haven't forgotten that sock drawer . . . [*He turns out the light. They leave.*]

SCENE TWO: "Her favorite color."

> A waiting room outside the Headmistress's office in a private school. A wooden bench, a straight chair, a low table with magazines. SEAN, in suit and tie, sits on the bench, flipping through a magazine and checking his watch. DAWN enters hurriedly, in a business suit. SEAN looks up–an irritated unspoken question.

DAWN: Don't ask. [*She sits down in the chair, breathless, hot, and guilty.*] She still in there?

SEAN: Where the hell else would she be?

DAWN: I don't know. Maybe she had to pee. Maybe she got bored and took a walk.

SEAN: She's six. She can't take a walk unless I'm with her. And if she were in the bathroom, I'd be waiting right there outside.

DAWN: They could have swooped her away on a tour or something.

SEAN: They don't take kids on the tour. The tour is for parents. You missed that too.

DAWN: Well, that's it then. I'm a rotten mother. I've messed up our child's life forever.

SEAN: Stop. [*Beat.*]

DAWN: How long has she been in there?

SEAN: About half an hour.

DAWN: Long interview for a six-year-old.

SEAN: They're getting to know each other.

DAWN: It's not like she's got an extensive resume. What's to know? She's six years old.

SEAN: We've been through this. It's a process.

DAWN: I'd just like to know what you talk about to a six-year-old for half an hour. It's a valid question.

SEAN: Try it sometime. You'd be surprised. [*Beat.*] They're watching her play.

DAWN: She'll really have a fun time playing with all those eyes watching her.

SEAN: That's how they make their judgment.

DAWN: I thought they used calipers to measure her head. [*SEAN looks at her, not laughing.*] God, I hate this shit.

SEAN: No! Really?

DAWN: Fucking elitist snobs.

SEAN: Language. Tone. Situation.

DAWN: Nobody heard. Unless the room is bugged. Which it definitely could be. Surveillance cameras everywhere so they can watch the parents fight.

SEAN: We're not fighting.

DAWN: Interacting.

SEAN: Let's just get her into the school, okay, and then we can fight about free speech or whatever as much as you want.

DAWN: You just said we weren't fighting.

SEAN: Interacting.

DAWN: I still wish we were sending her to public school.

SEAN: Well, we would be if it were 1953. But it isn't. We kind of want her to learn how to read and do arithmetic and not get raped in the stairwell before she's nine.

DAWN: That is so racist.

SEAN: Okay, it's racist.

DAWN: It's middle-class people like us who are effectively racist and therefore responsible for the collapse of the public schools—

SEAN: Can we talk about the state of public education another time?.

DAWN: That's all we'll do. Talk. We won't do anything. We won't put our money where our mouth is.

SEAN: That's such a stupid cliché, you know that? It's so irrelevant.

DAWN: It is exactly relevant, which is why it makes you angry.

SEAN: Money where our mouth is? What money? It's not money we're dealing with here, it's our child's life. Bet money, you win money or you lose money, who gives a damn? A child's life? You don't bet with that.

DAWN: It was just an expression.

SEAN: I don't use my daughter's life to make social statements.

DAWN: All I'm saying is it's a disgrace that educated people like us who have a stake in the future and could really do something about the school system—

SEAN: Then quit being a lawyer. Become a public-school teacher instead.

DAWN: Can't. Need to pull down the big bucks so we can send our daughter to private school.

SEAN: I make money.

DAWN: Oh God. Forget it. I'm sorry I said anything.

SEAN: I got something for that last story—

DAWN: I know you did. That was wonderful.

SEAN: And okay, maybe two adjunct teaching jobs don't pull in big bucks, but there's a chance of a regular position. I've got a proposal on my novel out to two publishers—

DAWN: Please, baby. I know. I apologize. [*Beat.*] Did they ask about me? You know, where I was or anything—

SEAN: I told them you were an attorney. They understood.

DAWN: What did they understand?

SEAN: The unending struggle for justice.

DAWN: I'm sorry! I'm sorry I was late! I'm sorry it was an uncomfortable situation because of me! I'm sorry I insulted your manhood! I'm sorry I'm me! Can't you throw me a bone here?

SEAN: Okay, okay, I'm sorry too. We're both a little bit nervous. [*Beat.*] Actually it wasn't an uncomfortable situation at all. It was rather pleasant.

DAWN: Because I wasn't there with my big mouth.

SEAN: They were very professional. We introduced ourselves and talked like civilized people. Nobody spoke in that stupid whiny voice some people use around children as if they were morons.

DAWN: Like my mother.

SEAN: I didn't say that.

DAWN: It's true. I hate it when my mother uses that voice.

SEAN: And she uses it all the time.

DAWN: I've talked to her about it. I've asked her not to. I've pleaded with her, "Talk to Pie like she's a human being, not a poodle!" She doesn't understand. Or won't. [*Beat.*] So what did you guys talk about like civilized people?

SEAN: Shakespeare's imagery in *King Lear*. [*She looks at him.*] I'm kidding. We talked about her likes and dislikes. Her favorite color and her favorite games and books. That kind of stuff. It went pretty well, I thought.

DAWN: Heaven be praised. She passed inspection. Well, as long as we can write out tuition checks that don't bounce none of this bullshit is going to matter.

SEAN: This school has a waiting list as long as my arm. You get what you pay for.

DAWN: And if you can't pay, you can go get raped in the stairwell.

SEAN: It's not like that. They value diversity here. They offer all kinds of scholarships to underprivileged kids—

DAWN: Who can play point guard and tap-dance.

SEAN: Maybe it was good you were late. Read a magazine.

DAWN: [*Leafing through the magazines on the table.*] Wall
Street Journal. Times Financial Page. Commentary.
Country Life. The National Review. I'll pass.
[*She takes out a stick of chewing gum and begins vigorously
chewing.*] I would have made it on time, but McCarthy kept
me going over the same damn contracts we've already been
over three times—

SEAN: It doesn't matter.

DAWN: I'm trying to tell you something here about my life,
okay?

SEAN: McCarthy is not your life. And there's nothing you
can tell me about McCarthy I don't already know. McCarthy
knew you wanted to get away, that you had something
important to do unconnected with the firm. McCarthy likes
to torture people who have a life. He likes to make them
insecure and screw up their relationships.

DAWN: I didn't realize you could see so deeply into people's
souls. Especially people you've never met.

SEAN: McCarthy doesn't have a soul, he's one of the
undead. He won't leave you alone until he's drained out
every last drop of decency and love, and you're the zombie
lawyer from hell. But at least you'll make partner. [*Beat.*]

DAWN: How was she when she went in?

SEAN: Scared a little, I think. But she put her game face
on.

DAWN: Poor baby.

SEAN: She has to learn that the whole world isn't Mommy and Daddy, Dawn.

DAWN: I think she already knows that.

SEAN: She is a little spoiled, you know.

DAWN: I wonder who spoils her.

SEAN: Maybe spoiled is too strong a word. You've got to admit we've been very protective. It's time she got into in a world where she'll be challenged.

DAWN: Somebody's projecting.

SEAN: Whatever.

DAWN: And I wouldn't call this place the world exactly.

SEAN: Which is what you want in a school. You want an environment where she'll feel safe, but you want her to feel challenged too. The only way she'll learn how to take risks is by not being afraid to fail. Or is that projecting too?

DAWN: What happens if she gets rejected by these bastards?

SEAN: Language. Tone. Situation.

DAWN: Oh cut the shit. What the fuck happens if she gets rejected?

SEAN: Actually I don't think it's going to matter much to her. Not at this stage. If she doesn't get in here, she'll get in somewhere else. Just as good.

DAWN: It'll just matter to us. Welcome to the private-school nightmare—competitiveness, cliques, paranoia—

SEAN: Well, in your racket you should be used to that.

DAWN: I'm not six. [*Beat.*] What did she tell them her favorite color was? It always changes.

SEAN: Black.

DAWN: Cool!

SEAN: There was a little sort of moment when she said that, but then we all had a nice laugh.

DAWN: Black is new. I haven't heard black before.

SEAN: Yeah, blue or green might have been better. But it didn't seem to set off any bells. I mean I don't think they're going to think she's like psychologically troubled or anything.

DAWN: You're cringing. Don't cringe. Who's in there, conducting this interview? The Headmistress and who else?

SEAN: Two teachers. No, wait, one of them was the psychologist. The other was her home-room teacher or whatever they call it. If she gets in.

DAWN: Headmistress, psychologist, teacher, and one little kid. Watching her play. It's sadistic. What did the psychologist say when she said black was her favorite color?

SEAN: He gave this sort of laugh.

DAWN: What kind of sort of laugh?

SEAN: I don't know. A laugh.

DAWN: I hate it when psychologists laugh.

SEAN: We all laughed. You had to be there. [*Beat.*] I didn't mean it like that.

DAWN: Did you bring the red bag? I left it for you guys in the foyer.

SEAN: No.

DAWN: But she loves the red bag! The red bag has all her favorite toys in it—

SEAN: They give her their own toys to play with.

DAWN: She can't even play with her own toys?

SEAN: They want to see how she plays with new stuff, how she reacts, how imaginative she is. It's what they do. They're professionals.

DAWN: She's incredibly imaginative.

SEAN: We know that. They are finding that out. [*He checks his watch.*] Think they would know by now.

DAWN: You can tell she's imaginative in like two minutes.

SEAN: We might be prejudiced a little bit.

DAWN: If she wasn't imaginative, I'd say she wasn't imaginative. I don't lie about my own child.

SEAN: Well, they've got a business to run. They can't just take our word for it.

DAWN: A school should be a school, not a goddam business.

SEAN: You've made your point. Repeatedly.

DAWN: So what's the worst case-scenario? They reject this intelligent, well-adjusted, deeply loving, highly imaginative child because—why? Her favorite color is black?

SEAN: Let's not get ahead of ourselves.

21

DAWN: She said her favorite color was black to protect herself. She knew people were judging her. It was her way of maintaining power over the situation.

SEAN: Who's projecting now?

DAWN: How am I not going to project with shit that happens to my only kid?

SEAN: Better learn.

DAWN: So what does it mean if she doesn't get in? I know what we do—keep on applying until the private-school god accepts us into private-school heaven somewhere—but what does it mean?

SEAN: It doesn't mean anything. It's just a selection process—

DAWN: I hate this. I hate it, I hate it, I hate it—

SEAN: Listen. Listen to me. This is only the first of many, okay? For the next twenty years, we'll be going through this stuff with her over and over again. It starts with what school, and then it will be what learning track she gets into, what activities, what sports, what high school, what college, what boyfriend, what boyfriend's family, what graduate school, what job—it's life, okay? It's one selection process after another. Sometimes she's going to be rejected. We've got to get used to it.

DAWN: Why does she always have to be the recipient of rejection? Why can't she be the one doing the rejecting?

SEAN: Christ. Of course she can do the rejecting too. I really look forward to a satisfying life full of my daughter rejecting people. I can't wait for the time when she's the president of some club or something and she rejects some other kid because—

DAWN: I get it.

SEAN: We can't live every one of these like it's the test of our worth to the world. We'll live through this, whatever happens. We'll deal.

DAWN: Obviously.

SEAN: She's a good kid.

DAWN: Obviously.

SEAN: We're good parents. [*Beat.*] What happened to obviously?

DAWN: You're right, you're right, I know you're right. About life, I mean. But not about this place. This is not a place I want to be. This shit is you, not me.

SEAN: Fine. This shit is me. [*Beat.*] Here she comes.

> DAWN quickly takes the gum out of her mouth and sticks it on the bottom of her seat. They stand and turn to the door, holding hands, smiling.

> BLACKOUT.

SCENE THREE: "The mercy rule."

> DAWN is pacing up and down the foul line as she watches a girls' softball game in progress. She wears sweats and a baseball cap. She is following the game and rooting intensely. (Her calls to the playing field are indicated in upper case, but should not be delivered in a uniform shout; she cajoles and coaxes as much as she shouts and upbraids.) She is also conducting a business call on a cell-phone. (Indicated in italics.) Dialogue with SEAN is indicated in normal type.

23

DAWN: C'MON, UMP! THAT WAS RIGHT DOWN THE MIDDLE! *That guy's never going to cave—I'm not buying it, I'm telling you*—YOU WANT HER TO SERVE IT ON A PLATTER? *No, no way, listen. He always plays coy like that, which is when you've got to hit him with a brick—[The crack of a bat hitting a ball.]* LEFT FIELD! LEFT FIELDER'S BALL! SOMEBODY CALL FOR THE BALL! JESUS, COACH, YOU GOTTA TEACH THEM TO CALL FOR THE BALL! *Tomorrow? Is that an English word? Because I don't understand tomorrow. I understand the word now. You want me to spell it? N-o-w.*

> During the above, SEAN has entered. He wears an open raincoat and he has loosened his tie. He watches the game from a little distance. When DAWN finally spots him there, she is surprised, but is in full sentence and doesn't address him until indicated.

DAWN: LET'S GO, D! ON YOUR TOES OUT THERE! [*Crack of a bat hitting a ball.*] POP-UP! THIRD BASE! WHO'S GOT IT? SOMEBODY CALL FOR THE BALL—PITCHER'S BALL! PITCHER! PITCHER! ALL RIGHT, PITCHER!! WAY TO GO, TEAM! NOW LET'S GET THOSE RUNS BACK! [*To SEAN:*] Excuse me, aren't you supposed to be in L.A.?

SEAN: Came to see the game. How's it going?

DAWN: It's going. [*Beat.*] *I want to hear from you in ten minutes, okay? Not fifteen, not eleven, ten!* C'MON NOW, LET'S KICK SOME BUTT! [*She disconnects.*] So what happened to L.A.?

SEAN: I suppose it's still there. What's the score?

DAWN: 8-1. No—GUYS! GUYS! EIGHT-ONE? NINE-ONE! WHEN THE HELL DID THEY—OH RIGHT—JESUS. It's 9-1.

SEAN: Not our day.

24

DAWN: What do you mean? We got 'em right where we want 'em.

SEAN: We have to hit two grand-slams just to tie.

DAWN: Sean, what are you doing here? Was the appointment cancelled?

SEAN: How long has Pie been pitching?

DAWN: She started. I pulled strings to get you that appointment. You didn't flake on me, did you? Oh God, you flaked.

SEAN: She gives up nine runs and she's still pitching. The coach has patience.

DAWN: McCarthy put his name on the line to get your script in front of that guy, Sean. That guy is a player. You are putting me in an extremely awkward position—ATTA BABY, GOOD EYE, WORK THE COUNT, LET'S GET SOME BASERUNNERS!

SEAN: What inning is it?

DAWN: Second. [*Her phone rings. SEAN waves at somebody and begins to move off.*] Yeah? No. [*She disconnects.*] Where do you think you're going?

SEAN: Pie just waved. I feel like a hug—

DAWN: Oh no, you don't! Are you crazy? She's the pitcher! You can't hug the pitcher in the middle of the game!

SEAN: Why not? Players hug one another all the time.

DAWN: Only if they're on the team and they're winning! You're not on the team! And you're sure as hell not winning.

SEAN: She's waving again. [*He waves back.*]

DAWN: Stop that! BOTH OF YOU! You're screwing up her game face.

SEAN: Such a pretty little face.

DAWN: Not when she's pitching it isn't! STRIKE? HE CALLED THAT A STRIKE?

SEAN: Looked like a strike to me.

DAWN: Whose side are you on? GOOD CUT! GOOD CUT!

SEAN: Easy. They're playing a game. It's not life or death.

DAWN: You bet it's life and death. That's what playing the game is. Win—you're alive. Lose—you're dead. OH MY GOD! UMP! GIVE ME A BREAK! [*To SEAN:*] You didn't even get on the plane, did you.

SEAN: Got my boarding pass. Then—I don't know. My feet just stopped going forward.

DAWN: You want to sit over here? Come on, sit over here. [*They move away a little and sit down. Beat.*] God. Look at you.

SEAN: What?

DAWN: I was afraid something like this—did you call the guy at least? Make up some excuse?

SEAN: I guess I should have done that, yeah.

DAWN: God, we are fucked. What am I going to tell McCarthy?

SEAN: Don't tell him anything. I'll call him myself and apologize.

DAWN: Apologize. Peachy. And that's supposed to make it all right? Let me think. [*The crack of a bat. DAWN jumps to her feet.*] LINE DRIVE TO THE GAP! GO FOR TWO! GO! GO! WHY ARE YOU GIVING HER THE STOP SIGN! SHE WOULD HAVE MADE SECOND EASY! THE RIGHT-FIELDER THROWS LIKE A GIRL!

SEAN: The right-fielder is a girl.

DAWN: There are girls and there are girls.

SEAN: They're behind eight runs, they need base-runners. The coach is playing it safe.

DAWN: Playing it safe is how you lose.

SEAN: Maybe you'd better lay off a little. The umpire kicked you out of the last game, remember, so you're already on probation—

DAWN: I can't believe you just stood up a Hollywood studio. Hollywood for fuck's sake! [*Her phone rings.*] I've got to take this. Pie's on deck. Give her some pep, okay?

> She answers the phone. During the
> conversation SEAN calls encouragement to
> their daughter on deck.

DAWN: *Yeah? No, I told the guy—when? Yeah—fine—that's what I'm saying—go for it, bring it on home.* [*She disconnects.*]

SEAN [*Overlap*]: Just keep your eye on the ball, sweetheart. Remember how we did it in practice, hands tight but not too tight, tense muscles are slow muscles. Look for her release point and stride into the ball. Take a few practice swings, that's my girl.

DAWN [*Overlap*]: WE GOT A RALLY GOING HERE! KEEP THE LINE MOVING! [*Crack of a bat.*] DIG IT OUT! DIG ! SHORTSTOP BOOTED IT! SHE BOOTED IT! FIRST AND

SECOND! WE GOT A RALLY! Okay, I've thought about it. We get you on the next plane and go with some story about weather and delayed connections-

SEAN: There is no next plane.

DAWN: Bullshit. L.A. is not Podunk. They fly out every hour on the hour—

SEAN: It's over, Dawn. I've been kidding myself. I'm not a writer.

DAWN: There's a desk full of manuscripts back home saying different. [*Crack of a bat.*] LINE SHOT! DIG! SHIT! SHORTSTOP SNARES IT! BACK! GET BACK! DOUBLE PLAY! SHIT! [*Beat.*] SORRY, UMP. I KNOW. LANGUAGE. JUST GOT CARRIED AWAY IN THE OLD HEAT OF THE MOMENT. WON'T HAPPEN AGAIN. SWEAR. [*To SEAN:*] Girl hits it on the screws and the same shortstop who can't pick a weak grounder, the same goddam kid, she snares a bullet and doubles up the runner WHO SHOULDN'T HAVE BEEN THAT FAR OFF THE BAG IN THE FIRST PLACE! [*Beat.*] SORRY, UMP.

SEAN: The girl made a great play. Doesn't matter what side she's on. NICE PLAY, KID!

DAWN: Oh, baby.

SEAN: What? It was a nice play.

DAWN: Don't quit on me, Sean. Please don't quit on me. As long as a product is there, there's opportunity. And I know we've got a product, a fabulous product—

SEAN: Product?

DAWN: Everything is a product. Don't you know that yet?

SEAN: I do. Finally. Which is why I'm going to get a regular job. Something where I show up every morning and deal with somebody else's goddam product instead of my own.

DAWN: Look, you don't have to make a decision now, take some time, I'll cover somehow with McCarthy—

SEAN: The decision has been made for me, Dawn! My feet wouldn't move!

DAWN: C'MON, ONE TWO THREE INNING, GUYS. [*Beat.*] What kind of job would you get?

SEAN: Drive a cab. Sell shoes. Slice salami.

[*DAWN's phone rings.*]

DAWN: *Yeah. I already talked to him. Ball's in his court now. Right. I'll be here. Where else would I be?* [*She disconnects.*] OKAY, LET'S GO, D!

SEAN: The worst thing is I was standing there in the airport—

DAWN: Maybe we should talk about this later, okay?

SEAN: —and I thought of everything you told me about how to pitch the script, and I said to myself, "Dawn is the person who should do this. Not me. She believes in the script, she could sell it." Which meant I didn't believe in it.

DAWN: You wrote it! Who the hell else is going to believe in it if you don't? [*Crack of a bat.*] THERE IT GOES. MAN. THAT'S OKAY, THAT'S OKAY. SOLO HOMER IS BETTER THAN A LEAD-OFF WALK—

SEAN: Exactly. I don't believe in it. Because I didn't write it. I assembled it. It's pre-fab—a screenplay product, made of used parts cobbled together to sell—

DAWN: So sell the motherfucker! Then you'll be in a position to do what you want. THROW STRIKES!

SEAN: I've been thinking about going back to school—

DAWN: Great. Another tuition to pay. Just what I need. Thanks.

SEAN: This wouldn't come out of your money. I'd take out a loan.

DAWN: On whose credit would you do that, darling?

SEAN: I just need to take a few courses to get my ABD, and then I could apply for better teaching jobs or get into administration—

DAWN: IS THERE AN OPHTHAMOLOGIST IN THE HOUSE? You'll be miserable if you don't write. You know that.

SEAN: I'm miserable when I do.

DAWN: She's totally lost the strike zone. That last shot totally broke her confidence. She's afraid to throw a strike. They're going to take her out.

SEAN: Then can I go over and give her a hug?

DAWN: No! Especially not then. [*Crack of a bat.*] Another shot. Man, those guys must be on steroids over there. We've got to get ourselves some fucking steroids.

SEAN: They're taking her out. Poor baby. THAT'S OKAY, SWEETHEART! DON'T LET IT GET YOU DOWN! IT'S JUST NOT YOUR DAY!

DAWN: Shut up! That's negative shit!

SEAN: I'm being supportive. Trying to make her feel better—

DAWN: I'm going home.

SEAN: We can't go home now. Now is when she needs us.

DAWN: Now is when she needs to stand on her own! Now is not when she needs her mommy and daddy to kiss it and make it better. Because we can't.

SEAN: THAT'S OKAY, SWEETHEART! YOU'LL GET 'EM NEXT TIME.

DAWN: I'm leaving, Sean. Do you hear me? I'm leaving.

SEAN: Well, I'm staying. EVERYBODY CAN HAVE A BAD DAY. NO SHAME IN THAT. Look at her. Aw. She's crying— [DAWN is crying too. SEAN doesn't notice.]

DAWN: Don't watch! Don't look at her!

SEAN: I don't understand—

DAWN: Yes, you don't understand. [Beat.] They're going to stop the game anyway.

SEAN: It's only the third inning. I thought they played six.

DAWN: It's called the mercy rule. Ten behind at the end of an inning. They don't let it get worse and become a massacre. The ump will invoke the mercy rule and stop the game.

SEAN: The mercy rule. I like the mercy rule.

DAWN: You would.

SCENE FOUR: "Grandma's Sweater Blue"

> A coffee-shop. DAWN is sitting at a small table, sipping coffee and studying paint chips. SEAN enters and seems surprised to see her.

31

SEAN: I don't have my day wrong, do I? This *is* Saturday?

DAWN: Thought I'd hang around after I dropped her off at her lesson. See how you were doing.

SEAN: But it's the same routine, right? I don't have to bring her back until tomorrow at five—

DAWN: You don't have to quote chapter and verse. You're always very punctual.

SEAN: I'd better be. One slip-up and you'd have me in court.

DAWN: Have a brownie. You like brownies.

SEAN: No, thanks.

DAWN: I bought Pie a brownie too. Don't let her eat it until after she has her lunch.

SEAN: She'll eat it as soon as she sees it.

DAWN: Well, don't let her. Exercise some parental authority for a change. [*He looks at her.*] Okay, hide it. Put it in your pocket and give it to her later.

SEAN: I'll forget it's there.

DAWN: I'll call you and remind you. Please sit down, Sean. I'm not going to bite you. You look like a frightened animal.

SEAN: I am a frightened animal. The species is "divorced father." [*He sits. Beat.*]

DAWN: Pie says your apartment is very nice.

SEAN: That's because she can slop around in it and do anything she wants. Dawn, what are you really doing here? You can't want money.

DAWN: I told you. I know you guys always have lunch here after her clarinet lesson. I wanted to see how you were.

SEAN: How am I?

DAWN: And I wanted your input.

SEAN: There's a first.

DAWN: [*She holds up two paint chips.*] This one or that one?

SEAN: What are we talking about here?

DAWN: For Pie's room. We're redecorating. [*SEAN has a delayed but very bitter reaction to this.*] What?

SEAN: Why are you asking me this?

DAWN: Because you have excellent taste in colors—

SEAN: Come on.

DAWN: You do! And she's being impossible about it. I need whatever help I can get.

SEAN: Even from me. Things must be bad at home. [*DAWN doesn't reply.*] Well, what happens if I accept your gambit and play? Say I pick this one—[*He touches a paint chip.*] —and she says it sucks. Then you get to say, "Daddy chose it." Uh-uh. No dice. You want to take the heat off yourself, shift the blame.

DAWN: Don't make everything so complicated. It's a simple request.

SEAN: You don't think it's just the least little bit cruel of you . . .

DAWN: Cruel? What's cruel?

SEAN: You kicked me out of the house, Dawn, out of my daughter's life. Except for thirty hours a week, that is, ten of which she sleeps. And now you're asking me for decorating tips?

DAWN: I didn't kick you out. We agreed. We've agreed on everything every step of the way. We wouldn't be talking so amicably if we didn't agree.

SEAN: Amicably.

DAWN: What's any of this got to do with the color of Pie's room?

SEAN: Everything. Everything has to do with everything!

DAWN: Give me a break. She wanted me to ask you. She demanded.

SEAN: Why hasn't she asked me herself?

DAWN: Who knows? She will. Or she won't. I'm trying here, okay? [*Beat.*]

SEAN: What color does she want?

DAWN: Black. [*SEAN laughs.*] Go ahead. You don't have to live with her.

SEAN: No, you took care of that. So paint it black. It's her room.

DAWN: I am not going to let my daughter live in a black room.

SEAN: A week or two of black walls and she'll probably change her mind. Then you can paint it again. [*Mockingly:*] Some more appropriate color.

DAWN: House painters do not come cheap. Not to mention the disruption –

34

SEAN: I'll pay the painters. Better yet, I'll come in and paint it myself if you'll let me. Painting one room is no big deal.

DAWN: It's already a big deal.

SEAN: That's because you fight her. It only makes her more stubborn. She's her mother's daughter after all.

DAWN: Will somebody explain to me why I always turn out to be the villain?

SEAN: Let me count the ways—

DAWN: The question was rhetorical. A black room is impossible. People cannot live in black rooms. And I don't play stupid placating games with people, even when they're willful adolescents acting out of spite.

SEAN: Which is why.

DAWN: Why what?

SEAN: You feel like a villain. How's she doing in chemistry?

DAWN: She's not taking chemistry.

SEAN: Not taking it—what do you mean? She signed up for AP Science. We talked about it. It was settled. There was a conflict between chem lab and field-hockey practice, and she was going to see the teacher about a change—

DAWN: Well, she changed. She's taking Global Culture now.

SEAN: Global Culture! What the fuck is Global Culture? No. Don't tell me. Some dimwit PC bullshit.

DAWN: Given her father's attitude, I'd say it's a good thing she's taking it.

SEAN: Why'd she do that? You should have had her call me before she did that. You should have told me. At least we could have talked about it. Shit.

DAWN: You don't want her to know about other cultures?

SEAN: We've been through this a million times. Courses like that are not a replacement for science and math. Science and math are the foundation.

DAWN: Communication arts—

SEAN: Okay, English too, writing, Shakespeare and shit. But Global Culture? Jesus! Even if it's taught right, whatever the hell it is, at best it can complement—

DAWN: Well, she's taking Global Culture as her foundation, and if she wants to she can take science and math someday to complement that.

SEAN: It doesn't work like that.

DAWN: Don't tell me how it works. You are not an expert on what works in this world. [*Beat.*] So how's the writing going? Are you working on anything new?

SEAN: I know you're not interested, so don't pretend you are, okay?

DAWN: That's not true. I've always been interested in your writing—

SEAN: Christ.

DAWN: Why are you being so nasty?

SEAN: Why the fuck are you suddenly so interested in my writing?

36

DAWN: Maybe because I don't have to listen to you whining about it every day! Maybe because I don't have to mentally calculate what you're making per hour—

SEAN: Four cents. And plunging.

DAWN: —trying to write some timeless classic you'll be too noble to try to sell.

SEAN: Noble. That's me.

DAWN: It is. You're so nobly sincere. That's so attractive in a man. You can be positively devastating because you're not trying to be, which makes you even more devastating. Sure toppled me once.

SEAN: You recovered.

DAWN: Sort of.

SEAN: You were pretty devastating yourself. Care to see my battle scars? [*Beat.*] I'm not writing at all. I'm full-time at the university now—

DAWN: Really? That's wonderful. What are you teaching?

SEAN: I'm teaching myself reality. I'm photocopying. I'm sharpening pencils and chasing people down to get them to go to meetings. I print out copies of department budgets and outline overrides in red. [*DAWN is looking at him uncomprehendingly.*] I'm in the Dean's Office. My title is "Faculty Coordinator." Don't get much time for writing.

DAWN: You're too creative for scut-work like that. It will just drag you down.

SEAN: Have to pay rent. Support checks.

DAWN: Sweetheart, your support checks barely keep her in sneakers! My lawyer and the judge worked out a token figure . . . look, what I'm trying to say is don't ruin your life to write support checks, okay? Keep your money. I won't sue. It's a promise.

SEAN: You always know how to make a man feel good about himself, don't you.

DAWN: Forget it. [*Beat.*] While we're on the subject of making you feel good about yourself—this is kind of funny actually in a tragicomic kind of way—or hell, maybe it won't matter to you at all—anyhoo—I'm going to get married.

SEAN: Married.

DAWN: Don't you feel relieved? I'm surrendering my fortunes into the hands of another to squire me through this wicked world. Fiddle-dee-dee. [*Beat.*] Reaction? None? Too many? What?

SEAN: That was quick.

DAWN: Not really.

SEAN: I didn't know you were even dating.

DAWN: Your permission for me to see other men was not part of the divorce settlement.

SEAN: May I ask who's the happy groom?

DAWN: I'm not sure I should tell you.

SEAN: Don't play games!

DAWN: Evan.

SEAN: Evan. Who's Evan?

DAWN: Evan McCarthy.

SEAN: Evan McCarthy. [*Beat.*] McCarthy?

DAWN: He's been really sweet since the divorce, and one thing sort of led to another and the next thing we knew, well. He's older and everything, but at this age what's a few years—

SEAN: A few decades you mean! McCarthy's had three wives already. He's fucked up every marriage he's been in.

DAWN: Marriage is a two-way proposition, Sean. It's rarely just the one person's fault. Perhaps that hasn't occurred to you yet. I admit I generally don't approve of mixing personal and professional relationships—

SEAN: But the head of the firm convinced you otherwise. So what is this all about? You're already partner, so you don't have to screw your way there.

DAWN: That was uncalled for.

SEAN: McCarthy. Jesus. I didn't think he had time for a personal life—oh Christ. You weren't having an affair with him all the time, were you? You don't have to lie to me anymore.

DAWN: Well, it's none of your business now, is it?

SEAN: Fuck it. Fuck it all. Fuck everything. Jesus, how could I have been so stupid? All those nights in your office working late—you're a fucking cliché! You're a fucking fucking-cliché.

DAWN: Pie adores him.

SEAN: Why hasn't she ever mentioned him then?

DAWN: She's her mother's daughter. She has a natural delicacy.

SEAN: The same kid who wants to paint her room black has a natural delicacy.

DAWN: That was a joke. Don't you ever laugh?

SEAN: I don't believe she even knows about this. You know what? I'm going to ask her about him.

DAWN: Leave her alone. Please? She doesn't need our bullshit.

SEAN: She'll tell me the truth, you know.

DAWN: The truth? What truth?

SEAN: The truth about her feelings. She doesn't conceal anything from me.

DAWN: Want to bet, dearest?

SEAN: You and McCarthy are why she wants to paint her room black. It's a protest.

DAWN: Just don't say anything to her about my getting married. Not yet. Okay?

SEAN: Why not? You said she adores the guy.

DAWN: She will. Give her time. Evan has a son by his second wife who's a little older than Pie and just the other day we went for brunch and they were so adorable together—

SEAN: Doesn't lying ever upset you?

DAWN: Look, fella. I've told you something I thought you should know before you found it out somewhere else. That's all. I probably shouldn't have said anything.

SEAN: I feel sick, physically sick.

DAWN: Life goes on, Sean. Sooner or later you'll meet somebody too, I know it—

40

SEAN: Give me those paint chips.

DAWN: What for?

SEAN: Give them to me! [*He snatches them from her.*]
Blue, green, pink. Marshmallow Bunny Pink. Lotus Flower
Pink. Once Upon a Time Green. Sea-to-Shining-Sea Blue.
How the hell do they come up with these names? No
wonder she wants black. You can't fuck with black.

DAWN: They're only paint chips.

SEAN: They're words! Words mean something. Words are
ideas, not just mood swings. Grandma's Sweater Blue. Now
there's an idea. That means something.

DAWN: It means that some English major couldn't find
another job except naming paint chips and had a grandma
whose sweater was that color and thought it was cute.

SEAN: It means comfort and warmth and security and
reassurance. All in a single color, Grandma's Sweater Blue.
All our lives together I was speaking in paint chips to you,
and you never understood a word.

DAWN: Quit bouncing in your chair. You're going to crush
Pie's brownie.

SEAN: You've got to let her paint her room black, Dawn.
Let her do it herself. Let her slop black paint all over her
walls and her clothes and her face and her hands and her
hair. It's the idea she believes in, damn it, in spite of us.
Because of us.

DAWN: I prefer Sheer Romance. It's a perfect blue for a
girl's room—

SEAN: Why not Mindless Slut Blue? It's a bit provocative,
but she'll grow into it.

DAWN: I'm out of here. Don't forget to give Pie her brownie after her lunch. I told her we're having pasta tomorrow night, so she shouldn't eat too much pizza. I know how much pizza you stuff into her. Could I have my paint chips back please?

SEAN: No. I have ideas to discuss with my daughter.

DAWN: Do what you want. [*She leaves.*]

SEAN: Grandma's Sweater Blue! Think about it! Think! [*Beat.*] On the other hand, black is good.

SCENE FIVE: "Perjury at the prom."

> An expensively furnished living room. DAWN sits on a sofa, sipping a drink. She wears casual, youthful summer clothes. A stereo with CD's, a coffee-table. The telephone rings.

DAWN: I've got it, Pie! [*She answers the phone.*] Hello? Pie, get off the phone! Get dressed! [*Beat.*] Hello again, sorry about that. MJ! What's up? [*Beat.*] Not a problem. She didn't get home from practice until late . . . what? Sure. It's going to be a long night for you guys anyway. You'll be sick of each other by midnight . . . I'm kidding . . . sure, I'll remind her. Absolutely. Tell the driver not to rush. See you in a bit. [*She disconnects and shouts.*] That was MJ! Limo's late, they're about twenty minutes behind, so take your time and make yourself gorgeous. If you need any accessory advice I'm here for you, girl.

> She gets up to put on a CD, flips through a few, finds one that makes her smile, and puts it on – a swing version of "It's Later Than You Think." The doorbell rings. She checks her watch, turns off the music, and opens the front door.

DAWN: That sure was a quick twenty minutes—[*SEAN stands there, in a rumpled summer suit and carrying a briefcase.*] Well, well.

SEAN: Hi, Dawn. Can I come in?

DAWN: Don't know if you can. Things are pretty frantic and girlie around here. If you want photos, I'm taking photos. You'll get copies.

SEAN: I'd really like to see her.

DAWN: You couldn't call first?

SEAN: I'm sorry. [*Beat.*] I was afraid you'd say no.

DAWN: I still can say no.

SEAN: That's true. [*Beat.*]

DAWN: Well, you're just letting the hot air in. Might as well come in where it's cool.

SEAN: Thanks, Dawn. I really appreciate this.

DAWN: I guess I didn't expect you, but now you're here I guess I'm not surprised.

SEAN: Scorcher for June. Nice in here though. [*Beat.*] Is your husband home?

DAWN: Nope.

SEAN: Business trip?

DAWN: Nope. [*Beat.*]

SEAN: I heard music when I was coming up the walk. Thought maybe the party had started already—

DAWN: "It's Later Than You Think."

SEAN: Beg pardon?

DAWN: Forget it. You want a drink? You look like you could use something.

SEAN: No, thanks. I don't want to take up your time. I just wanted to see her. You know, in all her finery.

DAWN: Well, it'll be at least ten minutes before she gets her finery down here, so you might as well have a drink while you're waiting. It used to be scotch-and-soda, plenty of rocks.

SEAN: I don't really drink Scotch any more—

DAWN: Well, there's beer, wine, vodka, gin—Evan doesn't drink but he stocks a world-class bar. I could make you one of my special martinis—Stoli on ice and I pronounce the word vermouth over it. [*She waves her glass.*] Tastes like an old band-aid, but it gets the job done.

SEAN: A Coke would be fine.

DAWN: Only Pepsi. Diet.

SEAN: Perfect.

DAWN: Ice and a glass? Or are you a straight-from-the-bottle dude?

SEAN: Ice and a glass would be great. If it's not too much trouble.

DAWN: [*Shouting as she leaves.*] Your old man's here to see you in your glory, Pie! So don't come down half-naked and disgrace the establishment. [*She leaves.*]

SEAN: [*Shouting too.*] Hi, beautiful! I'm here for the big night. Don't rush.

> He opens his briefcase, takes out a manila
> folder, and scans the papers inside. DAWN re-

44

enters with two glasses and he puts the folder on the table.

DAWN: One Daddy-special featuring ice. One Mommy—special featuring vodka. Now isn't this cozy? Sure you won't join me in a pacifying stimulant? I've got some Barbados rum that brings peace to the world—

SEAN: No. Really. I have to go back to work later.

DAWN: On a summer night? And they call lawyers workaholics. They sure get their money's worth out of you in that Dean's Office.

SEAN: I'm assistant to the President now. One of the assistants.

DAWN: In that case your suit needs pressing.

SEAN: Oh. Well. I'm behind the scenes. There's a dinner for the trustees and a reception afterwards. I make sure everybody has . . . whatever. [*Beat.*]

DAWN: Latest Prom Bulletin! The big show is behind schedule. Limo was late.

SEAN: How many couples are going together?

DAWN: Three. Derek and Julianne, Janey and Emily, MJ and Pie.

SEAN: Janey and Emily?

DAWN: It's a brave new world. Any objections?

SEAN: None at all. Good for Janey and Emily.

DAWN: Good for their parents.

SEAN: Good for the school.

DAWN: No virtue there, I'm afraid. They just know how not to get sued. I say if you've got to have a prom at all—and you've just got to, because it's another chance for ostentatious spending—you can at least let people go with who they want.

SEAN: People. They still seem like kids.

DAWN: They are kids. Get used to it, dad. I hope you didn't come over here to give your daughter a lecture. She doesn't need a lecture tonight, okay?

SEAN: I'm just here to see her dressed up. I promise. [*Beat.*] But now that you mention it—do you think she does things we don't know about?

DAWN: I didn't mention it, but what things?

SEAN: Things. You know.

DAWN: Oh, *things.* Absolutely. Every self-respecting girl does things her parents don't know about. It's called having a life.

SEAN: I'm not saying her life should be an open book, but—

DAWN: Take me, for instance. When I was Pie's age—hell, younger—my thoughts were in the gutter. There was this guy who lived down the block who had a motor-bike, little thing like a shop-cart that buzzed, what was it called, a Skidoo or something. He was skinny and sixteen, but he was Testosterone on a Harley to me. I could feel the buzz of that Skidoo up and down my spine from my toes through my you-know-what to the frizzy tips of my hair. The *things* I used to do to catch that boy's attention—you think my parents knew?

SEAN: Well, I know Pie wouldn't make a fool of herself over some boy.

DAWN: No. Never. Never in a million years. Not our Pie.

SEAN: Apparently you think she would. Any reason?

DAWN: Three reasons. She's seventeen. She's straight. And she's alive.

SEAN: But she's not stupid.

DAWN: Sex and seventeen can get pretty stupid. Chill, dad! You raise them as well as you can, and then they're on their own.

SEAN: Hardly on her own. It's just the Senior Prom. There'll be adult supervision—

DAWN: *Just* the Senior Prom? Haven't you seen any high-school movies? The Senior Prom is the climax of existence! Everything is down hill after this.

SEAN: Well, at least they're renting a limo, they're not driving.

DAWN: On the other hand, they are staying out all night.

SEAN: All night?!

DAWN: Didn't you know? Oh, I see. Beautiful didn't tell Daddy because Beautiful didn't want Daddy to get upset. Well, that's how it's done these days, dad. Proms are like these twenty-four-hour marathons of non-stop sex, drugs, and rock-and-roll. Be thankful I said no to a whole week-end.

SEAN: But where is she going to spend the night?

DAWN: At the Conroys' beach house out on the island. Don't worry. The Conroys will be there. Actually worry. The Conroys will be there.

47

SEAN: Jesus, Dawn. Don't you think all night is a little excessive?

DAWN: It's fucking insane. But what are you going to do about it? Show up at the Conroys' with condoms and black coffee?

SEAN: Condoms? Are you telling me that Pie and this boy—

DAWN: MJ.

SEAN: MJ—what's it stand for?

DAWN: MJ.

SEAN: Are you saying Pie and this MJ are having sex?

DAWN: Probably.

SEAN: Shouldn't you know? You're her mother.

DAWN: Let's see. What do I know as Pie's mother? I know that Pie is becoming a woman, and women are human beings, and human beings have sexual desire. Combine that with opportunity and a horny boy—

SEAN: But that doesn't mean she'll . . . you know. Let him.

DAWN: Let him?

SEAN: Maybe we should talk a little more quietly—

DAWN: Christ, Sean, haven't you ever thought that maybe your precious baby girl might want sex too? Why shouldn't she—[*Whispers dramatically:*]—"let him"? [*Regular voice:*] Maybe she jumps his bones whenever she gets the chance. She's young, she's healthy. Got a great set of boobs.

SEAN: God.

DAWN: Don't tell me you never noticed her boobs.

SEAN: Certainly I recognize that she has matured—

DAWN: Well, so have the boys around her, pal, which means they've noticed her boobs, not to mention the rest of her which is pretty good too. Better to be noticed than not to be noticed. I wish to hell Skidoo boy had noticed my boobs. Of course he would have needed a magnifying glass in those days.

SEAN: I'm not completely naïve, you know. I know things can happen on prom night. I just want her to use her head.

DAWN: As opposed to giving head.

SEAN: Your gift for putting things elegantly never ceases to amaze me.

DAWN: Well, I'm not an elegant kind of girl. What's this? [*She picks up the folder he has brought and opens it.*] "Having Fun, Staying Safe." What the hell?

SEAN: Read the whole thing before you say anything.

DAWN: You are not for real.

SEAN: Wait. Hear me out. It started out as this thing I was doing for freshman orientation at the university, and then I thought hey, you know, as parents, you and I might use it as reference points to talk to Pie about, we've never really had a formal talk about these things and she'll be going away to college soon . . . well, why not?

DAWN: You've even got three dotted lines where we can sign, along with the date.

SEAN: I thought if we presented it as a contract, she would see it as a mutual commitment and be impressed by the seriousness—my parents always used to write up contracts for us kids, you know, who's taking out the garbage during

49

the month of April and which three TV shows we could watch during the week—

DAWN: God, if it weren't so obsessive and fucked up, it would be kind of cute. Which, I guess, is you in a nut-shell. [*She tosses the folder down.*]

SEAN: You haven't read it through.

DAWN: I don't have to. She's not going to sign this. Neither am I. Of course I'm not the one going to the prom tonight.

SEAN: Why not?

DAWN: Because nobody invited me.

SEAN: I meant why won't you sign? Think of it as a starting-point of discussion.

DAWN: Why are you so clueless about this? You're around young people at the university—no, that's right, you're administration. You're paid to be clueless.

SEAN: The terms are perfectly reasonable. She agrees not to have sex, get drunk, or do drugs over the next year, and I buy her a car. In a medium price-range.

DAWN: And naturally she'll agree.

SEAN: Well then! Great! Terrific! Problem solved!

DAWN: And naturally she'll be lying. Hey, go whole hog and get it notarized! Make her swear before a judge! Then you can charge her with perjury at the prom.

SEAN: This thing works in her interest. She'll see that. She's smart.

DAWN: Yeah, but there's one tiny little catch. Say if she already has had sex, gotten drunk, and done drugs?

50

SEAN: Already? You know for sure then?

DAWN: I'm not going to rat out my own daughter. Sean, listen to me. You can't put a child, a person, in a position where she'll lie. You can't ask her to sign a contract that denies . . .

SEAN: Denies what?

DAWN: Life.

SEAN: There are more things to life than promiscuity and substance abuse—

DAWN: Maybe not when you're seventeen years old. Don't you see? Kids drink. They fool around. Dope is everywhere. If you get her to sign this, you're putting her in a position where she's bound to fail—and by bribing her you're guaranteeing that she'll lie about it.

SEAN: I don't accept your view that teen-age degeneracy is inevitable.

DAWN: Arrrgh! Stop with the committee-speak! We just have to be lucky. If she's the girl we think we raised, she'll be sensible. Basically. But things can happen. If she does get into some kind of trouble, we'll help her somehow. Whatever happens, she's got to know she can come to us. A contract like that would have the opposite effect. It would be a disaster.

SEAN: You say come to "us." You mean you and me?

DAWN: Who the hell else would I mean? We're her parents.

SEAN: What about her step-father?

DAWN: Let's just say she's not too interested in her stepfather's point of view on these issues—any issues. But that's another story.

SEAN: I wonder if we really have raised her to be sensible.

DAWN: Guess we'll find out, dad.

SEAN: But you don't have any specific reason to suspect she's sexually active.

DAWN: I suppose it's normal for fathers to be obsessed by their daughter's sex lives. Jesus! Aren't you listening? Now hear this! Your daughter is past puberty, Sean. She's interested in *things* that aren't SAT scores, her batting average, and the clarinet. Weren't you at seventeen?

SEAN: I played the French horn.

DAWN: That explains everything. Now put that damn thing away.

SEAN: Fine. [*He slowly folds up the contract, but doesn't put it in his briefcase* .] Maybe it would be different if you and I had stayed together. You know, if I had been in the house with her growing up, I would have seen her life more continuously instead of just on week-ends and things . . .

DAWN: It is what it is.

SEAN: She knows how to protect herself and everything?

DAWN: I've fitted her with a special chastity belt that goes all around her squinchum so nobody can get near her booch.

SEAN: I mean you've talked to her about sex, you've taught her.

DAWN: Taught her? What the hell do I know about sex? I know what can go where. Sort of. I can tell her about condoms like the rest of the world. But what do I really know about what kids are doing with their body fluids these days? What do I know about drugs? I smoked a few joints in college. Alcohol? I drink Stoli. Cheers. We're babies compared to these kids. They got money. Opportunity. A feeling of entitlement. Hormones. What have we got against that? Worries? Common sense? Get real. [*Beat.*] Her dress is gorgeous.

SEAN: I'm sure it is. She made it herself.

DAWN: Is that what she told you? [*Beat.*]

SEAN: This boy she's going out with tonight—

DAWN: MJ.

SEAN: MJ. Should we be worried?

DAWN: You mean about date-rape? Well, after they start taking E and chugging Southern Comfort, who knows? No, take it easy. I wouldn't worry about MJ. As far as I can tell he's a good guy. Actually you know him. He's that flat-headed kid who smashed into her with his bike and wrecked her razor-scooter.

SEAN: I remember that bastard. I don't see how smashing into a little girl with a bike qualifies him as a good guy.

DAWN: They were eight. Shit happens when you're eight. He's really grown into a decent kid. AP English, Math, Spanish. On the tennis team. Cute hairy legs. Says hello and smiles when he sees me. Most of them don't.

SEAN: That's just the kind you can't trust. How long has she been hanging out with this MJ?

DAWN: Listen to you! Hanging out! Way cool, the Seanster!

SEAN: I mean are they just friends or are they an item?

DAWN: An item? You just lost all your cool, honey. Well, if you're trying to determine the status of their relationship, I can't really tell. They have so many categories these days. It's not just cliques and boyfriend-girlfriend. There are cafeteria friends. Mall friends. Jock friends. Friends with privileges.

SEAN: What privileges?

DAWN: Finger-fucking and blow jobs. But they may be too old for that. [*SEAN starts to cough violently.*] Would you like another Pepsi? Perhaps something stronger?

SEAN: What kind of world are we living in?

DAWN: Good old US of A. Greatest country on earth.

SEAN: Do you think she's happy?

DAWN: Tonight? [*Beat.*] Yes. Yes, tonight I think she's happy.

SEAN: But do you think her life is happy? Overall. Essentially.

DAWN: You've got to lighten up, dad. You've got a healthy, smart, beautiful daughter. Fortunately not too beautiful. No eating disorders. She loves her parents despite their fuck-ups. And she hardly has any piercings at all.

SEAN: Piercings?!

DAWN: Don't ask. Better hide that contract. She's coming down.

SCENE SIX: "Malmsey."

> A typically messy student's room in a university dormitory. The door opens. SEAN enters, tired, unkempt, like someone in the midst of an ordeal that he knows is not yet over. He stands there for a beat, surveying the room. He musters up his courage and begins to pick through the contents of the room – books, clothes, papers – but he seems uncertain about

what he is searching for. Eventually he comes upon an old stuffed animal that stops him in his tracks. Energy and purpose drain out of him. He sits on the bed, hugging the stuffed animal. DAWN enters, weary but business-like, carrying several empty plastic bags.

DAWN: No rest for the weary. Can't quit now.

SEAN: [*He shows her the stuffed animal.*] Malmsey.

DAWN: She'll want that. Here, in with him. Come on.

SEAN: We can't put Malmsey in a bag. I'll carry him.

DAWN: The nurse said everything we bring should be put in bags and labeled. Otherwise it will get lost.

SEAN: [*Not yielding the stuffed animal.*] Good old Malmsey.

DAWN: God, what a pig-sty. And it's a single so we can't even blame her roommate.

SEAN: My room was a lot worse in college. At least there's no pizza under the bed. [*He finds a piece of pizza under the bed.*] At least it's not anchovy. [*He laughs; his laughter dissolves into weeping.*]

DAWN: Take it easy.

SEAN: I just found him here on her bed. She must still sleep with him under her arm. Like when she was three.

DAWN: She's going to be okay, Sean.

SEAN: It's not sure yet.

DAWN: Her temperature's down, and the referred pain in her arm is much less. The specialist says that means the new antibiotic is kicking in. She's turned a corner.

SEAN: [*Making a genuine effort to snap out of it.*] I know. I know. I know. Good signs all. Good signs. [*He breaks down again.*]

DAWN: [*Sitting next to him.*] Come here.

> She puts her arms around him. He sobs in her arms, and she soothes him until his spasm of crying stops.

SEAN: Wow.

DAWN: You okay now?

SEAN: Sort of lost it there.

DAWN: It's all right. It's the tension breaking. Now that she's going to be all right, you're beginning to break a little, that's all.

SEAN: You're not breaking. [*Beat.*] All this stuff. How will we ever sort through it?

DAWN: Look, maybe you should let me do this. The Student Center's right across the quad. Go get us some coffee. I'll have everything ready by the time you get back.

SEAN: I want to help.

DAWN: Coffee would help a lot.

SEAN: Can't we just stay together?

DAWN: Sure.

> DAWN starts to pick through the stuff in the room and put selected things in bags. SEAN doesn't move and sits there, holding Malmsey.

SEAN: She looked like she was dying.

DAWN: She was dying.

SEAN: How does a college kid, an athlete, get pneumonia and start to die overnight?

DAWN: She's not an athlete any more, Sean. She smokes. She eats God knows what. She had a sore throat, she wasn't taking care of it, her resistance was down, I never should have let her go on that ski trip—

SEAN: I told you that, goddamit.

DAWN: No fights, okay?

SEAN: I told her too.

DAWN: And she should have listened to you. We both should have listened to you. Truce. Please.

SEAN: How was she when you left the hospital?

DAWN: I left her like three minutes after you did. You saw. She was asleep.

SEAN: She didn't wake up and say anything?

DAWN: She was asleep, Sean. That's what she has to do now. Sleep, let the antibiotic work. When she wakes up, we'll get some food into her.

SEAN: I don't trust hospital food. We should bring her something good—

DAWN: One step at a time, okay? She'll probably only be able to take in some broth at first. I trust this new guy they brought in. Not the greatest bedside manner, but he sounds like he knows what he's talking about. You saw how she's not sweating like she was. Her face isn't gray any more.

SEAN: Thank God.

DAWN: Thank antibiotics.

        SEAN watches DAWN pick through clothes.

SEAN: Are you doing that according to some principle of selection?

DAWN: Mom's Nose Test. Eventually I'll do a load of laundry, but meanwhile she's going to need her bathrobe and some underwear and some socks—phew, maybe I'll buy her some new socks—and some T-shirts for when she starts to sit up—

SEAN: What would I do without you?

DAWN: Seems like you've done pretty well without me.

SEAN: But this . . . I wouldn't have made it through this. Never.

DAWN: Well, we're not quite through it yet. Still plenty to do.

SEAN: The university has been helpful. [*Beat.*]

DAWN: What has the university been?

SEAN: Helpful. Pretty much.

DAWN: The university has been for shit. If Evan hadn't known somebody at the medical school and pulled strings to get that specialist in, we'd be arranging her fucking funeral.

SEAN: Well, they did fly her down from Vermont –

DAWN: Which they shouldn't have. They should have contacted me right away. I would have been out there on the next plane and gotten her into the nearest first-rate hospital. Instead they brought her back through an ice-storm to that stupid infirmary where she almost died. The university could have killed her.

SEAN: Everything happened so fast. I think they were taken by surprise too—

DAWN: Let's not talk about the university, okay?

SEAN: I'm just saying I think it was a tough call. Not that I'm defending their decision, but I guess I can see these things from their perspective—

DAWN: What books do you think she'll want?

SEAN: You really think she's capable of reading?

DAWN: She will be. She's young. When the young start to heal, they heal fast. I don't want her to fall too far behind in her work.

SEAN: Maybe she should come home and convalesce for a while. I could take care of her. I know the Prez would give me a few weeks off if I asked—

DAWN: We'll see.

SEAN: Of course my apartment isn't big like your house, but I'd give her my bedroom and you could come over to visit whenever you wanted. I know your husband and Pie don't get along too well—

DAWN: We'll see how she is, okay? Meanwhile we'll bring her some books. What's she taking this semester? You always keep track.

SEAN: French of course, Developmental Psych, Fiction Workshop, and Post-Colonial Literature in Southeast Asia.

DAWN: Nice program.

SEAN: Bullshit program. Except for the French. That's real. Except she could always pick it up at a Berlitz—

DAWN: Or spend a year in France sink-or-swim. That's how I'd do it.

SEAN: Or spend a year in France sink-or-swim if her mother picks up the tab.

DAWN: All she has to do is ask. Not that she would ask me for anything.

SEAN: Unfortunately she doesn't consult me *before* she registers. Maybe because I'm the one who wanted her to take science in high school.

DAWN: Well, she consults you more than she consults me. She doesn't even deign to tell me what she's taking. I always have to find out from you.

SEAN: Consult is too kind a word. Let's say she informs me.

DAWN: Well, she's got an advisor. The advisor must have approved.

SEAN: Her advisor signs anything put in front of her. Not that an advisor's objection would ever stop our Pie, who happens to be a very headstrong person. I wonder where she gets that from?

DAWN: Our Pie is also a slob. I wonder where she gets that from?

SEAN: [*Breathing in and exhaling happily.*] Oh, isn't it wonderful! So wonderful!

DAWN: What?

SEAN: To be talking about her in the present tense. To be choosing books for her to read. To be doing her laundry.

DAWN: You do her laundry then. Be my guest.

SEAN: I will!

DAWN: Hah. [*Beat; Quietly:*] Yes. It's wonderful.

SEAN: We were losing her, Dawn.

DAWN: I can't talk about it yet, okay? I can only do the next thing, one thing at a time, or I won't be able to do anything. And she needs things to be done.

SEAN: I'll get in touch with all her professors.

DAWN: Great.

SEAN: I still wish I could get my head around the cause-and-effect of this thing. Who gets pneumonia these days? Sick people. Old people.

DAWN: Poor people.

SEAN: People with compromised immune systems . . . oh my God.

DAWN: What?

SEAN: Maybe she has HIV.

DAWN: [*Frightened.*] What? What are you talking about?

SEAN: HIV! Maybe her immune system is compromised, which is why it couldn't fight off whatever was giving her the sore throat—

DAWN: Oh my God.

SEAN: —and then she caught some other bug or something when she went skiing, which got into her lungs where it blossomed into pneumonia and—

DAWN: Stop. You stop it right there. They gave her blood tests in the hospital when she was admitted. They would have tested her for HIV, and somebody would have told us. The specialist never said a word about HIV, and he's such a cold competent bastard he would have said something because it would have figured in his treatment of her. Stupid fuck.

SEAN: The specialist or me?

DAWN: You, you stupid fuck.

SEAN: Why am I a stupid fuck?

DAWN: For scaring me. For scaring the shit out of me before I could think straight.

SEAN: I'm sorry. It occurred to me, that's all—

DAWN: Shut up and sit there. Don't do anything. Don't say anything. Pet Malmsey. [*Beat.*]

SEAN: Poor old Malmsey. All dirty and ragged.

DAWN: Malmsey is fine.

SEAN: When did we get Malmsey?

DAWN: Who knows. Malmsey's always been there.

SEAN: What would we have done with him if she had died . . .

DAWN: Will you shut up? Malmsey is going to the hospital to be with Pie.

SEAN: Would we have buried him with her, do you think? In the coffin?

Without warning DAWN physically attacks
SEAN, smashing him with her fists as hard as
she can. He protects himself by covering up and
lets her pound him until she exhausts herself.
Her anger finally turns to tears and exhaustion.
He catches her as she slumps.

DAWN: While I was watching her die—

SEAN: She's not going to die.

DAWN: While I was watching her die, I hated her for doing
this to me. For turning my life into helplessness. It was the
first time in my life I wished I had a soul because I would
have sold it to the devil to make her well. I'd have given
anything, my arms, my eyes, my sanity, my life, anybody's
life, just to have a chance—no guarantees, just a chance! —
to see her smile again, to see her get up out of that bed, to
be Pie, not a corpse. I never knew fear before, but I knew it
then. Fear chokes you. You can't breathe. Your teeth
chatter. I thought that was a myth, but I heard this loud
noise and felt the room bouncing around and it was my
own teeth rattling in my own head. You want to scream at
people so they're scared too, but your voice just gives out
this polite little kind of croak. You want to tell someone in
charge that the joke is over, buster, that it's time to stop
this shit and let it be yesterday again when everything was
fine. Love is awful, it's awful, I didn't know how awful. I
didn't know the world could go empty so fast. I didn't know
her feet were so skinny and her toes could get so blue.
There's a little scab on her ankle that was healing even
though she was going to die. And if she had died, I would
have been dead too, not literally, I guess, but worse than
dead, because I still could feel and there would only be
emptiness to feel and helplessness and the awfulness of
having loved.

SEAN: But she's not dead. She's alive. We're alive. We still
have her.

DAWN: We still have her.

> They embrace as if holding on to life itself. Malmsey falls out of SEAN's hand to the floor. They ignore it.

SCENE SEVEN: "The whistling groundhog."

> The bar of a trendy restaurant. DAWN and SEAN sit on bar-stools, studying menus and nursing glasses of red wine. DAWN is in a fashionable and rather daring dress; SEAN wears a conservative suit. Both wear reading glasses.

SEAN: Ostrich.

DAWN: Eel.

SEAN: Tapinade.

DAWN: Brandade.

SEAN: Farrotto.

DAWN: Quinoa.

SEAN: Fusion.

DAWN: Neo-nouvelle.

SEAN: Rip-off.

DAWN: Expense account.

> They put down their menus and take off their reading glasses simultaneously. They sip their wine.

SEAN: Good finish.

DAWN: Cherry under-taste.

SEAN: A bit.

DAWN: Too much. [*She swirls the wine in her glass and holds it up.*]

SEAN: Legs.

DAWN: Tree trunks.

SEAN: Glycerin.

DAWN: Robitussin.

SEAN: I thought Evan was coming.

DAWN: I thought you were bringing a date.

SEAN: Not if Pie's going to pick up the check. A place like this? With wine and tip? We're talking a hundred bucks a head at least. My male vanity isn't so fragile it has to be bolstered by some bimbo who's going to cost my little girl an extra hundred.

DAWN: I didn't know you were into bimbos.

SEAN: I'm not.

DAWN: What about simple female companionship?

SEAN: Female companionship is never simple. So where's Evan tonight?

DAWN: Haven't the faintest idea. Which is not quite true, but it sounds good. [*Beat.*] We've separated.

SEAN: No.

DAWN: Yes.

SEAN: When did this happen?

65

DAWN: Well, we haven't been living together for almost a year. But we haven't been sleeping together for—

SEAN: That's fine, enough detail. Pie never said a word.

DAWN: She doesn't know. No one has been informed except the principal parties who informed each other with a mutual boot up each other's ass. And now you.

SEAN: Why the big secret?

DAWN: No secret. Everybody at the firm knows, though they're too intimidated to say anything. And why bother Pie? Not that it would plunge her into terminal gloom or anything.

SEAN: She's been pretty absorbed in her job. Must take after her Mom.

DAWN: And her Dad. The hours you put in.

SEAN: Keeps me out of trouble. Do you really think she's putting this on her expense account? I didn't even know she had an expense account.

DAWN: Drink up. Our girl is a Success. God help her. [*Beat.*]

SEAN: So what happened between you and Evan?

DAWN: An old dull tale, signifying nothing.

SEAN: Porking his secretary.

DAWN: Actually I think she might have been the only exception.

SEAN: I'm sorry. That kind of . . . thing is degrading. You don't deserve that.

DAWN: I might. But thank you.

SEAN: So this is kind of like a date.

DAWN: What is?

SEAN: This. You and me. We can pretend to be a couple getting to know each other and—

DAWN: Hi, Sean, I'm your ex-wife Dawn, and our grown-up daughter is twenty minutes late.

SEAN: Okay, okay. With Pie, you know, you've got to figure on thirty minutes late at least. It's like everybody else is on Daylight Savings and she's on Standard. In which case you can tell yourself when she finally does come that she's half an hour early.

DAWN: What?

SEAN: Never mind.

DAWN: No, seriously. I have no idea what you're talking about.

SEAN: It's not worth explaining. Whenever I try to make a joke, it ends up that I have to explain it, which totally destroys it except it's never very funny to begin with. Which might be why I don't have a date tonight.

DAWN: Oh, I get it! Daylight Savings is an hour ahead, so Pie being late can seem like she's early if you count backwards. Sort of. That's very weird, Sean. Promise me you won't tell that joke to anyone you don't know.

SEAN: I promise.

DAWN: Couldn't get a date tonight, huh. Poor guy. So that deal about saving Pie money was really like this pathetic face-saver.

SEAN: Not that pathetic.

DAWN: Well, don't take it to heart. I'm just as pathetic as you are.

SEAN: I don't see how either of us is pathetic. Especially you. You're constantly traveling all over the world. I read about you on the Business Page all the time, representing big foundations, getting quoted—

DAWN: You read about me on the Business Page? For true?

SEAN: For true.

DAWN: That's so sweet.

SEAN: And I don't even understand the Business Page. But I always turn to it right away—well, after the Sports—and look for you. Whenever your name is mentioned, I read the whole article.

DAWN: Well, you must get pretty bored. I'm usually mentioned once, early on, and then I'm abandoned. I'm the snappy lead-in, jab and counter, then they bring in the heavy-weights for the kill.

SEAN: No. You're a player. When you speak, people listen.

DAWN: I think that line is under copyright for another firm, so I hereby disclaim any connection or complicity in your utterance of it and its assignation. [*SEAN laughs.*] At least you're laughing.

SEAN: You're funny.

DAWN: Am I? I forgot that. [*Beat.*] I Google you sometimes, you know.

SEAN: Really? Why?

DAWN: To see if you've written anything new.

SEAN: That's a laugh.

DAWN: Why? You're a wonderful writer. You just have to give yourself a chance.

SEAN: I'm not a writer. A writer writes. I don't even keep a notebook any more.

DAWN: But your imagination is still at work, you react to things differently from normal people, you see things, you hear.

SEAN: Not me. Deaf, blind, and dumb.

DAWN: Don't say that.

SEAN: It's true. I've become totally normal. It's a relief. You know the truth about me? I'd rather do a little thing well than try to do a big thing. Writing's a big thing. Too big for me. Or maybe that's just what I make it for myself. [*Beat*.] You're the one who does big things, Dawn.

DAWN: Nope. Pie maybe. If she doesn't fall in love with her expense account.

SEAN: Oh, that'll never happen—

DAWN: It's a vile seducer, an expense account. It makes you feel oh-so-important. Oh-so-in-control. Oh-so-loved.

SEAN: This bank job is just a stepping-stone for her. She's got her whole life before her, she can do anything she wants, be anything she wants. She's fluent in French, pretty good in Italian, Yale Law, she's going places. Hell, she's already gone to more places than I've ever dreamed of, Paris, Barcelona, Singapore, Hong Kong—

DAWN: She's never been in Paris.

SEAN: She's in Paris half a dozen times a year! She works for a French bank!

DAWN: She's never been anywhere. Just like her mom hasn't. We both travel to places all over the world, but we never get anywhere. Always in transit. Never there.

SEAN: Sure, okay, I see what you mean, hotels, conference rooms . . . elevators. Well, that's just globalization, right? You're still out there, in the great world. I'm stuck in one little office. You're just going through a bad patch. You'll feel better when the soap-opera stuff with Evan is over. Not to make light of it or anything. And Pie seems happy. She loves her life.

DAWN: She never thinks about it if that's what you mean. We've raised a success. [*Raising her glass in a toast.*] To Pie, our success story! [*DAWN drains her glass.*]

SEAN: Easy.

DAWN: Can we get another drink around here?

SEAN: I know you're upset about your marriage—or if you'd rather not talk about it, I understand—

DAWN: No, I don't mind. Evan and me? What is there to talk about? There was very little there to begin with, and what there was became nothing. *Voilá.* I talked about it. Questions from the floor?

SEAN: You're saying you left me for nothing?

DAWN: I left you for ambition and sex. Are they nothing? Maybe. [*Beat.*] Truth is I left you because of Pie.

SEAN: Because of Pie? How can you say that? Our divorce shattered Pie—

DAWN: Yeah. But it had to be. You couldn't win for losing. And I wanted Pie to feel . . . oh-so-loved.

70

SEAN: But I love Pie!

DAWN: Not the way an expense account loves a girl. You have no idea. [*She picks up the menu again.*] What's a "*siffleux*"?

SEAN: What?

DAWN: The name of this restaurant is *Le Siffleux*. What's a "*siffleux*"?

SEAN: A whistling ground-hog.

DAWN: How do you know that?

SEAN: I asked Pie when she told me where we should meet.

DAWN: See that? She talks to you. She doesn't talk to me.

SEAN: I asked her! [*Beat.*]

DAWN: How does a ground-hog whistle?

SEAN: Like this. [*He whistles Beethoven's "Ode to Joy" from the Ninth Symphony.*]

DAWN: A ground-hog whistles like a ring you download for a cell-phone?

SEAN: So I'm told.

DAWN: And they whistle because why? They can't get the tune out of their heads? They're dwarfs marching off to work?

SEAN: Because they're afraid.

DAWN: Oh. [*She very deliberately whistles "The Ode to Joy." Beat.*]

SEAN: Dawn, let's get married.

DAWN: What?

SEAN: Let's get married! We can announce it to Pie when she gets here. This can be our engagement party. I'm serious! Pie comes and we pretend business-as-usual. But I tell the waiter to bring us a bottle of champagne like a couple of minutes after she arrives—it comes—we pop the cork—we tell her we're engaged. Surprise!

DAWN: Why do you want to marry me?

SEAN: Because you're my wife.

DAWN: Excuse me?

SEAN: Well, I've always felt you were my wife, no matter who you were married to.

DAWN: You're out of your mind.

SEAN: I love you, Dawn and I'm lonely without you! Every woman I've ever spent any time with since we broke up has known that. Why don't you know it?

DAWN: This is our first date. You're not allowed to say you love me. It's not fair.

SEAN: It's not our first date. I think you love me too. We're a part of each other. Don't you feel that?

DAWN: You don't tell a girl you love her when you know she's afraid. It's unfair, like blowing away a groundhog with an Uzi when he's whistling Beethoven.

SEAN: We're both groundhogs whistling Beethoven.

DAWN: Just because we're whistling doesn't mean we're in love.

72

SEAN: There's no one else in the world I'd rather be with than you right now. Is there someone else you'd rather be with?

DAWN: It's not fair! [*Beat.*] Are you proposing to me because of me or because of Pie?

SEAN: Pie's got nothing to do with this.

DAWN: Are you sure about that?

SEAN: There's no you and me without Pie. We can't deny reality.

DAWN: But we can turn it into romance? You're still a writer, Sean. You're writing a story about you and me, and this is your happy ending.

SEAN: Well, we don't have to announce anything tonight. I just want us to think about it.

DAWN: Oh, baby. Can't you see? It's not me you want to marry. You want Pie to have her mommy and daddy back again. I left you once because of Pie, Sean. At least that's what I told myself. But I'm not going back to you because of her.

SEAN: You're talking in riddles. Maybe this is not the time to discuss it, but let's keep the dialogue open at least. We'll have a real date, just the two of us, where we can relax and talk about things—

DAWN: Things. Well, it's a pretty thought.

SEAN: It's not just a thought! What about dinner tomorrow night? Just the two of us.

DAWN: You know what would happen if we did?

SEAN: We'd have fun.

DAWN: We'd spend the whole night talking about her.

SEAN: Well, that's fun, isn't it? Who better to talk about? [*DAWN looks at him.*] Fine. We won't talk about Pie. I can accept that. I promise you I won't even mention—

DAWN: You're very sweet and you're very sincere and you're very persuasive, which is why I should get the hell out of here. Now. [*DAWN gulps down SEAN's glass of wine and gets up to go.*]

SEAN: Where are you going?

DAWN: Home.

SEAN: Home? You live in an empty house.

DAWN: Emptiness has its advantages.

SEAN: What advantages?

DAWN: It leaves you alone.

SEAN: But you can't go now. Pie has been looking forward to this for weeks—

DAWN: And sure as hell she'll give me shit about it tomorrow. It's better this way, dad. Without me.

SEAN: Don't say that. Why say that?

DAWN: Because Pie is the only woman in the world who can give Dad the female companionship he prefers. For him she keeps it simple. [*She leaves.*]

SCENE EIGHT: "Class."

> An airport sitting-area. SEAN, embarrassed, is
> wheeling a small carry-on suitcase away from

74

the Executive-Class Lounge, where DAWN is
haranguing someone off-stage.

DAWN: I know, you're just doing your job, but something
tells me you won't be doing it very much longer.

SEAN: It's all right, Dawn. Forget it.

DAWN: [*To the official:*] One last thing: here's my card. I
have your name and you should know the name of the
person who's going to turn your life into a living hell.

SEAN: Leave it. He's right. I don't have an executive-class
ticket.

DAWN: No reason I can't buy you a drink in the executive-
class lounge. I'm not allowed to have a guest? What's
executive-class about that?

SEAN: Not when the guest is economy-class. And I don't
want a drink.

DAWN: Well, I'm not going to sit out here in meaningless
existentialist hell. It smells like popcorn.

SEAN: Well, go back to meaningful executive-class heaven.
I'll see you in Paris.

DAWN: I know! We'll go to the desk and upgrade you. It's
on me.

SEAN: That's very generous. No. Thanks.

DAWN: It's nothing! Nothing! If I'd known we were going to
be on the same plane, I would have had my secretary do
this from the get-go. Nothing!

SEAN: But I don't want to fly executive-class.

DAWN: You don't want to drink champagne and get a great meal and stretch your legs out in a bed? You want to sit up all night scrunched up like a pretzel, gnawing on pretzels?

SEAN: I like pretzels.

DAWN: That's cannibalistic. The truth is you don't want to be with me.

SEAN: Hey, who's the one who told me to stop calling her?

DAWN: For a date! For fantasy games!

SEAN: Yeah well, water under the bridge. Look, I'll make you a counter-offer. Stay with me here until our flight's announced.

DAWN: How is that a counter-offer? What do I get out of this?

SEAN: Popcorn. You used to like popcorn.

DAWN: You'll buy me popcorn?

SEAN: I'll buy you popcorn.

DAWN: Deal. [*She sits down. He goes to buy popcorn.*] I hate popcorn.

> DAWN takes out her Blackberry and checks her messages. SEAN returns with popcorn. They both nibble at it during the remainder of the play.

DAWN: No extra butter?

SEAN: You don't like extra butter.

DAWN: Aw. You remember! [*Beat.*]

SEAN: Where are you staying in Paris?

DAWN: I don't know. Where I always stay. Ask my secretary.

SEAN: How do you know where to go when you get off the plane?

DAWN: I follow the guy who holds my name up on a card. We get into a car. I get out at a hotel. How about you?

SEAN: Metro.

DAWN: I'm impressed.

SEAN: Actually a bus first, then the Metro—

DAWN: Sounds like an adventure! Tell you what. You let me upgrade you to executive-class, and when we get there I'll ditch my driver and go with you on the bus and Metro.

SEAN: Counter-offer: I don't accept the upgrade, but you pay for the bus and Metro—

DAWN: No deal.

SEAN: Let me finish—and we only take public transportation during the rest of the trip, for which you pay and I serve as your personal guide.

DAWN: Can you guarantee me a seat on the Metro during rush hour?

SEAN: No.

DAWN: Promise me no one will have B.O. and pinch my ass?

SEAN: No.

DAWN: Swear to me that no one will tread on my Manolo Blahniks?

SEAN: No.

DAWN: Then no deal.

SEAN: [*Laughing.*] You've sure come a long way since your Legal Aid days.

DAWN: I give a hefty annual donation. Seems to make them happy.

SEAN: Not to mention your tax accountant.

DAWN: I like to spread cheer wherever I can. [*Beat.*]

SEAN: I take it our future in-laws didn't invite you to stay with them either.

DAWN: Why should they?

SEAN: Oh, I don't know. Gesture of family solidarity? We're going to be the grandparents of the same children some day. Hopefully.

DAWN: We'll hate each other on sight.

SEAN: Think positive.

DAWN: They'll critique us through their big French noses oh-so-intellectually behind our backs, and we'll just have to take it. No! I know how we can get back at them.

SEAN: How?

DAWN: We let them take us out to dinner at some chic Parisian restaurant and we order fried clams and coleslaw and a couple of brew-skis—The Crillon! That's the place.

SEAN: Should have guessed. Well, I will not be staying at the Hotel Crillon.

DAWN: It's a dump.

SEAN: It's the best hotel in Paris.

DAWN: It would be. Hey, stay with me! It'll be fun. They always put me in this huge suite. Sitting room. Flowers. Fruit. Two queen beds. We can throw fruit and discuss our in-laws across the divide. I promise I won't make sexual overtures.

SEAN: Maybe I'll make sexual overtures.

DAWN: Goody. How about you jump out of the closet and throw me down on the bed while I scream rape in a little tiny voice?

SEAN: Someone might hear through the walls and call the gendarmes.

DAWN: They won't. The French understand these things. You really want to fuck me?

SEAN: Jesus, Dawn. Language, tone, situation—

DAWN: More to the point: do I want to fuck you?

SEAN: Do you think you could possibly lower your voice—

DAWN: You know, you have asked me to lower my voice seventy-four billion times since the day we met. I've made a very exact count. Are you ashamed of me? Sometimes I'm ashamed of me, but it's not because I talk too loud in public.

SEAN: We're both a little on edge, I guess.

DAWN: You mean because our little girl's marrying a ratty Frenchman.

SEAN: Rudolphe is not ratty. And be good. This is a French flight. There are French people all around us.

DAWN: Surrounded by frogs! Well, if they think I'm going to kiss them—

SEAN: Shush.

DAWN: Seventy-four billion and one. I hate airports. I hate France. I hate Europe. I hate in-laws. Who are these people that I have to take them seriously just because their ratty son has the hots for my daughter and wants to put an ocean between us?

SEAN: More than the hots. He loves her.

DAWN: Rat, son of rats.

SEAN: Please remember that Pie will have to live with them, we don't. We get to leave, but she's going to stay.

DAWN: So don't foul her nest. Yeah, yeah. I'll be on my best manners. Rudolphe. Jesus.

SEAN: Seems like an okay guy. Likes American sports. Well, wears a Lakers cap. Prefers soccer of course, but that's only natural. His team is Marseilles, who are not very good apparently, so he suffers a lot. Seems to make decent money as an editor-translator. His translations are inspired, according to Pie, but she would say that. Listens to classic jazz, Coltrane, Miles. Likes hip-hop, but you can't have everything. Drives an old tin-can Renault with the shift on the dash. Skis—

DAWN: Eurotrash.

SEAN: No.

DAWN: So if he translates shit, why can't they live in the States?

SEAN: He translates Russian into French.

DAWN: Commie rat. So how come you know so much about this guy? You two go to summer-camp together?

SEAN: Sort of.

DAWN: Meaning?

SEAN: Well, last summer I was over there for vacation—

DAWN: I didn't know that.

SEAN: Just for a week, ten days, you know how I do. So this time I stayed with Pie because she has that new big apartment in the twentieth arrondissement—very up-and-coming neighborhood—

DAWN: Cut to the chase.

SEAN: Well, the first few days she was working most of the time, but she left me maps and itineraries so I learned the Metro and got myself oriented. Then she took some time off and we went places and did stuff and that's when she introduced me to this guy, Rudolphe. I knew right away.

DAWN: What right away? What?

SEAN: That it was serious.

DAWN: How did you know? She didn't cook for him, did she?

SEAN: He cooked.

DAWN: Fairy rat.

SEAN: I figured out that they'd been living together in Pie's new place, and he had very politely got out of the way for me before I arrived. There were signs of a man around— you know, after-shave and sneakers and stuff—but it was none of my business, so I didn't say anything. After we got to know each other, I told them I'd be happy at a hotel, but they wouldn't permit it. Pie spent the last few nights I was there at his place. They'd drive me back to hers at the end of the day, and then they'd go off to his, which I actually did get to see once. A real rat-trap.

DAWN: Hah!

SEAN: I don't know why they were so shy at first about living together. Or maybe they were just shy about sleeping together with me in the next room. Maybe Rudolphe's a moaner.

DAWN: Or Pie is.

SEAN: Whatever.

DAWN: Well, we're the ones who are getting screwed. She's going to be a lousy ex-pat, which is such a boring precious thing to be, and she's going to have lousy denatured ex-pat kids who will speak with a creepy accent, and they'll live thousands of miles away and I'll never see them except on fucked-up special occasions when I'll be their American grandma with blue hair and a garbage mouth, and they'll roll their eyes behind my back.

SEAN: She's chosen her life. Which is what we've raised her to do. And you'll never have blue hair, Grandma.

DAWN: But they will roll their eyes, Grandpa.

SEAN: What do you care?

DAWN: I must be a tiny bit self-conscious, don't you think?

SEAN: But why? You're a class act. You have nothing to feel self-conscious about.

DAWN: I need a drink.

SEAN: You don't need a drink. Why are you so uptight about meeting these people? Would it be different if they were Americans? It's three thousand miles from coast to coast, and it's three thousand miles across the Atlantic. She'd be just as far if she lived in some far corner of the States—

DAWN: Mileage statistics don't cut it with me, Sean. Americans are Americans. Even if I hated their politics or loathed their accent or resented their car, she'd still be in my world. I wouldn't be losing her as bad.

SEAN: I suppose you always lose your child a little when she gets married—

DAWN: Not the same. She's rejecting us. She's rejecting our world.

SEAN: No. She loves us—

DAWN: Yeah, yeah, she loves us, we're her parents, blah blah blah. But she's choosing to become someone else, someone we'll know less and less. Oh, I'll understand the business side of her life—the spreadsheet's the universal language. But her food, her clothes, the TV shows she watches, the way she'll gab to friends over the phone, the way she'll talk to her kids' teachers and they'll talk to her, it'll all be stuff we can't really understand. And it's not just the language. She'll be somewhere else. Somewhere we can never be. Where even the love is different.

SEAN: Love is love wherever it is. She'll love her children the way we've loved her. She'll be their mom.

DAWN: Their *maman.*

SEAN: It's the same. On the other hand, she might not even have children.

DAWN: Which would be the worst rejection of all.

SEAN: It's not about us. It would be their choice. But something tells me they will want to have children. And those children will be very happy to have a crazy American grandma and grandpa. They'll think we're funny. Especially you.

DAWN: Thanks.

SEAN: They'll come over and visit us and I'll make out endless itineraries and you'll make them laugh and we'll buy them fast food and take them to Disney World and—

DAWN: They have fast food in Paris and Disney invaded France long ago.

SEAN: Okay, Yankee Stadium.

DAWN: It's just a great big mall now. Nothing's real in America.

SEAN: The Grand Canyon! The Maine coast! The big sequoias of the Pacific Northwest!

DAWN: What are you, selling vacation packages now? Why don't we just sing them "America the Beautiful" on Skype and save air-fare?

SEAN: We'll buy them popcorn. [*Beat.*]

DAWN: Maybe I will fly coach. [*Beat.*] No. That would be socialist.

SEAN: You've earned your executive-class. Enjoy it.

DAWN: Champagne and room to stretch out.

SEAN: And I've earned the right to be a pretzel.

DAWN: At least we're going to the same place.

SEAN: And get to see our Pie! [*They kiss.*]

DAWN: Your lips are salty.

SEAN: So are yours.

They hold hands and sit silently, looking out.

END

Alien Hand Syndrome
By Michael Erickson

Michael Erickson's plays have been produced at the Ensemble Studio Theatre, NYC, A Director's Theatre, LA, The Empty Space, Seattle, Mixed Blood Theatre, Minneapolis, the Cleveland Public Theatre, the Imaginary Theatre co., St. Louis, and many other theaters. His *Apologies from the Lower Decks*, a commission with Malashock Dance & Co., toured the country and was filmed for PBS. He has been awarded an NEA Playwriting Fellowship, California Arts Fellowship in Playwriting, and the Mobil International Prize in Playwriting, Royal Exchange Theatre, Manchester, England. He holds an M.F.A. in Theater from the University of California, San Diego. Presently, he teaches playwriting and dramatic literature at Webster University in St. Louis.

Alien Hand Syndrome was first produced by MadLab Theatre in Columbus, Ohio, as part of the Theater Roulettte series, a national new play competition, April - May, and again in August, 2009, as part of the best of the Roulette.

Alien Hand Syndrome also won the 15th Annual Moving Arts one-act competition and was produced at the Son of Semele Theater in Los Angeles, October – November, 2009.

For rights contact Michael Erickson at ericksmi@earthlink.net, or 314-961-1954.

Characters:
Mark, late 20's
Emily, late 20's
Mr. Smalls, Dr. Carmody, 30's to 50's
(can be played by same actor)

Setting:
Various locations. Mark's home, an office, a bus stop, a movie theater, etc. Alien Hand works best with a simple, flexible set design for quick changes.

SCENE ONE

> Mark's home. Mark, dressed in a t-shirt, sits in a straight back chair in front of a kitchen table. He stretches his hands out in front of him and examines them. He places his hands palm down on the table top.
>
> Mark looks from one hand to the other. He wiggles his fingers. Stops. Wiggles them again. Stops.
>
> The index finger of his right hand rapidly taps the table top, then stops abruptly. Frightened, Mark stares at his right hand. His breathing is shallow, rapid. The fingers of the right hand begin to spasm. Mark concentrates hard, willing his hand to stop. It does. Mark relaxes, worn out from the effort.
>
> Suddenly, Mark's right hand jerks to life. It's fingers dance a macabre jig on the table.

MARK: Stop!

> He tries to seize his right hand with his left hand. It evades the left and slaps his face.

MARK: Goddammit, stop!

> After a bizarre chase, the left hand manages to catch the right hand, pinning it to the table top. Mark leans over weight over his left hand. He is breathing hard. Sweating.
>
> He looks out at the audience. A realization, then terror.

> BLACKOUT

SCENE TWO

> Mark's office. He wears a wrinkled jacket and
> carries a cubicle watering can in his right hand.
> He's on his way to water his ficus.
>
> A young woman, Emily, stops him and begins
> signing excitedly. Mark stares at her
> bewildered. Emily stops and waits for a reply.
> She smiles and nods expectantly.

MARK: Um...I....

> Emily enthusiastically re-signs her message to
> Mark. He backs up a bit, gingerly holding the
> watering can.

MARK: I'm sorry, I don't know...

> Emily smiles and waves a hand to start over.
> She signs as she speaks.

EMILY: You...know...American...sign...language...

MARK: No. No, I...

EMILY: Yes! I saw you! [*She points.*] I'm in the next
cubicle. Catty-corner.

MARK: Where?

EMILY: [*Holds out her hand.*] I'm Emily.

> He juggles the watering can and shakes her
> hand. She seems to tingle at his touch.

EMILY: Oh, my. You're not deaf?

MARK: No. I'm Mark.

EMILY: You have a very sexy hand shake.

MARK: I do?

EMILY: Yes. Are your parents deaf?

MARK: Not really.

EMILY: Shoot. I thought we could make jokes about our deaf parents. You know. Commiserate. Not that I don't love 'em. But they can drive you batty.

MARK: My dad's a little hard of hearing.

EMILY: Oh. You have a deaf girlfriend.

MARK: No.

EMILY: So how do you know ASL?

MARK: I don't.

EMILY: Yes you do. I saw you cuss out the assistant divisional manager behind his back. It was brilliant.

MARK: What? I couldn't have. How could I?

> Mr. Smalls, the Assistant Divisional Manager, can be heard screaming "Mark" from off-stage. Mark freezes.

> Mr. Smalls enters, furious, panting, out of breath. He is a middle aged man stuffed into a white shirt. He waves several sheets of paper at Mark. He starts to speak, says nothing. Starts again. Nothing comes out.

> Emily squeezes Mark's arm and tiptoes away.

MARK: Mr. Smalls?

SMALLS: Assassin!

MARK: Sir?

SMALLS: Murderer! Traitor! Now I have to answer for this!

MARK: I don't understand.

SMALLS: Tell me you didn't write these emails! "Incompetent." "Worst manager ever." "Small man complex." "Foot fetishist!" "Eats his own snot!"

MARK: I didn't write that!

SMALLS: Liar! All from your email address. [*Rifles though the papers.*] And this one. A hand written note on the cafeteria bulletin board. Is this not your handwriting?

MARK: Well, it looks like my...hand...but I didn't write it!

SMALLS: Suggesting people contact me to start a wife-swapping club! On the cafeteria bulletin board! Posted without prior approval!

MARK: I swear to God, sir. I didn't write that...any of that.

> His right hand wants to throw water at Smalls. He wrestles with his hand.

SMALLS: That and the sign language. Oh, you think I didn't hear about that? Very funny. Well, you've just laughed yourself out of a job. What are you doing?

MARK: [*He struggles with his hand.*] Please, sir, there must be some mistake.

SMALLS: Stop that. What is that? Some kind of fit?

MARK: Oh no, oh no!

SMALLS: [*Backing away.*] Don't you even think about it!

MARK: [*To his hand.*] STOP!

BLACKOUT

SCENE THREE

> Bus Stop. Mark sits on a bus stop bench. On his knees he holds a cardboard box filled with his cubicle possessions: a couple sickly plants, a stuffed donkey, etc. He stares ahead, in a daze.
>
> Emily enters wearing an overcoat. She sits beside him. He doesn't notice her.

EMILY: Mark? [*Beat.*] I heard what happened. I'm...I'm sorry.

MARK: Oh, hi...Emily.

EMILY: [*Simultaneously with the above.*] Emily. [*Beat.*] I just wanted you to know...that I thought what you did was...great.

MARK: What did I do? [*He stares ahead, puzzled.*] I'm not sure I know.

EMILY: You took a stand. Made a statement.

MARK: Did I?

> A long silence. Mark's right hand takes Emily's hand. She looks down, pleased. Unaware, Mark closes his eyes and leans back. He presses his left hand to his forehead.

MARK: I don't understand what's happening to me...

> His right hand begins to caress Emily's neck and cheek. She leans into his touch.

94

MARK: It's like something's taken control of me. I don't know how to explain it.

EMILY: Yes. Lately, I've had the same feeling.

> She takes his hand and kisses his fingers, then presses his hand to her heart. His hand begins to undo her coat. Mark opens his eyes.

MARK: Like I find myself doing things, and I don't know why I'm doing them. Like those emails. The note. I have no memory of that. And yet, I must've done those things. [*Beat.*] Oh, look. A pigeon.

> The hand moves its way down to her lap. It begins to caress her thigh. Emily takes a deep, shuddering breath.

MARK: It's all so peculiar. Like I'm there but not there. Like the left hand doesn't know what the right hand is doing.

> Emily moans and presses his hand closer to her. Mark turns to look at her, sees his hand buried in her crotch. He jumps up, spilling his box.

MARK: Oh my God! I am so sorry. I, I, I don't know how that happened. Please, please, please, don't think that I'm like that.

> Emily stands, embarrasses and flustered.

EMILY: NO no no! It's...

MARK: You must think I'm a, a....

EMILY: It's nothing. Really. I didn't mind. So much. I mean. Oh, God, what am I saying?

MARK: It's like my hand has a mind of its own. Honestly. It's not me.

EMILY: Oh. Okay. [*Beat.*] Well. I should, you know, get back.

MARK: Oh sure, sure, sure. Again...I'm sorry. The hand. I don't know...

EMILY: No, really. Not a problem. In fact...

MARK: What?

EMILY: This is going to sound weird. No. I should go. Okay. Well. Good luck.

> She turns to go. Mark stoops to pick up his box. She turns back to him. A short pause.

EMILY: Mark?

> He looks up at her. She smiles.

BLACKOUT

SCENE FOUR

> A doctor's office. An x-ray of a hand appears in the dark.

> Lights up on Dr. Carmody examining Mark's right hand. He has an avuncular demeanor and wears a white lab coat.

> He sits on a stool next to Mark and writes something in a chart.

DR CARMODY: Mark, the good news is it's not MS or Parkinson's.

> Mark exhales with relief.

DR CARMODY: X-rays, blood work, and the physical examination reveal nothing. However, your symptoms point to something very rare. Very rare. Mark, I believe you are suffering from what we call "alien hand syndrome."

>Mark takes in a sharp, terrified breath. His right hand suddenly snakes out and takes a pen from Dr. Carmody's pocket. The doctor takes back the pen and re-pockets it.

>Mark's hand begins to roam wildly.

MARK: Did you say, "alien hand syndrome?"

DR CARMODY: We call it that because the afflicted hand begins to behave in a transient manner. As if it's being controlled by some "alien entity."

MARK: You're kidding.

DR CARMODY: I assure you, men from Mars are not controlling your hand.

MARK: But...what is this? How did I get this?

DR CARMODY: We don't know exactly. The cause could be neurological.

MARK: What!?

DR CARMODY: Perhaps an aneurysm. A few more tests might reveal the culprit.

MARK: OhmyGod.

DR CARMODY: Mark, this is rarely fatal. Inconvenient, yes.

MARK: How long could this last?

DR CARMODY: We don't know, exactly. Case studies suggest five to twenty years. Often longer.

MARK: Longer?

DR CARMODY: I'm sorry, Mark. I know you wouldn't want me to sugar coat this.

MARK: I think I'd prefer it if you did.

DR CARMODY: Here's what we know. In some rare cases, a hand begins to act independently of the conscious mind. Why? We don't always know. [*Beat.*] The hand begins to create an independent life for itself. It writes letters, fixes meals, even works without the person, the owner, knowing.

MARK: That's exactly what happened to me. I was fired for writing emails I didn't write.

DR CARMODY: Ah. With many degenerative diseases the afflicted limb becomes less useful as the illness progresses. Here, we have almost the opposite. Ah, Mark? My cell phone.

> Mark looks at his hand. The hand has taken the doctor's cell phone. Mark takes the cell phone away and gives it to Dr. Carmody.

MARK: Damn you!

> The hand slaps him. He fights with the hand. Dr. Carmody breaks up the fight. Mark pins his right hand under his left arm.

DR CARMODY : You must try to remain calm. Fighting with yourself will only exacerbate the problem.

MARK: I'm sorry. [*He begins to tear up.*] Dr. Carmody. How could this be happening?

DR CARMODY: I am sorry. But try to look on the positive side.

MARK: What positive side?

DR CARMODY: Some people learn to accept their alien hand. Make peace with it. An alien hand can bring new talents, new abilities to the host. Think of it as a misbehaving child. Keeping the hand occupied seems to help. Busy work.

MARK: What if I can't control it?

DR CARMODY: There are other options. One could bind afflicted limb. Strap it to your body. Limit its mobility.

MARK: Oh, God. There must be other options.

DR CARMODY: Well, case studies in Brazil indicate that amputation often alleviates the problem.

MARK: Amputation! I could never—

DR CARMODY: We're not there yet, so don't let's panic. Why don't I write you a prescription for something to help calm you? Now what did I do with my pad?

> He feels around in his pockets for his script pad. It's gone. Mark sees his hand with the script. He takes it and gives it to the doctor.

DR CARMODY: Mischievous rascal. Thank you, Mark.

> He reaches in a pocket for his pen. It's gone. Mark takes the pen from his right hand and gives it to the doctor.

DR CARMODY: Thanks.

MARK: Sorry.

As the doctor writes a prescription, Mark glares at his hand. Its fingers curl into a menacing claw.

BLACKOUT

SCENE FIVE

Mark's home. Mark is dressing for a date. He tries to put on a blue shirt. His right hand doesn't like it and begins to take it off. Mark brushes off his right hand and tries to get back into the blue shirt. Again, his right hand starts to pull off the shirt. Mark wrestles into the wrinkled shirt.

MARK: I already told you. I'm wearing the blue shirt. [*His right hand holds up a black turtle neck sweater.*] No. I already said no to the turtle neck. [*The hand insists.*] I don't care what you think. [*The hand pleads.*] Look, it's my body. I decide what I wear. Okay? [*The hand goes limp.*] You understand? Good. [*Beat.*] I haven't been out with anyone in months. And no sarcastic gestures. [*The hand tries to look innocent.*] Oh, don't give me that. I know what you're thinking. Now, I gotta get going.

He begins to tuck in the shirt. At first, the right hand cooperates, then suddenly it pulls out the shirt tales and rips off the shirt.

MARK: Goddammit!

A violent struggle follows. Finally, Mark gains the upper hand. He pins the hand under his knee.

MARK: You are not the boss of me!   Do you understand that? You are not the boss of me!

BLACKOUT

100

SCENE SIX

> At the movies. Dim, flickering light. Tinny
> sound of movie music. Emily and Mark sit
> facing the audience. They share popcorn.
> Mark is wearing the black turtle neck sweater.

MARK: ...and then the lady on the bus slapped me.

EMILY: Oh, Mark.

MARK: Yeah, like wham. "What do you think you're
doing?" And I say, "It's not me!" And they're all looking at
me "like what an asshole." [*Beat.*] Why can't I have a nice
alien hand? You know? One that helped out. Did good
things, wrote thank you notes, held doors open, instead of
flipping off people, or touching their boobs.

EMILY: [*She takes his right hand and holds it to her.*] I'm
sure it's good. It wants to be good. [*She stokes it.*] He's
just misunderstood.

MARK: He?

EMILY: Well...you know.

MARK: Right.

EMILY: [*Beat.*] You look good in the sweater.

MARK: Thanks. It picked it out for me.

EMILY: Oh.

> She pets his hand. The hand responds.

MARK: Emily, it's fighting me...for me.

> Somewhere in the dark a voice shushes them.

EMILY: [*Whispering.*] I'm sure it's not.

101

MARK: It's gotten it's own FaceBook page. Don't ask me how. It's getting hundreds of emails from people I've never even heard of. [*He clamps his eyes shut. This is hard for him to say.*] It's...it's started doing puppet shows.

EMILY: What?

> The hand begins to caress Emily. She begins to respond.

MARK: Somehow it writes these little plays...these little Charles Dickens like plays about orphans and lost and recovered fortunes. With costumes and everything.

EMILY: Really? And you don't know about it?

MARK: Well, I find out. Eventually. It does shows for the neighborhood kids.

EMILY: Mmmmm...that's nice.

MARK: It knows how to sew. How does it know that? [*He takes a breath to compose himself.*] It had a party yesterday.

EMILY: [*Gasps.*] Oh.

MARK: It invited it's friends over. People just started showing up. People I'd never seen before. I had to go along with it. I had no choice.

> Emily kisses his hand, then presses it to her heart.

EMILY: Poor thing.

MARK: Well, at least it seems to like you.

EMILY: Yes.

MARK: Thank God it hasn't come between us. I don't know what I'd do if...

> She kisses him on the cheek. Then guides the hand to her lap. The hand is eager to comply. It unbuckles her belt.

EMILY: [*Softly.*] I think it likes me.

MARK: Dr. Carmody says I need to be patient. Give the hand things to occupy it. Busy work.

EMILY: Yes. Yes.

MARK: Try to understand it.

EMILY: Yes. Good idea.

MARK: He even suggested it may bring new experiences into my life.

EMILY: Mmmm...

> The hand is gently making love to Emily. She sprawls luxuriously in her seat.

MARK: It's certainly done that. Victorian hand puppets? FaceBook? What's that about? [*He munches some popcorn.*] It's like it's not even my hand anymore. We have nothing in common.

EMILY: [*Breathing heavily.*] Don't...worry...about...it...

MARK: Is this the movie or the previews? I can never tell with these foreign films. [*Beat.*] If we shared some interests. You know, could laugh and have a beer. But it just does its own thing. And I'm supposed to just live with it? Just go along with it? Without me it wouldn't exist. It's not the other way around. I'd like to see how it'd get by without me. That I'd like to see.

Emily suddenly throws herself on Mark and kisses him passionately. He seems surprised.

EMILY: Take me home. Now!

A swell of romantic movie music.

BLACKOUT

SCENE SEVEN

Dr. Carmody's office. Several x-rays of a human head are illuminated in the dark. The brain tissue appears as soft swirls of gray. Lights rise a bit. Dr. Carmody appears with a stethoscope and a chart.

DR CARMODY: [*To us.*] Nothing. [*He turns to the x-rays.*] We found nothing. Nothing apparent. No lesions. No aneurysms. [*To us.*] This is good news, Mark. Now, perhaps, we can look for other causes of your alien hand syndrome. I know. I know. This is disconcerting. I realize that. But you're young. You're healthy. You can overcome this. And do you know what? You'll be a better person for it. [*He smiles.*] You will be a better person for having overcome this. I'm sure of it.

BLACKOUT

SCENE EIGHT

Emily's studio apartment. Sound of love making in the dark. A woman climaxes again and again.

MARK'S VOICE: I can't do this!

EMILY'S VOICE: Don't stop!

MARK'S VOICE: This is wrong!

Sounds of a struggle. Squeaking bed. Emily
turns on a lamp next to a pull-out sofa bed.
She pulls a sheet around her as Mark struggles
into his clothes.

EMILY: What? What are you doing, Mark?

MARK: Leaving! [*His right hand reacts. Tries to stop him.*]
Stop it! Stop it! [*He swats at his right hand with his left.*]
I'm getting out of here!

EMILY: Why?

MARK: [*Stares at her in disbelief.*] Why?!

EMILY: Yes, why?

MARK: [*Holds out his right hand.*] Because of this! That's
why.

EMILY: Mark—

MARK: Don't think I haven't noticed.

EMILY: It's not what you think.

MARK: Oh, right. I've seen you two together. I know what
you're doing.

EMILY: No, Mark, no. You're mistaken.

MARK: It's like I'm just along for the ride. Good old Mark.
Just lay there in the dark while you and the hand get it on!

EMILY: What are you saying?

MARK: Isn't it obvious? You're in love with my hand. Not
me. Admit it.

The hand vehemently shakes a denial.

EMILY: No. It's you. I want you. I've never been with anyone like you.

MARK: You mean my hand.

EMILY: No.

MARK: I'm going.

   He starts to go. He slaps his hand away.

EMILY: Don't go! Please. Don't. Okay, yes. It's the hand.

   He stops and turns back to her.

EMILY: Look, I'm sorry. [*Deep breath.*] What your hand can do...it's magic. I've been with a lot of men and no one can do what you can. Believe me. The pleasure you can give a woman is beyond anything I'd ever imagined.

MARK: But it's not me!

EMILY: Yes, it is, love. It is you. You've been given a special gift. Why not accept it? [*The hand nods enthusiastically.*] Mark?

MARK: I don't know. This is too weird.

EMILY: [*She holds out her arms to him.*] Come back to bed, love. Please?

   The hand begins signing to Emily. She nods
   and signs back.

MARK: What was that?

EMILY: He says he wants to make peace with you.

MARK: Really?

EMILY: Give it a chance.

> Mark sits on the edge of the bed. The hands signs happily to Emily. She signs back.

MARK: What's it saying?

EMILY: He says his name is Hank.

MARK: Hank? It has a name?

EMILY: He says he's always been in you. Trying to find a way out.

> She kisses the hand as it signs gently on her lips.

MARK: Oh my God.

EMILY: He says he's loved me from our first touch. Remember that shiver of excitement when we first shook hands? Hank says that we are soul mates. Oh, Mark! He promises to make us both happy. Happier than we've ever been!

MARK: This is insane.

> He tries to pull back his hand. She holds on to it.

EMILY: I'm not going to let you pull us apart.

MARK: Let go of me.

EMILY: I can't, Mark. Not until you realize the importance of what we're saying to you.

MARK: We?

EMILY: Yes. There are three of us in this relationship now. And we have to be kind to one another. Do you understand that?

MARK: No, I do not. Now let me go.

> He tries to stand. She pulls his hand. Mark struggles with both his hand and Emily.

EMILY: You can't leave. Hank doesn't want to go.

MARK: "Hank" doesn't get to decide what I do. Emily, let go.

EMILY: You can't separate us.

MARK: Are you insane?

EMILY: You can't do this to us. We belong together! No! No! Please, Mark!

> He pulls away from Emily. She sprawls across the rickety sofa-bed in tears. Mark stands looking over her in horror. His hand is firmly clamped under his left arm.

EMILY: Hank!

BLACKOUT

SCENE NINE

> Mark's home. Mark, dressed in a t-shirt, sits in a straight backed chair in front of a kitchen table. His arms are stretched out on the table top. Long pause while he looks from one hand to the other. The right hand does not move on its own.

MARK: I'm not falling for it. You think I don't know what you're up to, "Hank"? [*The hand doesn't move.*] Come on.

Do something. [*Nothing.*] Hank? Hello? Hank? Are you there? [*Nothing.*] Ah...you know what's coming. Don't you? Think you can trick me. But you can't. [*No response.*] This is the end, my friend. Where we part company. [*He laughs.*] We'll see how well you manage on your own.

> He reaches under the table and raises a butcher's knife. His right hand remains remarkably passive as he holds the knife over his right arm.

MARK: Let's see. Should we take you off at the wrist? The elbow? Why take any chances? [*Grimly.*] Take the whole arm off.

> He stretches out the length of his right arm out on the table and raises the butcher's knife with his left hand. Suddenly, his right hand leaps up and seizes the left hand. Mark's hands fight for control of the butcher's knife.

> Mark twists and turns his body as he stands and tries to force his right hand down. His right arm delivers several staggering blows to his head. He stumbles, in shock, dropping the butcher's knife on the table. Both hands dive for the big knife. It is knocked off the table and slides downstage. Mark lunges over the table, landing on the floor. Both hands fight and reach for the knife. But it's the right hand that finally comes up with the butcher's knife. Mark scrambles to his knees, his left hand out defensively. His right hand holds the knife menacingly close to his throat, triumphant.

MARK: Now, Hank, you know I was only kidding. I wouldn't have done it. No. Hank? You know that. [*He slowly backs away from the knife.*] Hank? Let's call Emily. Would you like that? [*His right hand eases the knife off a bit.*] Yeah, we'll go to her. We'll never be apart again.

Would you like that? [*The butcher knife begins to droop.*]
Anything you want, Hank. From now on. Scout's honor.
[*He makes the scout salute with his left hand.*] You're
calling the shots, Hank. That's it. Good. Let's drop the
knife and go see Emily. Won't that be nice? From now on,
everything will be better.

> Mark makes a sudden grab for the knife with
> his left hand. His right hand easily evades the
> left.
>
> The butcher knife is raised for the last time.
> Mark knows that this is it. He shrieks in terror
> as the huge knife swipes at his throat.

BLACKOUT

SCENE TEN

> Emily's home. A funeral reception. There is a
> black framed portrait of Mark on a stand.
> Emily enters dressed in black. She carries a
> tissue. She pauses before the portrait of Mark
> and wipes away a tear. She's lost in thought.
>
> Dr. Carmody enters wearing a dark suit. He
> carries a small plate with a wedge of white cake
> on it. He too stops at the portrait of Mark.
> Beat.
>
> Emily reaches out and touches the portrait.

DR CARMODY: Such a tragedy.

EMILY: [*Startled.*] Oh. [*She turns to Dr. Carmody.*] Yes.
[*Beat.*] Were you a friend?

DR CARMODY: No. I was Mark's physician.

EMILY: Dr. Carmody?

DR CARMODY: Yes. And you are?

EMILY: Emily. Girl friend.

DR CARMODY: Oh, I am sorry. [*She looks quizzically at him.*] I meant sorry for your loss. He seemed a nice young man.

EMILY: Yes. I'll miss them. Him.

DR CARMODY: I'm sorry?

EMILY: Mark. He was more than any one man could ever be. To me.

DR CARMODY: I was, alas, not on intimate terms with him. I was treating him for a rather unusual condition.

EMILY: Alien hand syndrome?

DR CARMODY: Yes. I must confess that's why I came today. The strange circumstances of his death. That, and the fact that I attend most of my patients' funerals.

EMILY: Very thoughtful of you.

DR CARMODY: The least I can do. [*Beat.*] Um, I hope you don't think me rude, but I have a rather delicate question I'd like to ask you.

EMILY: Yes. Yes, it was the most incredible sex I've ever— [*She looks at him, suddenly realizes her mistake.*] Oh, I'm so sorry. Yes?

DR CARMODY: I was wondering if...they...if they ever found his...hand.

EMILY: No.

DR CARMODY: The entire right arm?

EMILY: Gone. Severed at the shoulder. [*Tearfully.*] He bled to death.

DR CARMODY: How ghastly. To cut off his arm like that. What pain, what torments could have driven him to such an extremity?

EMILY: Oh, Hank. [*She cries into a tissue.*]

DR CARMODY: Hank?

EMILY: Gone. The right hand and arm. Never found. How could that have happened, doctor? And they're calling it suicide.

DR CARMODY: No, this wasn't suicide. I believe Mark was driven to it. No, if anything, this was a young man's last desperate act to save himself. This was the act of a man who wanted to live.

EMILY: But what could have happened to his right hand? It couldn't have just crawled away. Could it?

> She breaks down. Dr. Carmody hugs her, careful not to drop his cake.

DR CARMODY: There, there. He's gone to a better place. A place where he can be whole again.

> He exits with his cake. Emily blows her nose, then makes her way to the couch. She sits, alone and miserable. Long pause.

> Hank emerges from the cushions of the sofa. The hand begins to gently stroke her arm, then face.

> It takes Emily a moment to realize it's Hank. Then joy. She takes Hank in her hands.

EMILY: Oh, Hank! I knew you'd come back.

Her fingers intertwine with Hank's fingers. She bends and kisses Hank's fingers one by one. Johnny Mathis' *Stranger in Paradise* plays (production must obtain rights). Slow fade to black.

END

Besides, you lose your soul
or the
History of Western Civilization
by Julia Lee Barclay

Julia Lee Barclay is a writer and director originally from New York City now living in London. She has had her work published, produced and been given awards and fellowships internationally. She is the founding Artistic Director of Apocryphal Theatre, which has been running exploratory theatre labs and producing shows since 2004. Along with writing and directing, she also teaches workshops in the techniques created in her labs in New York and London. She has recently been awarded a practice-as-research PhD from University of Northampton entitled *Apocryphal Theatre; practicing philosophies*, which includes this play, both as text and in performance.

Apocryphal Theatre's production of *Besides, you lose your soul...*premiered at Camden People's Theatre (CPT) in London in February 2009. The show was a co-production with CPT and was funded in part by Arts Council England and Camden Council.

Director/Writer: Julia Lee Barclay
Players/Creators: Bill Aitchison, Zoe Bouras, Rachel Ellis,
Player/Visual Artist: Birthe Jorgensen
Assistant Director/Sound: Lucy Avery
Lighting Design: Boris Kahnert
Special Guests: Fred Backus, Alison Blunt, Theron Schmidt
Sound Engineer: Martin Williams
Producer: Clare Maloney

Special Thanks: Nesta Jones at Rose Bruford College, Peggy Ramsay Foundation, Royal Victoria Hall Foundation, Chris Goode, Matt Ball at Camden People's Theatre, Paul Burgess, Kelina Gotman, Robin & Tom Schmidt, Jane Bacon and to those who helped develop performance: Lukas Angelini, Maggie Cino, Jane Munro, Daniel O'Brien, Robin Reed, Julie Shavers, and Eva van Dok.

A note to readers, directors and ensembles:
    This play, as with all my stage texts, does not suggest what players should take which lines or how the text itself should be embodied. I came to writing from directing and hope that this

format can give latitude to directors and actors alike, as it has done for the companies with which I have worked as a writer and director. As this text was written originally for my company Apocryphal Theatre, which like most ensembles has developed its own language and tools, there are terms in the stage directions which may not make sense to you, but you should feel free to allow the terms to evoke in you whatever images or resonances that emerge, as the words we use in our labs and rehearsals are working definitions, not meant to pin anything down as much as stimulate ideas and imagination.

Each Apocryphal performance is unique, as we do not decide on any one way to perform any text, using it instead as a springboard for new improvisations each night, using certain flexible internal structures but no rigid rules. The only thing that does happen during each performance is that we make it through the text and each free-form improvisation suggested in the text is attempted. However, if you are interested in directing this text, you should feel free to create a more predetermined performance score if that works better in your circumstances. I am interested to see what other directors and/or ensembles do with this play, and invite you to create your own wild ride through these kaleidoscopic fragments of Western Civilization.

A note on formatting:

As per formatting norms, the deeply indented lines are meant to be stage directions not spoken text. As per this text, the slightly indented and italicized text indicates where the player is either (a) quoting directly from a pre-existing text directly, (b) cutting up pre-existing text or (c) is commenting on one of those texts in the voice of 'one who quotes from authorized texts.' Make of this what you will.

Setting:

In the room are strewn many old classic books of Western
Civilization, preferably from college or university level of
courses, with underlining and highlights, crumpled pages,
etc. There can also be a sense of an interrogation of some
nature going on, something shadowy and not quite right –
no literal indication of this, but a tone that pervades, like
an odor from the basement you can't quite disguise –
perhaps if possible there is a floor covered in a grey ash-like
substance about 6 inches thick. If any recorded music, it
should be something like the homemade CD I was given by
a man who worked at a Kurdish restaurant of dirges sung
by an older Kurdish man. CD player and any and all
means of production visible, including any documentation
or film and video technology, such as Super-8 film loops or
projections from laptops, the text itself and any
improvisational structures. The audience should ideally be
seated throughout the space.

In the original production, the text was projected onto the
wall and there were over 1,000 pre-WWII books in stacks on
the floor, regarding literature, philosophy, politics or
religion that were arranged and re-arranged each night by a
visual artist who treated the space as an ever-shifting
installation. The audience was encouraged to move around
and read the books throughout the show, and the chairs,
which the actors and audience moved throughout the
performance, created in the end a thrust stage space for the
last scene.

Performers begin with a cut-up of quotations/questions mostly from Shakespeare's Hamlet, and one from Edward Albee...working through as usual the levels of address and presence...when it feels as if some kind of shift has occurred begin the text that follows, which is of course somewhat of a cut-up-riff itself – and as per usual, if something comes out of this improvisation that seems somehow apt, you can intersperse throughout.

And yet to me what is this quintessence of dust?

What's Hecuba to him or he to Hecuba,
That he should weep for her?

And for my soul, what can it do to that,
Being a thing immortal as itself?

Alexander died, Alexander was buried, Alexander returneth to dust; the dust is earth; of earth we make loam; and why of that loam whereto he was converted might they not stop a beer barrel?

Who's afraid of Virginia Woolf?

NB: for anyone who has not experienced cut-ups: the 'rule' is that once cutting up, you cannot add new words not in phrases, but they can be cut up in any way, so for example, we might end up with "he should weep for a beer barrel?" or "earth is immortal her." These cut-ups can be created individually or as a group, where one person could begin a phrase and another finish it.

***

Besides, you lose your soul.

119

Be-sides

You

Lose

You lose

You

Yours truly,

A soul

Lost

Loser

Losing

Lost

Loved once and lost

A soul

> *Being a thing immortal as itself*

> *What's he to Hecuba, or Hecuba to him?*

Sold.

You sold it?

Yes.

I mean no.

I mean.

Mean?

120

Mean.

Quintessence of dust.

Soul. A mean soul, sold for cheap.

Mean as in *mean*?

Yes, as in 'mean'.

Where are we now, England or the U.S.

England, I think. Where mean is *mean*.

As in cheap.

As in quintessence of dust.

Soul-less?

Maybe

Where does the soul come from?

Soul?

Yes, soul.

Not sure.

What is it? This thing you can lose?

This thing you can lose when you torture people you mean?

Right, yeah, that's right, *that's* what he was talking about I think.

But he said you couldn't—remember? Just now...it's immortal. How can it be lost?

Who?

The other guy, before, the famous one, who wrote a lot—
English guy.

About torturing people?

No, well yeah, but no, not the same guy.

About Alexander stopping beer barrels?

Yeah, that guy.

Yeah, but I'm talking about the other guy—the ex-FBI guy—
who was talking about torturing people. He was saying it
wasn't that efficient in the end, because people will say, you
know, anything, if you torture them long enough.

So you might not get the right information?

Right, you might not get the right information.

And besides, as he says, you lose your soul.

Right, you lose your soul.

Aren't we kind of, well, repeating ourselves a lot here?

Well, yeah. But some things, you know, well, they kinda,
well, *bear repeating* don't you think?

Maybe.

Yeah, maybe.

But the English guy, he was writing before America was
even like something real—it had just been found by other
English guys but no one was really you know *sure* of it, not
really sure if it *meant anything.* Could that make a
difference? With the idea of an immortal soul, I mean...one
that you know, can't get lost?

Not sure I follow you...

You know like maybe it was more secure then, that idea about souls...that they kind of couldn't get you know lost...but then they were suddenly kind of well more you know less um well I don't know, less like fixed or something?

Um, maybe...I guess...

Maybe that's why he was so obsessed with stopping beer barrels?

Maybe...

Yeah, yeah, because he was beginning to *sense* it – that something wasn't right...that something was about to get really, you know, *lost.*

So, you mean in finding something new something else gets lost?

Yeah, something like that...

Wow.

Yeah.

> Maybe here everyone starts looking for something metaphorically or literally, and without any success...something important that can't be found...like keys, a wallet, identification, a wedding ring, an idea that was great in the bathroom, a dream you just forgot...then below begins the interrogation of S/He Who Has Lost That Thing Which Was Important

OK, then...so before we lose it

—if you haven't already lost it …

Yes, right if you haven't already Lost it!

Me?

Yes, You!

How do you think Western Civilisationstarted?

WHAT????

Well, how do you think it started?

How the fuck should *I* know?

I don't know, I thought maybe you had, you know, like, a *theory* or something...

A theory?

Yeah, you know, a *theory* as to how Western Civilisationmight have started. Doesn't everybody?

Um.

Well?

I mean, everyone *we* know?

What do you mean everyone *we* know?

You know what I mean.

No I don't. I haven't a fucking CLUE what you mean!

Yes you do.

No I don't.

Yes you do.

No *we* don't!

Aha, there, caught you!

It was a joke for Christsakes....

Maybe there?

What?

The beginning, of Western Civilization.

Um, I don't think so...I think we'd at least have to go back to the Greeks or—

SEE, I *knew* it, you DO have a theory!

It's not a theory.

Yes it is.

No, it isn't.

Yes, it is.

No, it's just, you know, *fact.*

Fact? You're joking, right...I mean we, the people *we* know, do you think *we* believe in simple 'fact' anymore?

Um, maybe? And who do you think I know that you know that makes us a 'we'? Just out of curiosity, you know, *Idle Speculation...*

Well, I think you do, I mean *we* do...it's all of us, those of us who find ourselves *here.* And those we *already know.* The people who count. The people who *know things.* Them, who of course are now we, or at least I hope so...I mean, I think, really, I've done enough work here by *now* to be counted one of *we* rather than *them*. Don't you think? I mean, really?

> *and why of that loam whereto he was converted might they not stop a beer barrel?*

I'm kind of lost.

That's such a lie.

No it's not.

Yes it is.

No it's not.

Yes it is.

SHUT UP!!!!!!!

Make me.

Make you?

Yeah, make me.

This is a joke right?

Maybe. Maybe not.

How can you be so FUCKING childish?

I don't know, how can YOU be so FUCKING childish?

Or how can *we* be so-

STOP, please DEAR GOD, STOP!

> *In the beginning was Oedipus, and God said, that is good, and in seven days, someone rested and we were all happy. The word was Aristophanes, and*

126

Aristophanes was the word. There were birds in the heavens and he said it was good. Sometimes there were women around, but they usually had a supporting role, unless of course they were fucking everything up, in which case they became crucial to the plot points...but I digress...

Excuse me.

Yes?

Who are you?

I am he who tells stuff that ye shall believe what I say because I said so....Amen

Do you really think that stuff works anymore? I mean aren't we kind of like, well, beyond that?

This is the very word of Thou wretched, rash, intruding fool

That's enough.

What, the fair Ophelia?

Amen.

Pretty Ophelia!

Amen.

Good night ladies, good night. Sweet ladies, good night, good night.

Amen.

[*Beat.*]

Is it all like that?

I'm afraid so, more or less, give or take, etc.

OK, let's start again then.

Again?

Yes, again.

We can't do that.

Why not?

Because we already started.

Who says?

They do.

Who is they?

Them, you fool. *Them.*

Oh, come on, who cares about *them*???

Well, we should.

Do you think so, I mean really? Isn't this one of those, you're either *on* the bus or you're not kind of things? Or shouldn't it be? I mean aren't *they* supposed to be part of *we*, I mean seeing as we're in the same room and all? Like you said before?

I never said that.

Yes you did.

No I didn't.

Yes you did.

No, I didn't. I think *you* said that, if you want to be accurate with the facts.

But you said there were no facts!

I most certainly did not.

You are such a liar.

Yes. I am.

Finally, the truth.

Is it?

> At this point there could be any number of responses, for instance: dancing, gesture-texts from labs that come from moments of training/disciplines, some way of responding to this whole tiresome 'truth-lie' contradiction that resolves the paradox without recourse to linear narrative...by resolve I don't mean 'solves' but resolves into action somehow...

That's scary.

Is it?

It can be.

Why?

Because it's not moving anything forward, not getting us anywhere.

Where on earth do you want to GO?

I don't know, somewhere.

WHERE?

Well, somewhere.

Somewhere BETTER?

Well, yeah, maybe somewhere better. Is that so bad?

Could be. Could be one of those horrible utopian type things that leads to fascism and world wars and god knows what else!

Or not.

How do you know?

I don't. I'm just saying, sometimes wanting to go somewhere better can be, you know, good. It's not always bad. It could mean getting out of somewhere bad and going somewhere, you know, better.

But do you really think it's a matter of going somewhere???

Maybe.

I'm not so sure. I think that usually makes things worse.

Maybe.

But maybe not.

Ok, whatever.

Whatever?!

Yeah, whatever.

> *So this early Dionysiac ritual was a cathartic that took man out of himself—*

A cathartic?

> *That's what it says, right here, in this book on Myths.*

130

It sounds like an enema.

Yes, it does. You're right. Shall I go on?

Ok, for a bit...

and purged his irrational impulses, or directed them into a special channel...Yeah, I know, I know...but listen to this, it gets better: These were the times when the religious sanction had become guilt instead of shame (page 167)-

So what's on page 167?

OK, here's something: Clytemnestra, tormented by a snake-dream that is a gift to psychoanalysts-

Excuse me? Were there psychoanalysts in ancient Greece?

Well, no.

So what's That all about?

I think the author is trying to be clever.

Great.

And anachronistic.

Well, yeah.

I mean, is there a SOUL yet or not? Is anyone talking about souls??? Isn't that the point here???

Shall I go back to the original reading?

OK, let's try again.

and some of the Greeks, their old clan solidarities weakened, were finding it difficult to bear their new

burdens of individual responsibility...blah blah blah....
orgiastic rites... blah blah...snake handling... blah
blah...Mediterranean fertility cults...oh but this is good, it
all relates to the ecstatic rattlesnake cult of the Holiness
Church in Kentucky!

Wow.

Who knew?

Kentucky?

Yeah. Kentucky.

Wow.

Yeah.

Wow.

> *Men will know that I am the LORD*
> *when I execute judgment upon her*
> *   and thereby prove my holiness,*
> *I will let loose pestilence upon her*
> *   and bloodshed in her streets;*
> *the slain will fall in her streets,*
> *beset on all sides by the sword;*
> *then men will know that I am the LORD.*

Lord is always in all caps, isn't it?

> *Yes.*

So, is this it then? How they justify the torture and all, do
you think? God's will, that kind of thing?

Some believe this to be the case yes.

Some? Is 'some' different than 'we'?

But of course.

132

So 'we' don't believe this then, am I to presume?

Right. 'We' are smarter than that.

Oh, good, well, that's a relief.

So, what is it that 'we' believe then? Just you know again, out of *idle curiosity*?

Oh, we! We don't believe Anything!

We don't believe in Anything?!

Right, we're Smarter than that! I mean More Clever than that...in America they or we say 'smart', in England you or I say 'clever' depending on who is saying this line that is... I am *trying* to be culturally *sensitive*...

That's impossible.

That I'm trying to be culturally *sensitive*?

No, that 'we' don't believe anything!

Of course it's possible!

No, it's not.

If I say I don't believe in anything then I don't.

It's not that simple.

Of course it is.

No, it's not. Even the denial of belief is a statement of belief, and even if it weren't, you certainly believe in Something.

Prove it.

OK, do you believe that we should discriminate against people based on race, for example?

No, of course not.

So, there you go.

What?! I just said I didn't believe in something.

Right. But the opposite is a belief: I believe that we should not discriminate against people based on race.

Yes, but that's just *common sense*, it's something *we* all agree on! It's not a *belief.* A belief is something unreal, unprovable, irrational... Wrong.

In other words, something you disagree with.

Right, I mean wrong, I mean it's just because it's just *common sense.*

I rest my case.

That's just sophistry.

No, it's not. Good try, but it's not. And anyway, the sophists weren't all bad, they got a bad name, but –

Please stop before I have to resort to violence.

Violence?!!

Yes, violence.

Are you thinking of torture perhaps?

Maybe.

> *I left you as ashes on the ground*
> *for all to see.*
> *All among the nations who knew you were aghast:*

134

you came to a fearful end and shall be no more forever.

That's kind of harsh.

That's Ezekiel "Prophesies against foreign nations" to be exact. From The New English Bible (with Apocrypha).

> *A figure like your father,*
> *Armed at point exactly, cap-a-pe,*
> *Appears before them and with solemn march*
> *Goes slow and stately by them. Thrice he walked*
> *By their oppressed and fear-surprised eyes*

Yeah, I know that onc.

Ghost.

Soul?

Ghost.

> *People who say they will first die and then arise are mistaken. If they do not receive resurrection while they are alive, once they have died they will receive nothing.*

Gnostic guy?

Yeah.

Which one?

Valentinus. The Gospel of Truth...according to Wikipedia.

Ahhh.

Well, I had to start somewhere. To look for the soul.

Hm.

You got a better idea?

No, not really, but there are certainly a lot of BOOKS written about it, that you don't need to be on a Web to look up, etc., etc...

Yeah, yeah, I know. I have them too. But I was looking for, you know, the Origin of the word. Where it comes from? How can I lose something I haven't found in the first fucking place? You know?

Yeah, I guess.

OK then.

OK.

What about Lucretius?

What about him?

He didn't believe in a soul.

True. It didn't exist yet. At least not written down anyway, at least according to Wikipedia, and other sources that shall remain nameless, until they are deemed nameable, because I – I mean 'we' – decide that – but of course as 'we' all know there is no 'real' anyway, so citation is like, fascistic or something, right...?

Right?

Right?

Um, I'm not sure.

I wish you'd get over your patriarchal need for Definition!

Yeah, I'll work on it.

Good. It's really a bother.

A bother???

136

Yes.

A bother??? How long have you been in England now?
Have you lost your Identity Already? You never would have
said 'bother' before! Do you know that?

Oh, leave it.

Leave it?!

Yeah, leave it...What do you want me to say: can it? bag it?
Fuck it? etc.

That's better.

It's had its chips!

NO!!!!!

America the Movie brought to you by Some American Writer
You've Never Heard of Before! Better????!

Oh, nevermind. I'm just trying to Help.

Great. Stop. It's not Helping.

OK, OK....

I consider it a great privilege to have had such a father—

Oh stop quoting Nietzsche, it's tiresome, and well, all of
them and their Father this, Father that business....

You're being quite literal. You do know that, don't you? I
mean this tiresome cod feminism...

Cod feminism?

Well, yeah.

COD Feminism???

You heard me. It's boring, B O R I N G…boring.

> *Some have located the soul in this possible difference*
> *between the mind and a classical computer.*

Wikipedia again?

Yeah. The scientist bit.

Oh. Them.

Yeah, *them.*

> *Researchers, most notably Ian Stevenson and Brian*
> *Weiss have studied reports of children talking about*
> *past-life experiences. Any evidence that these*
> *experiences were in fact real would require a change in*
> *scientific understanding of the mind or would support*
> *some notions of the soul.*

That reminds me of that story—remember?

Yeah, the one about the little kid. Yeah, the little girl who
wanted to talk to her brother who was a baby—alone.

Yeah, and her parents were totally freaked out and thought
it was one of those little kid homicidal moments or
something, so they said 'yeah, sure you can talk to Bobby
alone'

Bobby, was his name, Bobby?

Oh, I don't remember, does it matter???

Just checking…

Anyway, so they said yes, and then put on those walkie-
talkie things…you know the little kid intercom things so

they can hear what's going on in the room when they're not there—

You mean like *spies* do?

No, not like that!

What's the difference.

In this case it's because they're *concerned*.

Oh.

So anyway, the little girl goes into little Bobby's room and the parents are listening over the walkie talkie thing and she says to him "Hey, Bobby, can you tell me about God again, I forgot."

Wow....
She forgot?

Yeah, she forgot.

But then how did she know to ask?

I guess because she hadn't quite forgotten but was afraid she would, or maybe she had a *feeling* of something she couldn't remember.

Did the baby tell her anything?

I don't know. They didn't get that part on the walkie talkie bit.

Thank God.

You can say that again.

I mean it.

Yeah, me too.

Season your admiration for a while
With an intent ear till I may deliver
Upon the witness of these gentlemen
This marvel to you.

"For God's love let me hear!"

Well done, that was the next line of the play!

He knows; because now He knows that Christ is born,
which means the same thing as Christ will be born.

False!...I mean Correct!

Ding ding ding...you win the "I've read the Summa Theologica Award" – at least page 158.

Yay!! I'd like to thank my Mother and my Father and All the lovely people from the Shop....

OK, enough...Enough!

Hearts and flowers, hearts and flowers....will anyone ever love me on Valentine's Day?

What???

Oh, sorry, just a diversion.

Are you sure?

Yes. I don't want to seem, you know, cheesy.

Cheesy?

Yeah, cheesy. Can we move on?

Um, ok, I guess...

But what about the diversions? Are they always? Aren't you maybe Avoiding something?

Maybe.

> Here perhaps performers could talk about that which makes them uncomfortable, i.e., beliefs that go against their 'beliefs' – where the personal and political for example don't link up...and as always, no one will ever ask you what is 'real' or not here...but there's something interesting in the 'official story' and the emotional usually derided as 'trivial' one... as per usual you can work with levels of address/presence/ verbs, etc.

Speaking of inconsistencies, why isn't the soul mentioned in the Bible?

Didn't exist yet.

Oh.

Who invented it?

I think Aquinas might have. Well, there was Plato first of course, then the reinterpretation by Aquinas.

Oh.

Why do you think they did that?

Who?

Whoever – invented the soul?

I don't know if anyone invented it. Maybe it was there all along and then discovered!

Like America?

Right, like America.

Be serious.

What?

America was already here.

I know that's my point.

But it wasn't 'America' was it?

Sure it was.

No it wasn't. It was just a bunch of land with some people here and it was not called 'America'. Get it?

Ummm.

Like with Freud and the idea of psychology, same thing. Dreams used to be visitations, messages, whatever, then they became something to be interpreted. Looked at. *Used.*

Yeah, so?

So, before that they were Something else!

What?!

I don't really know!

Why not, you seem so fucking sure of everything else.

I don't know because I was born after Freud, not before.

Oh, how tedious.

Tedious? Our entire identity, what we're doing here on earth, all that, tedious???

Well, it can be talking to you.

142

Why?

Because you're so Sure of Yourself. It's boring.

So I should pretend to not know stuff for your amusement?

No. Nevermind.

What does She think?

Oh, not Her again.

Well, She does creep into it now and again, doesn't she?

Why?

Because it's *unavoidable.*

Why?

Because she's *here.*

She's here?!

Yes. Always.

Like the Soul???

Kind of. Yeah, like the *soul.*

> *What Napolean failed to recognize was that the antipathy shown by the Spaniards toward their ruler did not necessarily imply a corresponding enthusiasm for rule by the French.* —Get it?

No, not really.

Well, try.

Do we have to?

Yes, *you* have to.

> Long pause...any number of things could be
> happening here, but the following text comes
> after a length of time appropriate to the
> condensation of Western Civilisationinto a cut-
> up.

OK: despite the improvised character of these forces,
with handmaids bearing loaves, ending the Inquisition,
during the seven years that I taught Greek, Men will
know that I am the LORD, the eating of the bleeding
goblets, those "things utterly non-human and immoral"
knows that an annunciation is sometimes true.

Therefore, the knowledge of God is not speculative.

The ship sailed on, out of the Ocean Stream, then stood
by weeping while the flame burnt through The way of
heaven—

That wasn't Western!

What!

The last bit, "the way of heaven".

How do you know?

Trust me. She tells me things.

She *tells* you things?

Yeah.

OK, so where is it from then?

Lao Tzu. Eastern guy.

Right. Eastern guy.

144

But Jesus was supposedly influenced by—

Yeah, yeah, Buddhism, we know, we know...

But there's no Proof, is there?

Proof?! You must be joking. You're asking for proof, at this stage?! When we know there is no such thing. I can't believe we're back *here* again.

Therefore, God has a speculative knowledge of all things.

Wait, before you said He didn't.

Right, but I never said He. You did? You're assuming God means He.

Yeah, but I bet that guy does too...and you're diverting me...How does God now have this knowledge?

A lot of words.

Words?

Words words words

Yeah, a lot of words. Quoting other people, and then what was true is not, and what is true now won't be later. That kind of thing.

Great.

It gets better...Apparently, according to the same guy, "God is not operable."

Wow, like there's a problem?

He doesn't seem to think so.

But it sounds like a toy that doesn't work right when you buy it. Like that Mister Potato Head she got for her birthday once that didn't have the plastic potato. Remember?

Yeah, that was a drag.

All those little parts, noses and eyes and whatnot and no potato.

Right, no potato.

Like God?

Yeah, lots of little parts, something you can guess about maybe—some ornamentation at best, but no Potato. In the end, He's not operable.

I really doubt that's what this guy meant.

Doesn't mean we're not onto something.

True, true...

What did her mother do when the potato wasn't in the box?

She shrugged and said, Oh well. Maybe?

You don't remember? No, and neither does she.

She was a Child then, remember? Very small. Too small to remember very much except a laundromat, an IGA food store and some tar outside. And that box with little plastic pieces and no potato.

That was back in the 60's right?

Yeah, back in the 60's.

There was a lot more important stuff happening then.

146

Yeah, it's true, but she was like 4 or 5 max.

Still.

Yeah.

Lost. She was lost.

She was lost or she *felt* lost?

Does it matter when you're 4?

What are we talking about now? The car and being left there and not knowing where anyone was and crying? And crying... And crying..

Something like that. Is she still there?

Sometimes, yes, sometimes she's still there.

Is She?

No. and yes. She was always there, but sometimes she didn't know it.

Is She the soul?

Not exactly.

Who is She?

Can't say exactly, not without problems.

> *I am always equal to accidents. I have to be unprepared to be master of myself.*

One of those, then. An accident. But one that works in your favor.

She is a favorable accident?

If you like.

And you have to be unprepared to see Her.

There is no murky pit of Hell awaiting anyone.

No?

No.

As for all the torments that are said to take place in the depths of Hell, they are actually present here and now, in our own lives.

Same guy?

Yeah. Roman guy. Lucretius.

Not so bad really.

No, not so bad. Plus he's right. About that anyway.

Why are they all men?

Gee whiz I have No idea.

Copyright problems?

Yeah, something like that.

> *...this is not the System, it hasn't the slightest thing to do with the System. I wish all good on the System and on the Danish shareholders in the omnibus; for it will hardly become a tower.*

Kierkegaard.

Oh *him.*

Yeah, him.

148

You know his nephew tried to keep them from burying him in the churchyard. That's the first recorded act of non-violent civil disobedience.

You don't say.

It's true.

Did it work?

No.

Figures.

Yeah.

But he *tried.*

That's true. He tried.

His nephew that is.

Right, the nephew. But so did *he.* Kierkegaard, that is. Tried. He really did *try* to get heard even though he wasn't *saying anything*—that is saying anything anyone wanted to hear.

What was he trying to say?

That's a little hard to explain actually.

Well, try.

OK.

OK.

OK.

> Here, performers have the option to attempt to say by doing and/or speaking and/or dancing,

playing music etc. something which demonstrates how to be 'a witness not a teacher'—something which bears witness to something hard-won—as Kierkegaard says regarding the true knight of faith: 'what he won, he did not win on the cheap so he does not sell it on the cheap'—perhaps this has something to do with moments of discipline training where you transcended yourself somehow, or it could be a conversation or description of some kind of experience you have had that does not 'fit the box'—I believe you are dealing here with grid level of address quite consciously—though can take the mask of other levels—this is not a facile moment, but needs to be somehow challenging to oneself on a deep level. If this seems impossible at this moment, witnessing others is fine—so is silence and/or stillness.

The full quotation, from Fear and Trembling, not to be said, but known by players is:

"The true knight of faith is a witness, never a teacher, and in this lies the deep humanity in him which is more worth than this foolish concern for others' weal and woe which is honoured under the name of sympathy, but which is nothing but vanity. A person who wants only to be a witness confesses thereby that no one, not even the least, needs another person's sympathy, or is to be put down so another can raise himself up. But because what he himself won he did not win on the cheap, so neither does he sell it on the cheap; he is not so pitiable as to accept people's admiration and pay for it with silent contempt; he knows that whatever truly is great is available equally for all."

*He foresees his fate will be to be completely ignored; has
a dreadful foreboding that the scourge of zealous
criticism will more than once make itself felt.*

Yeah.

Yeah.

Yeah.

She loves you, yeah, yeah, yeah...

A love like that

You know it will be fi-ine.

Or is it: She will be mi-ine...

> *Good luck and prosperity one and all.*

Something like that.

Timeless tales of Gods and Heroes.

Back to Western Civilization?

No, to "timeless tales of Gods and Heroes."

Oh.

> *And it was the Goddess of Love who brought about what
> next happened.*

Which was?

Zeus raping Europa, you know turning into a bull, all that
kind of thing. Then she bears famous sons not to mention
having a continent named after her.

Wow, so getting raped by a god is a good thing?

Apparently. Except when it isn't.

Right.

She loves you, yeah, yeah, yeah....

With a love like that,

You know you will be fi-ine...

A Letter from A Gentleman to his Friend in Edinburgh.

What?

An Enquiry Concerning Human Understanding!

Oh.

We have already observed, that nature has established connections among particular ideas, and that no sooner one idea occurs to our thoughts than it introduces its correlative, and carries our attention towards it, by a gentle and insensible movement.

Kind of like this?

Kind of, except all this stuff is from books on a floor, not anyone's thoughts per se.

Per se?

Yeah, per se. Got a problem with that?

No, I guess not.

Good.

...were we to attempt a definition of this sentiment, we should, perhaps, find it very difficult, if not an impossible task.

152

Yeah.

Kant's own attempt to get out of this difficulty often appears to his readers an addition of insult to injury.

Kant? I thought it was Hume.

Yeah, yeah...

It's kind of a collage, don't you see???

Kind of a way to get At something, you know, Larger than the individual thoughts...

A kind of connection?

Yeah, a kind of connection.

When you say 'larger', what do you mean?

I mean larger.

But larger than what!

Larger than individual ideas.

What makes you think there is something Larger than individual ideas?

I don't know, um, intuition? Life? Something like that.

Sounds fuzzy.

Fuzzy?

Yeah, fuzzy.

Fuzzy wuzzy was a bear. Fuzzy wuzzy had no hair. Fuzzy wasn't very fuzzy wuz he?

> *In action we are, as we never are in scientific research, 'up against reality'*

Yeah, well we are here, aren't we!

> *Whilst in ordinary life every shopkeeper is very well able to distinguish between what somebody professes to be and what he really is, our historians have not yet won even this trivial insight. They take every epoch at its word and believe that everything it says and imagines about itself is true.*

Marx, right!

Yes!

Bracing stuff.

Yes.

True.

Yes, true.

> *...if I wish, I can become the friend of God at this very moment.*

What???

That's also true.

So? What does that have to do with Marx? That's St. Augustine!

I don't know!

So why mention it.

Because I don't know!!! That's why!

Thus the whole body of materialistic elements has been removed from how sordid I was, forcing me upon my own sight this whole semblance that, the more bitterly I hated myself, or the 'general interest', refusing to see myself, the historical method, which reigned in Germany, they had agreed upon it, as soon as it is no longer necessary to give me chastity and continence, but not under empirical conditions, which I did not explore but opposed out of malice.

Ah, now I see.

Good.

Still no women.

Right, no women. Striking that.

Yes.

Do they have a soul? Women?

Not sure. It's usually something given to 'man' or 'Man'.

Or 'the idea'

Right, 'the idea'.

Or a victim, some men do refer to women as victims, slaves, etc.

Right, yes, like that guy in college who told her she shouldn't be playing that Rolling Stones song because it was mysogynist.

Yeah he just came into her room uninvited, to tell her she was a victim of false-consciousness.

And thank God, he did. I mean, what would have become of her otherwise?

Yeah.

Like when she wasn't allowed Barbie dolls or Betty Crocker ready-to-bake ovens because they were patriarchal.

Yeah, like that.

Wow, that's annoying.

Yeah. It is - uh was - uh is.

It's truly incredible how everyone seems to know what's best for womenandchildren.

Right womenandchildren.

Watch out, here come some Womenandchildren, be careful, don't say anything too loudly or they might just all Fall Apart or get blown up or be corrupted or something...

Unless of course she's prime minister. Right unless she's prime minister. But then she is a man-women, you know, not quite right. Something's Wrong. Plus she was of course a victim of False Consciousness. Right, right. Of course she was.

> Whenever a woman acts like a human being she is
> accused of acting like a man.

Simone, Simone, Simone...

Yep.

And if you do that, you're not allowed to want flowers on Valentine's Day.

Right. These things cannot take place at the same time. You are liberated or you are not. That's that.

Right.

156

That's that.

> *To remove the mystical appearance of this "self-determining concept" it is changed into a person – "Self-Consciousness" – or, to appear thoroughly materialistic, into a series of persons, who represent the "concept" in history... Thus the whole body of materialistic elements has been removed from history and now full rein can be given to the speculative steed.*

That's nice: speculative steed.

But somehow it all feels oppressive.

Yes, it does. Like a well-constructed prison almost.

Yes.

Almost exactly.

Almost exactly.

Identical even.

Perhaps, yes.

Any escape routes?

Let's check.

OK.

> Check for escape routes...this can be literal, metaphoric, symbolic, verbal, physical, visual, musical...etc.
>
> Then begin repeating and cutting up the following sentences from philosophers – each person take one and work through levels of address (to the self, each other, audience, grid, i.e. rules of the room):

157

I have always thought that the two questions of God and of the soul, were the principal questions among those that should be demonstrated by rational philosophy rather than theology. (Descartes)

Consequently, the objective reality of these concepts (viz., that they are not mere chimeras) and also the truth or falsity of metaphysical assertions cannot be discovered or confirmed by experience. (Kant)

The philosophers who have examined the foundations of society have all felt the necessity of going back to the state of nature, but none of them has reached it. (Rousseau)

Even my experiences with people with whom everybody has bad experiences bear witness, without exception, in their favor: I tame every bear, I even make buffoons behave themselves. (Nietzsche)

A pathos is a destructive or painful act, such as deaths on stage, paroxysms of pain, woundings, all that sort of thing. (Aristotle)

Witnessing
hostages
explosions
war
terrorism
exiles
journey

gaps

How did we get here?

How did you get here?

Is She here?

Is He here?

Have you lost your soul?

All copyright should remain with yourself

It's your work after all.

After

All.

It's your work.

Your

Work.

If you could notify me before I am grateful,
I am old-fashioned enough
to get some ideas.

> *Love comes on strong,*
>
> *consuming*
>
> *her*
> *Self*
>
> *She risks*
>
> *Everything and*
>
> *Asks for*
>
> *Nothing*
>
> *Without cause,*
>
> *Give it back.*

Again.

Love is reckless, not reason
Reason seeks a profit.

Somewhere between East and West?

Yes.

Not taught in school?

No.

"the reality construction machinery"

School?

Sometimes.

"Why were you not more like Moses?"

That's not the question!

I know, I know.

What is it then?

Why were you not more like you?

Can you answer that?

Will you be able to answer that?

Will anyone ever be able to answer that?

Why the past tense?

It happens after you're dead.

How do you know?

I don't.

Then why ask it.

Because it can help now.

Help what?

Help us figure out if we're where we want to be.

We?

Ok, you, whatever, me...I don't care.

You should.

Ok, ok, whatever...

Why are we torturing people? Why is that?

I'm not torturing anyone.

Yes you are.

No, I'm not. I'm here with you, right now. Not torturing anyone. None of us in this room is torturing anyone.

But we are.

Oh, come on!

I'm serious.

You mean self-righteous.

No, I don't think so.

Well you wouldn't, would you? She said you were self-righteous, remember?

Yeah, so? Who gives a fuck what she thinks?

Oh, Now we don't Care what she thinks!

Depends on who we're talking about, doesn't it, especially since we're talking in this kind of annoying code.

Yes, but it's to make it emblematic, you know, so people can read into it, create their own meanings, see the construction of signifiers and all that.

Oh, God, how tiresome.

Yeah, well....

But this is a digression, isn't it?

Isn't all of it?

Well, yeah...

But the torture thing.

What about it?

Why are we torturing people?

Don't we have to agree it's 'we' first?

Yes, but where do we get if we say 'they'?

Somewhere else?

Right, we get to a place where they are they and we are we and can pretend 'they' torture while we sit around and deconstruct, as it were. Fiddling with semiotics while Rome burns and all that.

Is Rome burning?

You know what I mean.

No, I don't.

Yes, you do. Rome, as in 'our ethics', 'our ideals as a democracy', 'any sense of common decency or the rule of law', 'that which should be good about Western civilization' etc.

Burning?

Right, with each person being tortured right now in 'our name'.

Someone's using our name?

Oh stop being an idiot or trying to be clever. It's annoying!

Which one?

Both!

It's hard to stay here, isn't it?

Yes.

OK, so let's try. Let's take a moment and consider that at this very moment someone is being tortured, having their toenails pulled out, or their genitals electrocuted or their teeth pulled or almost drowned in the name of 'democracy' and 'freedom' and perhaps the person doing the torturing believes he or she is doing the will of God. The person being tortured may believe the same. The person being tortured may be completely innocent or may be planning to blow up the Tube or Eiffel Tower or New York. Either way, they are being held without trial or recourse to any outside justice. You probably have a better chance of knowing or recognizing the torturer than the one being tortured. The person being tortured may die and be thrown into a shallow grave and we'll never know. Or even if we do know, we probably won't care for very long. It'll be a news photo, a momentary 'tragedy'. A *pathos*, 'that sort of thing.'

See if it's possible.

> Very, very long and most likely uncomfortable
> silence—there can be many ways to attempt to
> squirm out of this and the only 'rule' is: no
> words and to try to remain still, but any
> discomfort can be—should be—allowed to be
> visible

And for my soul, what can it do to that,
Being a thing immortal as itself?

Is it?

I hate choice.

What?

She hates choice.

Does he?

Ask?

Do you?

Yes.

No.

Maybe.

That's the problem right there!

It's where it all goes Wrong.

Choice?

Yes. Choice, the illusion of, p. 94.

What book is that?

164

It's figurative for Christsakes. Jesus.

Oh, that again.

It's a Figure of Speech.

It's a damn sight more than that!

OK, OK...

Think about what you say, for Once, just Think first before saying, writing, whatever the fuck it is you're doing.

> *Alexander died, Alexander was buried, Alexander returneth to dust.*

Nietzsche. Yes.

What? That was Shakespeare.

It was Nietzsche. He said that thing, in that last thing he wrote about the Four Great Errors, that you can't condemn anyone for anything they've done because it's never actually a choice.

Nietzsche said that?

Yeah, something like that....wait here it is:

> *The error of false causality.*

What?

You know when you think a caused b because they happen one after the other, but they might not have anything to do with each other....

No, no you mean the Other error...here it is:

> *The error of free will.*

Yeah, yeah, that's the one...where he talks about how the will to hold accountable by intentions is the will to punish, right, that one!

> *One is necessary, one is a piece of fate, one belongs to the whole, one is in the whole—there exists nothing which could judge, measure, compare or condemn our being, for that would be to judge, measure, compare, condemn the whole...But nothing exists apart from the whole!*

Hard to argue with that.

Yes, it is.

Hard to argue.

With that.

> *....thus alone is the innocence of becoming restored.*

But what about the torturers?

What about them?

Can't we judge them?

Isn't that what they're doing?

What?

The torturers are judging. That's what they are doing. They are part of that 'moral order', aren't they?

But what about us?

What about us?

Shouldn't we judge them?

166

From where?

From here!

But Nietzsche said it already, we are *part* of the whole. How can we *judge* any of it if we're *in* it?

So we just accept it, just let people do horrible things and sit around and agree with Nietzsche?!

What's Nietzsche to Her or She to Nietzsche
That she should weep for him?

But we *have* to accept it.

Why?

What choice do we have???

The choice to judge! To act! To condemn! To write stupid email petitions, something!

That's kind of pathetic.

Yeah, I know.

I would really like to interject something here, something you know *clever* but I seem to be unable to do that.

Maybe ask God for something?

I tried that already.

Oh. Shit. Then we're on our own???

Afraid so.

Shit.

Yeah.

Quick, everyone, search!!!! NOW!!!!

> A frantic search ensues with audience invited to join through all the books of Western Civilisationfor an Answer. You can read out what you find, no matter how absurd and then repeat it, work through levels of address and then cutting up might be good... and keep doing this until you have hit the 'grid' and something has shifted—a paradoxical moment of both shift and acceptance, a shift that somehow manifests from acceptance.

the innocence of becoming restored...?

Maybe.

> *Without cause God gave us Being;*
> *without cause, give it back again.*

Rumi?

Yes.

That's different.

Yes.

We're not coming up with a consistent thing here, are we?

> Long pause to stare at whoever said that (or wrote that, esp. if you are the person who got stuck saying it)

I guess not.

> *Here now again he lay, waiting for dawn,*
> *while in the great hall by Athena's side*
> *Odysseus waited with his mind on slaughter.*

> *Presently Penelope from her chamber*

stepped in her thoughtful beauty.

So might Artemis
or golden Aphrodite have descended.

What does that have to do with anything?

What do you think?

She wrote a note next to this when she was young.

Oh yeah, what does it say?

It says "all threads come together." Written in pencil.

Hmm. So maybe she wasn't sure?

Maybe.

Probably she was identifying more with Odysseus than Penelope, though...

Odysseus, the great tactician

Choice, maybe?

Maybe, or maybe he's just sneaky.

Hmm.

What if all the threads don't come together? What then?

They stay apart.

Yeah, because she knows she's a she but then she can't imagine stepping anywhere in thoughtful beauty—

Was she referring to Penelope and her weaving do you think? The whole 'threads' thing?

Maybe...but then again she definitely couldn't weave. The only class she ever failed was home economics, and even then she was pissed off she couldn't take shop and learn how to make wooden things with saws—

Yeah, but she wanted all the threads to come together, that we know.

Yes.

Did they?

No.

They couldn't. They didn't even come together in *her!* How could they come together in Odysseus?

Have they?

No. Not in that way anyway...

Will they ever?

Probably not.

There is no end here, is there?

No, not really.

There usually is, you know, that word, that way, that phrase that sums it up, in a poetic, yet open ended way.

Yes, there usually is.

> *With a sudden intensity, as if she saw it clear for a second, she drew a line there, in the centre. It was done; it was finished. Yes, she thought, laying down her brush in extreme fatigue, I have had my vision.*

But as he said about classical music once:

> *It gives you the illusion that you can own your own
> home.*

Right he did say that. And so what did *he* do?

Composed silence.

Among other things.

Ah.

Perhaps we should try that.

Compose silence?

Among other things, yes.

OK.

> Perhaps here you do this, in whatever form that
> makes sense, if the 'opposite' of classical music
> is silence, what are other ways of 'acting', 'art',
> 'dance', 'writing', 'speaking', etc...that do not
> give us the illusion of being able to own our
> own home...

Are we trying to find the end?

Maybe.

OK.

Hey, that's a construct you know! Beginning, middle and –

Yeah, we know. But we have to figure out a way to end
anyway, as we're all here in the same construct.

Tick. Tock. Tick Tock. Tick Tock.

The mouse ran up the clock.

The mouse ran down.

The clock struck one.
Hickory Dickory Dock.

The mouse ran up the clock.....

And continue...

So, no end then.

Right, no end.

No end.

No end.

No end.

World without end...

—ing.

Right "—ing." End-ing.

Not quite the way it used to sound, but then what is?

Do souls end?

No, I don't think so, if they exist.

Ghosts?

Not so sure. Maybe they fade away. Eventually.

And us?

Depends.

Yes it does. It does Depend.

On what?

On who we are, what we are, etc.

This is like one of those conversations you have with someone on a sidewalk (in New York, that is – if it was London it would be a pavement...) and you just don't stop. Even though you've said a million times you have to Be somewhere, or Do something.

Yeah, it is.

OK, so I'm going to pretend the conversation is actually over now.

You're going to do WHAT?

Pretend this is actually coming to an end. See, here I am, waving goodbye.

Goodbye!

Goodbye!

Goodbye!

> At least one person walks out of the immediate space.

Exeunt a player.

No, it's exit a player. Exeunt players. It's Latin.

Oh.

Let's keep pretending stuff, it's fun.

OK, I'll pretend that we're leaving too. Here I am, waving goodbye.

Goodbye!

Goodbye!

Goodbye!

Another person walks out.

Exit a player.

I am the King:

> *Stay, give me drink. Hamlet, this pearl is thine.*
> *Here's to thy health. Give him the cup.*

I am Hamlet:

> *I'll play this bout first; set I by awhile.*
> *Come. [They play.] Another hit. What say you?*

I am Laertes:

> *A touch, a touch; I do confess't*

I am the Queen:

> *He's fat and scant of breath.*
> *Here, Hamlet, take my napkin, rub thy brows.*
> *The queen carouses to thy fortune, Hamlet.*

I didn't know Hamlet was fat.

Me neither.

Queen dies.

Laertes falls.

King dies.

Laertes dies.

Hamlet dies.

Horatio lives and puts Hamlet on the stage.

> *Go, bid the soldiers shoot.*

Exeunt.

Go on, then.

But we're just pretending.

Right.

> *I have had my vision.*

> Rest of the players leave.

> Below is audible but not visible, and maybe getting further away:

Where should we have our thanks?

Not from his mouth,
had it th' ability of life to thank you.
He never gave commandment for their death.

Right, I forgot about that.

Hmm...

Ouch. That hurts.

Sorry.

END

Laying Off

By James McLindon

In the past year, James McLindon has had 14 plays produced in theaters across America, 13 of them world premieres. His plays have been produced or developed at the Lark Theatre, PlayPenn New Plays Conference, Abingdon Theatre, Samuel French Ten-Minute Play Festival, CAP21, hotINK Festival, Irish Rep, Estrogenius 2009, Penguin Rep, Victory Gardens, Stage Left, Prop Thtr, Theatricum Botanicum, Colony Theatre, Circus Theatricals, Grove Theatre Center, Ashland New Plays Festival, and Seven Devils Playwrights Conference. He has also won or been a finalist for numerous awards including the Heideman Award, the Kaufman and Hart Prize for New American Comedy, a Joseph Jefferson Citation Nomination, the John Gassner Memorial Playwriting Award (New England Theatre Conference), the John Gassner New Play Festival (Stony Brook University), the Jane Bingham Prize, the Siena College International Playwrights Competition, the Hudson River Classics Showcase Theatre's W. Keith Hedrick Playwriting Competition, Arch and Bruce Brown Foundation Playwriting Competition, Eileen Heckart Full-length Drama competition; and many others.

Laying Off has been produced by the Fusion Theatre at both the Samuel French Off-Off Broadway Festival and at The Seven Short Play Festival, by Eastbound 2009, and by the Briefs Festival. It was developed at Humble Play, the 2008 Appalachian New Play Festival.

The rights to perform Laying Off may be obtained by contacting the author at jamesmclindon@yahoo.com.

Characters:
Meddie, a middle manager, late 30's
Rick, another middle manager, Meddie's rival, around 30.
Robert, their CEO, 50's

Setting:
The play takes place entirely in the conference room of a large corporation. The time is the present. The conference room setting may be minimally depicted or realized in thorough-going detail. What is essential is a conference table and chairs, and a door to the conference room located either Stage Left or Stage Right. Some hideous corporate art adds a nice touch.

SCENE ONE

> Morning in an office conference room. A single
> folder sits on the otherwise clear conference
> table. MEDDIE, late thirties, a middle manager,
> sips coffee, staring moodily out the window at
> the company parking lot. She is quiet, but not
> someone to trifle with. After a few moments, she
> sighs wearily.

MEDDIE: Scary.

> RICK, around thirty, her colleague and rival,
> ENTERS, carrying a folder.

RICK: Wow. I'm parking just now, and the guard, the real
old one, tells me to put it in one of those big SUV spots.
"You don't want that new Audi getting dinged," he goes. I
mean, he's not even in my division, and he's sucking up to
me.

MEDDIE: Ten years ago, if you didn't get here by 8:30, you
had to park on the grass, the lot was so full.

RICK: Well, I guess that's the upside to layoffs. More
parking spaces.

MEDDIE: If you'd gone through one of these before, you
wouldn't be so glib.

RICK: Well, sorry I'm not as old as you.

MEDDIE: [*Beat.*] Ouch.

RICK: C'mon, Meddie, it's just capitalism. If we don't stay
efficient, we go out of business, which, correct me if I'm
wrong, means everyone gets laid off.

MEDDIE: I'm just saying.

RICK: And there's another upside, and you know it. Layoffs are like ... forest fires. They clear out the deadwood and let in the sun to nourish the hardy saplings. Like me.

MEDDIE: The preferred term is "reduction in force." Euphemisms are of critical psychological importance at a time like this.

RICK: I don't think someone who just got pink-slipped gives a shit what euphemism they're using this week.

MEDDIE: I'm not talking about their psychology.

RICK: What, it's for management?

MEDDIE: It's for the market. "Layoff" says your business is tanking. "RIF" says you're getting more efficient.

RICK: Whatever. But c'mon, a little, you gotta like RIF's too, unless you're stupid. And you're not stupid.

MEDDIE: Thanks, Rick.

RICK: You know what I mean. I liked Tom, but for the first time in two years there's an opening up above, permitting a shaft of light to shine down from the very vault of heaven all the way to ....

      RICK spreads his arms wide.

MEDDIE: Us?

RICK: Me. Okay, us.

MEDDIE: Tom wasn't deadwood. What he was, was 54.

RICK: Come on, that had nothing to do with it.

MEDDIE: Are you stupid?

RICK: He'd been here 30 years, that's what had to do with it. If he'd been your age with 30 years in, they still would've fired him. [*Laughing.*] Of course, he would've had to start here when he was 12—

MEDDIE: Eight.

RICK: I would've had to start here in utero.

MEDDIE: You know we're on the line, too.

RICK: No shit we are. This whole thing is a test to see which of us gets Tom's job and which gets RIFfed. Man, I wish I was black. No, crippled. No, black <u>and</u> crippled. [*Beat.*] So ... who are you recommending?

MEDDIE: Who are you recommending?

RICK: Ladies first.

> THEY stare at each other. Then MEDDIE takes a sheet of paper out of the folder on the table and offers it to him. RICK reaches for it, but she withdraws it, and nods to the folder he holds.

RICK: Meddie! And after I caught you in the trust fall at the retreat last summer. I should've dropped you.

> MEDDIE is unmoved. RICK shrugs, removes a sheet of paper from the folder, and offers it to her. As she reaches for it, he pulls it back.

RICK: Uh-uh. Together.

> After a moment, they exchange papers simultaneously.

RICK: Crap, I knew it, identical. Wait ... You didn't put Patricia Thatcher down?

MEDDIE: No.

RICK: Uh, yeah! How could you not?

MEDDIE: She's valuable.

RICK: She's expensive.

MEDDIE: She adds more value than she costs.

RICK: Long term, maybe, but not for this quarter's numbers. This quarter's all they care about.

MEDDIE: She's also got two kids in college.

RICK: Are you shitting me!?

MEDDIE: I mean, her kids are gone, so she's got nothing to do but the job now. She costs more, but we're going to get a lot more hours out of her than somebody younger with kids or breakups or wedding plans.

RICK: Dump the big salaries is the first rule. Why else is Tom gone, he was great—You're scamming me. Aren't you? You are, you know something. Don't you? Do you?

            THEY return the proposals to each other.

MEDDIE: No. Rick. Let's just make this whole mess a little better.

RICK: How? There's nothing we can do.

MEDDIE: We can save one person's job. If we make it a joint recommendation.

            MEDDIE holds out her proposal. RICK
            considers it.

MEDDIE: They'll find another way to pick between us.

RICK: What, is she a friend of yours? She is, isn't she?

183

MEDDIE: If you don't go along, I can just add her to my list and we tie.

RICK: Yeah, you can. Will you?

MEDDIE: What do you think? C'mon, Rick.

> MEDDIE holds out the proposal again. RICK considers it, then shrugs, starting to relent. The door opens. ROBERT, a big presence, walks in, breaking the moment. RICK turns away from MEDDIE.

ROBERT: Morning.

RICK: Morning, Robert.

MEDDIE: You're in a good mood, all things considered.

ROBERT: I appear to be in a good mood. The tone we set filters down. If we walk around looking clinically depressed, we'll scare the crap out of everyone.

MEDDIE: They're already scared.

ROBERT: Of course, they are, so let's not make it worse. Okay, what've you got for me?

> MEDDIE turns to RICK, her proposal in hand.

MEDDIE: What've we got for him?

> A pause. Then RICK hands ROBERT his proposal.

RICK: Here's mine.

MEDDIE: [*Beat.*] And here's mine.

ROBERT begins to study the two proposals.
MEDDIE waits calmly. RICK can't. After a few
moments:

RICK: Creating a 10% reduction in telephone center
personnel without increasing hold times by more than 5%
is a tall order, but my proposal focuses on eliminating more
expensive personnel in favor of younger, and frankly more
energetic, productive—

ROBERT: These are the 15 highest salaries?

RICK: Yes. It forecloses any age discrimination suits
because it's strictly by salary and only coincidentally by
age.

ROBERT: And Meddie, you seem to agree—wait. Who's
Patricia Thatcher?

RICK: Night call supervisor, 12 years in the Call Center, 23
with the company. The most expensive one down there, a
no-brainer RIF.

ROBERT: Yeah. [*Surprised.*] You disagree, Meddie?

MEDDIE: She practically built the Call Center from the
ground up.

RICK: And now it's built.

MEDDIE: She wrote most of the scripts that the customer
service reps use.

RICK: And now they're written.

MEDDIE: She gets the need to maintain a modicum of
politeness while moving the calls along. She can teach that
better than anyone.

RICK: Maybe, before she wrote it all up for us in the
procedures handbook. Now, my dog could.

185

MEDDIE: It's a hard job that she knows how to do well and efficiently. That'll be key given how shorthanded they're going to be.

ROBERT: But with her, you don't make the numbers.

MEDDIE: Just by a little. It's the right trade-off.

ROBERT: We have to hit our numbers. We miss one quarter, and the Street just kills us.

MEDDIE: If another division comes in a little better, it'll even out.

ROBERT: And if I let you slack off, every other division will, too. [*Puzzled.*] You know this, Meddie.

RICK: It's inevitable. Well, I guess we're done here.

          RICK gets up to go.

ROBERT: We have to stay profitable, and I don't mean a little, I mean a whole lot, so that this is where investors with lots of options want to put their money.

RICK: That's exactly what I was telling her—

ROBERT: This Patricia. She trained you, didn't she?

MEDDIE: When I started here, yeah.

ROBERT: Look, nobody likes this, Meddie. I couldn't even fall asleep last night, ended up watching some History Channel documentary. This Hungarian had been forced to fight for the Nazis and he's ordered to execute some partisan they've caught. He can't do it, asks to be relieved, so the German C.O. takes his rifle. Now, you think he's just going to execute the partisan himself, show 'em how it's done, but instead, he shoots the Hungarian. Then he asks the other Hungarians for another volunteer, and they just

186

about knock each other down to do it. Now I know we're supposed to view the Hungarian as a hero and all, but I couldn't help thinking, is it that simple? Didn't he just take the easy way out of a very complicated moral choice? I mean, the partisan still got shot, right? In fact, the Hungarian basically forced some other poor guy to do it. Plus now his wife is a widow and his kids are orphans. It was a grand gesture, sure, but that's quite a price to pay, and for what? All he really gained was a bullet behind the ear.

MEDDIE: He gained immortality. Sixty years later, you're still telling his story.

ROBERT: And therefore?

    Beat.

RICK: If we're done, I'm late for a meeting.

MEDDIE: I've got an alternative proposal.

    MEDDIE pulls another report out of her folder and hands it to ROBERT.

RICK: What alternative? [*Beat.*] What alternative!?

ROBERT: [*Thumbing through it.*] I don't get it. This is everyone, the whole Call Center.

MEDDIE: Except Patricia. We'll need her to get the new one in Bangalore up and running. She's by far our best trainer.

    MEDDIE hands ROBERT another sheet.

MEDDIE: It will cut our costs by 60 to 65% the first year, a little more each year after that once the start-up costs are over.

ROBERT: Can Indians really handle this?

MEDDIE: The studies in there all say the key is the manager. Patricia will make them good enough.

> ROBERT stands up, still thumbing through her proposal.

ROBERT: Wow. I think I've been selling us short. I'm going to bump the required cuts to 15%. See ya.

> ROBERT exits. Beat.

RICK: FUCK!

MEDDIE: Rick—

RICK: No, fuck you for sandbagging me! Is this my punishment for not joining your little crusade?

MEDDIE: It's business. You did well, I did better. [*Beat.*] Tell marketing you want a lateral move. They'll be happy to take you and dump someone more expensive.

RICK: They've already made their cuts.

MEDDIE: They've got to hit 15% now.

RICK: Why are you helping me?

MEDDIE: I owe you. I didn't have the balls to recommend the whole call center when I walked in here, even though that meant we'd probably tie and you'd get Tom's job because you're younger. So I was just going to make my hopeless pitch to save Patricia on my way out, to make myself feel ... noble.

RICK: so why didn't you, and leave me the job!?

MEDDIE: Because you're right, it is inevitable. Because they don't make documentaries about heroic middle managers. Someday soon someone else would figure out how we could dump the call center, right? I might as well save Patricia, and get the credit, not the pink slip behind the ear.

RICK: [*Beat.*] You. You are the most cold-blooded person in this whole building.

MEDDIE: We're all laying people off.

RICK: That's not what I mean, that's just the way it is and if my time comes, I hope I take it with some class.

MEDDIE: [*Imitating him.*] FUCK! [*Herself again.*] Like that?

RICK: I mean, even though you think it's wrong, you not only do it anyway, you do it bigger than even Robert dared dream of. Cold. Blooded.

> RICK starts to leave, then turns back.

RICK: Oh, can I get a recommendation for marketing?

MEDDIE: After that, you want a favor?

RICK: So shoot me for being aggressive. I'm a valuable corporate asset, and this is just business. Like you said.

> Beat.

MEDDIE: Draft me something.

RICK: Thanks. [*Beat, then bowing with his fist to his chest.*] My Dark Lord.

> RICK smiles. MEDDIE smiles back. RICK EXITS. MEDDIE's smile fades. She stares out over the parking lot again and sips her coffee.

MEDDIE: Scary.

> Lights down slowly.

CURTAIN.

Safe

By James McLindon

In the past year, James McLindon has had 14 plays produced in theaters across America, 13 of them world premieres. His plays have been produced or developed at the Lark Theatre, PlayPenn New Plays Conference, Abingdon Theatre, Samuel French Ten-Minute Play Festival, CAP21, hotINK Festival, Irish Rep, Estrogenius 2009, Penguin Rep, Victory Gardens, Stage Left, Prop Thtr, Theatricum Botanicum, Colony Theatre, Circus Theatricals, Grove Theatre Center, Ashland New Plays Festival, and Seven Devils Playwrights Conference. He has also won or been a finalist for numerous awards including the Heideman Award, the Kaufman and Hart Prize for New American Comedy, a Joseph Jefferson Citation Nomination, the John Gassner Memorial Playwriting Award (New England Theatre Conference), the John Gassner New Play Festival (Stony Brook University), the Jane Bingham Prize, the Siena College International Playwrights Competition, the Hudson River Classics Showcase Theatre's W. Keith Hedrick Playwriting Competition, Arch and Bruce Brown Foundation Playwriting Competition, Eileen Heckart Full-length Drama competition; and many others.

Safe has been produced by the Boston Theater Marathon, Circus Theatricals, Love Creek Productions, Riverside Cultural Consortium, Salem Theatre Company, Eastbound 2008, and the Briefs Festival. Safe was a finalist for the 2009 Heideman Award.

The rights to perform Safe may be obtained by contacting the author at jamesmclindon@yahoo.com.

Characters:
Joyce, a graduate student, nearly 30
Luke, a graduate student, Joyce's Fiancé, 30

Setting:
The play takes place entirely in the living room of a modest
bungalow. The time is the present. While the living room
may be realized in thorough-going detail, only the following
is essential: The room contains a number of moving boxes,
some open, some empty, although it is already fully
furnished. That is, while LUKE is just moving in, JOYCE
has been living here for a while. There should be a couch
center stage. Also necessary are some bookshelves, only the
bottom half of which are filled with books. One or two
chairs (perhaps old and overstuffed) are probably present. A
six-pack of beer sits on one of the boxes. In a fully realized
set, the décor should be serious-female-graduate-student,
not too expensive, but tasteful enough.

SCENE ONE

> The living room of a modest bungalow. JOYCE,
> a graduate student, nearly 30, is unpacking
> books from a box and filling the empty top
> shelves of a bookcase with them. She is
> somehow all on the surface and yet secretive,
> all at the same time. Other boxes, opened and
> unopened, lie scattered about. LUKE, a
> graduate student about the same age, is heard
> trudging up the basement steps. He ENTERS,
> tired.

LUKE: Good thing that was the last load cuz your basement's about full.

JOYCE: You're all moved in. [*Beat.*] Yay.

> JOYCE hugs LUKE and they kiss. Her
> enthusiasm is a bit forced. She tries to break off
> the embrace, but LUKE holds her.

LUKE: "Yay?" That sure didn't feel like "Yay."

> JOYCE wraps her arms around him again. He
> reciprocates.

JOYCE: I'm just tired. You know how I am with change.

LUKE: You suck with change.

JOYCE: A little.

LUKE: No, with change, my girl sucks a lot.

JOYCE: Okay, a lot. This is just weirding me out a little.

> JOY and LUKE let each other go.

LUKE: Hey, Joyce, is it okay that I put some of the heavy stuff on that big metal thing with the plywood on top?

JOYCE: Oh, the safe? Sure.

LUKE: A safe? Really?

JOYCE: Yeah. Look, I put your books on the bottom two shelves.

LUKE: Oh. I was just going to splice them together alphabetically with yours tomorrow.

JOYCE: Oh. Okay.

LUKE: Is it okay?

JOYCE: Well, it's a little OCD. No, it's fine, I was just tired, it was easier to leave them separate for tonight.

LUKE: So what do you keep in the safe?

JOYCE: Nothing. The old owners left it when they moved out.

LUKE: What did they need a safe for in Northampton?

JOYCE: No, they just brought it here when they closed their business. Their kids didn't want it when they sold to me. I sort of like it.

LUKE: What was in it?

JOYCE: I don't know. The kids couldn't find the combination.

LUKE: They never opened it up?

JOYCE: Why do you want to open it? I like the mystery, the potential?

LUKE: You'd like the money in it more. What if there's money?

JOYCE: There's no money in that safe.

LUKE: You don't know that. The parents could've kept money, stock certificates, jewelry in there.

JOYCE: Then they would've told their kids.

LUKE: Maybe they were estranged. Were the kids all like, "Thank God they're gone?"

JOYCE: I don't know, they didn't seem all that close. Like, they didn't know where the trash barrels were kept. Shouldn't your kids know where you keep your trash?

LUKE: There's no better way to say "I love you, Mom." Yeah, they probably wouldn't have just left it if they thought there was anything in there.

> Beat.

JOYCE: Except, I don't know, the kids already had tons of money. The daughter flew up to the closing from Boca Raton and the son couldn't even make it because he had this big business thing going on.

LUKE: So maybe they were so rich they didn't care about the safe. Maybe the manufacturer could give us the combination.

JOYCE: I sort of already have it. The kids also left this old file cabinet in the attic full of old tax returns, mortgage applications, stuff like that. And a file marked "Safe."

LUKE: So you did open it.

JOYCE: The combination was in code.

LUKE: They encoded it?

JOYCE: Sort of. It said, "Clear the dial and then three times to the right to your day, two times to the left to mine, and one time to the right to ours."

LUKE: Your day ... our day. What's that mean?

JOYCE: It's obvious. It's in a woman's handwriting, so it means three times to the right to his birthday, two times to the left to her birthday, and one time to the right to their anniversary.

LUKE: How is that obvious?

JOYCE: What else could it mean?

LUKE: Lots of things, like, like ... lots of things. Crap, how do we get those dates?

JOYCE: It was pretty easy. Their birthdays were on the mortgage application. She was the 17th and he was the 30th.

LUKE: C'mon, their anniversary wouldn't have been.

JOYCE: No, that was harder. They weren't in the City Hall index. They probably got married somewhere else.

LUKE: Whoa. You really worked at this.

JOYCE: I didn't really work at this. Okay, I worked at it a little. It was a fun little puzzle.

LUKE: Why didn't you ever tell me?

JOYCE: Well, now you're moving in, so I am telling you. My neighbor said they were still like these old sweethearts. He sang "The Way You Look Tonight" to her at their 50th anniversary party. That was their song.

LUKE: You're a little obsessed.

JOYCE: No, I'm not! Their karma or whatever is probably still in this house, I just like knowing they were happy.

LUKE: Well, except for their emotionally distant kids who didn't give a damn about their own parents' trash. So when was their anniversary?

JOYCE: He didn't know. He remembered that the party was in the summer, but that was just to accommodate the kids' schedules.

LUKE: Crap. Maybe we could call the kids. No, what if they get suspicious. They might claim the krugerrands—

JOYCE: I have the date. [*Beat.*] The paper always does a story on 50th wedding anniversaries. It took a few hours, but I went back through their microfiche and found it.

LUKE: [*Beat.*] You're a whole lot obsessed.

JOYCE: I'm not obsessed! Okay, I'm a little obsessed.

LUKE: Why are you making me drag this out of you?

JOYCE: I don't know. Part of me wants to tell you. And—

LUKE: And part of you doesn't. Fine. So, would part of you tell me what was in it? [*Beat.*] Oh, come on, you looked, you totally looked, anyone would look.

JOYCE: Except me.

LUKE: Why? [*Beat.*] Well, what's the date? I'll look.

JOYCE: No! You can't.

LUKE: Why not?

JOYCE: Because … I don't know. I just like having it in the basement.

LUKE: We'll leave it in the basement—

JOYCE: Not the safe. The mystery.

LUKE: It's probably empty, Joyce.

JOYCE: So, then I'll have given up the possibility of something for the certainty of nothing.

LUKE: Unless it's full. Of Krugerrands.

JOYCE: Then, it'll be full of Krugerrands next year.

LUKE: Why do you need a small mystery more than a small fortune?

JOYCE: I need ... the potential. I turn 30 this fall, Luke.

LUKE: I turned 30 last winter. It's not that big a deal.

JOYCE: Yes, it is. Before, I didn't have to be anything except all this potential and possibility. But now I'm thirty, now I've really got to choose what I'm going to be. And what I'm never going to be.

LUKE: Well, yeah, but, so what?

JOYCE: I once was in Italy and I had three days left on my Eurail pass, which meant I had time to go to Spain or to Greece, but not both, and I chose Spain and I loved it, but I never got to see Greece. I hate that. I'm starting graduate school in history, but I'm passing up graduate school in English and now I'll never write a thesis about the Bronte sisters.

LUKE: But you saw Spain. You'll write about Gladstone and Disraeli.

JOYCE: I'm engaged to you, and you're moving in, and now I'll never date or marry anyone else.

Beat.

LUKE: Not necessarily. [*Beat.*] It would've been more efficient to have had this discussion, oh, maybe, before I moved all my stuff in—

JOYCE: I don't want to marry anyone else, Luke.

LUKE: You just don't want to marry me?

JOYCE: I mean ... I loved Spain, I love history, I love you. Why do you have to lose something to get something?

LUKE: I don't know, maybe because bigamy is a crime is why, Joyce!

JOYCE: Doesn't it bother you?

LUKE: No. It's just how you define yourself. If you never had to choose, you'd be everything, which is the same as nothing. Are you a Republican or a Democrat, Methodist or Buddhist, Red Sox or Yankees? Your choices are who you are. Choosing is just growing up.

JOYCE: Yeah, well, then growing up just ... sucks. Now do you understand about the safe?

LUKE: Yeah. [*Beat.*] No, I don't understand a God damn thing about the safe.

JOYCE: I just want what's in that safe down there to be able to be anything. And if I open it, it can't be.

LUKE: Well, it can't be anything now, it's too small for it to be a rental truck. Which I've got to get back to U-Haul before 10.

LUKE gets up off the couch and heads to the door. Just as he reaches it:

JOYCE: April 21st. That was their anniversary.

200

LUKE: [*Beat.*] Are you sure?

JOYCE: Yeah, the paper did a big story—

LUKE: I don't mean about the date.

JOYCE: [*Beat.*] Yeah. I'm sure.

> LUKE studies her for a moment, then heads toward the basement stairs. He stops at the head of them for a few moments. He returns to the couch slowly.

LUKE: This is your house, Joyce. I don't need to know that badly.

JOYCE: Thank you.

> JOYCE suddenly stands and heads to the basement door.

JOYCE: But now ... I do.

> JOYCE EXITS, and is heard descending the stairs. When she is out of sight, LUKE celebrates with a victory dance.

JOYCE: You'd better not be doing that stupid dance.

> LUKE stops, sheepishly. After a few moments, JOYCE is heard climbing the stairs. She ENTERS, carrying a large book and two passports. LUKE is disappointed.

LUKE: So, the Krugerrands were too heavy to carry up?

JOYCE: Sorry. [*Thumbing through one of the Passports.*] It was only their passports and—Oh, fine!

LUKE: What?

JOYCE: She got to go to Greece!

LUKE: What's in the album?

> They sit on the couch and JOYCE opens the album.

JOYCE: "To Mom and Dad, on your 50th wedding anniversary." [*Flipping the pages.*] Wow, it's photos of their whole life.

LUKE: Whoa. She was a hottie.

JOYCE: Shut up.

> JOYCE suddenly kisses him passionately, then releases him and returns to the album.

JOYCE: This is our house.

> JOYCE settles in with the book on the coach. LUKE thumbs through a passport.

LUKE: Huh. She got to Greece ... but she never got to Spain.

> LUKE closes the passport and joins JOYCE in gazing at the photos.

> LIGHTS DOWN SLOWLY. CURTAIN.

The Boston Forty-Nine Flamingo
By K. Biadaszkiewicz

Fiction, poetry, and drama by K. Biadaszkiewicz have been published in Asia, Europe, and the U.S. Her plays have received special recognition from outstanding performing arts programs including Wayne State University, Tisch School of the Arts, Sumter Opera House and College of Charleston (both South Carolina), University of Louisville, Institute for Southern Studies, and the International Institute for Documentary and Drama in Conflict Transformation.

BOSTON FORTY-NINE FLAMINGO was first performed at the Love Creek Short Play Festival in the Nat Horne Theater, New York, New York and the Centerpiece Lunchtime Series in Roanoke, Virginia. The play earned designations in several national competitions, including TheatreWorks, University of Colorado; Playwrights Theatre of Baltimore; Writers Network Competition, Beverly Hills, California; and the George Kernodle National Playwriting Competition, University of Arkansas.

The first draft of BOSTON FORTY-NINE FLAMINGO was written during a fellowship at The Millay Colony for the Arts, Austerlitz, New York.

For production rights, send an email to the author at isoperhaps@yahoo.com

Characters:
Winslow, a pathologist
Nell, a visual artist
Scott, a slick art dealer

Setting:
A studio apartment, a delicatessen, and an art gallery in
New York.

The present.

ACT ONE

SCENE ONE

> The tiny kitchenette of a studio apartment in
> New York. A small table and paint-spattered
> stool. The morning paper. A one-burner stove,
> toaster oven, beverage refrigerator.
>
> AT RISE, NELL, in bathrobe, stands at the stove
> preparing breakfast: soft boiled eggs. As SHE
> struggles with the task, SHE speaks to
> WINSLOW, off.

NELL: Winslow? Winslow! Listen...The person I was—and
the one I am now—met each other last night, okay? [*No
response.*] It was a bomb. There. I said it...The person I
was...She was having a bad day, all right? Okay, she was
rude and loud and boring...And you never even said a word.
Why didn't you say something? Wait. Let me guess. Perhaps
she wouldn't let you. That's what you're going to say. Is that
what you're going to tell me? Is it?

> SHE takes a soft-boiled egg out of the boiling
> water, spilling some of it, not concerned.

WINSLOW'S VOICE: Are they done?

NELL: What?

WINSLOW'S VOICE: Are they done?

NELL: Oh. Cut to the chase. Stick to the really important
information, Nell. Shut up about what's churning inside.
Ignore the torment, the passion, the regret...

WINSLOW'S VOICE: What?

NELL: The person I was, she would still be asleep. She
would still be in her place of refuge. The Wonderland of cozy
comforters and sweet—

206

WINSLOW'S VOICE: [*Cheerful.*] I'll be there in a minute.

> SHE cracks the egg. SHE opens it a different way every morning.

NELL: —Dreams.

> SHE scoops the egg into a dish. Some of it spills. No matter. She retrieves it with HER finger, licks it off. SHE salts and peppers the egg.

WINSLOW'S VOICE: I'll be right there.

NELL: You want me to take yours out?

> WINSLOW, a man of medium height wearing a conservative suit, white shirt, brown shoes, and an extremely loud tie, enters.

> HE gives HER a kiss on the forehead. Almost imperceptibly SHE pulls away.

> WINSLOW checks HIS watch, picks up a spoon, examines it closely, and takes HIS position at the stove.

WINSLOW: Mmm. There's nothing I like better in the morning than the smell of toast toasting.

> As HE hovers over the stove, NELL chops HER egg with HER spoon. The toaster oven buzzes. NELL takes out the toast and looks for a dish, burning HER fingers. WINSLOW is positioned at the stove, spoon poised, ready to extract the egg. HE hesitates, notices that the timer is not set.

WINSLOW: The timer's not set!

NELL is busily buttering HER toast.

NELL: Uh uh.

WINSLOW: You didn't set the timer?

NELL: Uh uh.

WINSLOW: When did you start it?

NELL: I just said I didn't start it.

WINSLOW: I mean the egg. When did you put it in?

NELL: With mine.

SHE adds some jam to the toast.

WINSLOW: What time was that?

NELL: When?

WINSLOW: When you started cooking them.

NELL: [*Eating.*] I don't know.

WINSLOW: You mean you forgot.

NELL: I didn't forget. I just didn't notice.

WINSLOW: You didn't notice?

NELL: If you don't take it out, it'll be hard-boiled.

Exasperated, WINSLOW takes the egg out of the boiling water and puts it aside. HE gets a fresh egg from the refrigerator. HE is going to do it the way it should be done.

NELL sits on the stool, balancing HER breakfast on one knee and the newspaper on

the other. SHE looks through the paper
absently as SHE nibbles.

Meanwhile, WINSLOW places the new egg on
the spoon, and lets it hover above the boiling
water as HE studies HIS watch: HE could be
timing an important track meet or the pulse of
a patient in intensive care.

WINSLOW: Eight...seven...six...five...

NELL: You could save yourself some trouble if you'd—

WINSLOW: Shhh!

NELL: It's a lot easier if you just put it in cold water and
take it out when it starts to boil.

WINSLOW: When it starts to boil. Oh, that's precision, isn't
it.

NELL: Sometimes a little after.

WINSLOW: After what?

NELL: A little after it starts to boil. I do that sometimes for
Extra Large.

HER irreverence for precision has once more
distracted WINSLOW, causing HIM to lose
count. Exasperated, HE begins yet again, the
spoon still poised above the boiling water.
Suddenly, HE thrusts the cold egg into the
boiling water.

HE sets HIS watch. The tension melts from HIS
face.

WINSLOW: There.

> Noting the label on the bread package, HE
> selects two slices of bread, places the slices into
> the toaster oven. HE smoothes out the bent
> fastener and neatly re-closes the bread
> package. HE wipes up some crumbs NELL left,
> and puts them—and HER eggshells—into the
> garbage. HE consults HIS watch and checks on
> the egg, seems pleased that it is still boiling in
> the pan where HE left it. HE finds the
> necessary materials and lines them up neatly: a
> dish, clean spoon, salt, pepper, napkin, toast
> dish.

NELL: Have you decided?

> When WINSLOW pauses below, it will be to
> think of the worst abomination, then, with
> some venom, HE will continue.

WINSLOW: There's nothing to decide.

NELL: You mean it?

WINSLOW: Absolutely. I would rather have...cold flounder
for breakfast than an egg of unknown doneness.

NELL: I meant about my show.

> WINSLOW'S watch goes off.

WINSLOW: Hold that thought.

> HE deftly extracts HIS egg and places it in the
> dish. HE breaks the egg and slides it out of its
> shell. HE places the shell into the garbage.

NELL: The pictures.

WINSLOW: Oh, that.

NELL: How to display them.

WINSLOW: You'll have to use wires.

HE fetches HIS toast.

NELL: Oh, <u>that</u>?

WINSLOW: I know your frames and I looked at the walls in there, and the only way it's going to work is with wires.

NELL: But I told you I don't want to mess with wires.

WINSLOW: You don't have to, honey. I'll do it.

NELL: I'd rather you didn't...

WINSLOW: No problem. I'll take care of everything, so you can forget about hanging them up and just concentrate on what you need to concentrate on.

NELL: Which is how to display my work.

WINSLOW: Me: display your work. You: not to worry.

NELL: But I don't need any help.

WINSLOW: But you just said—

NELL: I paint pictures, Winslow. I'm a big girl now. I don't need anybody to clean up my pictures or hang up my mess. I mean ... You know what I mean.

WINSLOW: Pass me the jam?

SHE does not pass HIM the jam just yet.

NELL: Do you know how long it took me to the point where I don't have to beg them to let me display my work next to the salad bar? Do you know how much farther I have to go before I can get my foot into Fifty-Seventh Street?

211

> Pause as THEY try to focus on THEIR breakfasts.

WINSLOW: Do you think I could have some jam?

> Clearly angry, SHE picks up the jam and puts it down in front of HIM.

WINSLOW: Is something wrong?

NELL: Wrong?

WINSLOW: Yes.

NELL: Why would you say that?

WINSLOW: I don't know. Sometimes I just—

NELL: Wrong? What could possibly be wrong?

WINSLOW: That's what I was thinking, but—

NELL: I don't know where you could possibly get the idea that there is anything wrong, Winslow. I really don't.

> SHE throws what is left of HER toast across the room, startling WINSLOW. A crumb catches in SHE starts to cough. SHE coughs a lot.

> WINSLOW gives HER something to drink. SHE still coughs. HE pats HER on the back. SHE coughs more. Finally HE pulls both of HER hands over HIS head. SHE stops coughing.

WINSLOW: Straightening out the trachea does it every time.

> HE proceeds to tidy up the mess made by HER toast on the floor.

NELL: Graduating from the salad bar to the dining room may not sound like much to you, but it is to me.

WINSLOW: I think you're overreacting.

NELL: I never over react!

WINSLOW: You should relax when you're having your breakfast.

NELL: I am.

WINSLOW: You don't look like it.

NELL: An "I'm sorry" might help.

WINSLOW: A what?

NELL: An "I'm sorry."

WINSLOW: I don't know what that is.

NELL: It's when one person tells another he is sorry.

WINSLOW: Sorry for what?

NELL: Oh, it's just an expression. A tiny little concession to someone who might be prone to overreacting.

WINSLOW: Are you making fun of me?

NELL: Winslow, fun is at the bottom of my list right now.

WINSLOW: It shouldn't be.

NELL: Should I throw my dish against the window?

WINSLOW: Why?

NELL: Oh, I don't know. To relax a little?

WINSLOW: ...You want me to apologize? I'm sorry. There. Feel better?

NELL: You'd do anything to protect your Lenox china.

WINSLOW: If you broke it, you'd feel bad. You'd miss it.

NELL: I don't know.

WINSLOW: You would.

NELL: You once told me I'd miss the days when I had to beg for space, and I was glad to get an easel by the john.

WINSLOW: You know what I miss? I miss the days when I'd get out of lab early and you used to be glad to pack up and spend weekends with me in the Poconos...

NELL: Don't start on that. You know I had to stay here to get ready for this show.

WINSLOW: ...Remember the time we got snowed in at the lodge and all we had was chocolate cookies and canned peaches?

NELL: Don't romanticize, Winslow.

WINSLOW: Who's romanticizing? I almost froze to death trying to find that can opener in the snowdrift.

NELL: I couldn't help it if it slipped out of my hand, okay? My fingers were stiff from holding the brush for hours and hours.

WINSLOW: Those are still my favorite landscapes. They were good.

NELL: They should have been good. All I did the whole week was paint.

WINSLOW: I was working on a paper.

NELL: Your thesis.

214

WINSLOW: That's what it was. And the deadline, looming ahead of me like—

NELL: I spent forever on that series.

WINSLOW: We found time to talk, though.

NELL: We certainly did. About germs.

WINSLOW: Germs?

NELL: Yes. You described all that stuff you saw in your microscope. Streptosomething, and staphlosomething.

WINSLOW: We talked about ties, too. Don't forget them.

NELL: How could I? It was my "tie" period: "Untitled with Stripes"; "Untitled with Polka Dots"; "Untitled with Peaches"...

WINSLOW: That was the time I tore up my hand trying to open a can of peaches with the screwdriver.

NELL: Served you right for breaking my manicure scissors.

WINSLOW: Those must've been <u>some</u> scissors, the way you carried on. I was the one who was bleeding, but you used up all the Kleenexes.

NELL: It wasn't the scissors. I was crying because you informed me that the only way my work would ever be successful was if I could paint germs.

WINSLOW: I never said that.

NELL: You did too.

WINSLOW: I believe the term was "as full of the potential for life as a bacterial spore."

NELL: I was too busy trying to find a Band-Aid for your finger to pay that much attention.

WINSLOW: I still have a scar.

> HE shows HIS finger, but receives no sympathy.

NELL: You never did apologize.

WINSLOW: I bought you a very expensive manicure kit.

> SHE glares at HIM.

NELL: The trouble with you is, you spend too much time staring into microscopes looking at things nobody else can see.

WINSLOW: Why are we having this discussion again?

NELL: We're not having a discussion, Winslow; we're having a fight.

WINSLOW: But I don't like to fight.

NELL: I think you do.

WINSLOW: I do not. There's no reason to. We have a lot in common. Germs, ties, the smell of paint...

NELL: No we don't. It's your germs, your ties, and my...paintings.

WINSLOW: Six of one, half a dozen of the other - the significant factor is that they all involve fascinating patterns.

NELL: [Shaking HER head.] Well, as long as we can identify the significant factor, there's no problem, is there?

WINSLOW: Patterns of nature and patterns of art. We are two like-minded spirits. You told me we were.

NELL: In general, maybe. But there's one tiny little difference, Winslow. You <u>collect</u> your germs and put them on slides and photograph them.

WINSLOW: Of course I do. That's what you do with germs.

NELL: You <u>collect</u> your ties, too, don't you?

WINSLOW: Sure.

NELL: Well I <u>make</u> my paintings. I create them. Without me they wouldn't exist.

WINSLOW: Well they aren't alive.

NELL: I'm working on it.

WINSLOW: Maybe you ought to get back to landscapes.

NELL: Well maybe, you ought to try cold flounder for breakfast. It might be less fishy than when it's warm.

WINSLOW: They told me that flounder was fresh.

NELL: [*Quickly.*] They told me that flounder was fresh. Try it fast.

WINSLOW: [*A good sport.*] They told me that flounder was fresh. They told me that flounder was fresh ... They told me—

NELL: [*Interrupting.*] Do you really hate my portraits?

WINSLOW: No.

NELL: Then why did you just tell me to go back to landscapes again?

WINSLOW: I just like them better.

NELL: You've got to be kidding. The Lake Champlain Series, was a disaster. The Berkshire Series? Garbage.

WINSLOW: [*Fond recollection.*] How about the Pocono Series?...

NELL: Nobody wanted them, either.

WINSLOW: I wanted them.

NELL: You wanted me.

WINSLOW: Well, yes. Yes I did.

NELL: I knew it. Me and my work: a package deal.

WINSLOW: I didn't mean it like that. Why do you always do this?

NELL: You never liked my landscapes at all.

WINSLOW: I did too.

NELL: You never liked my paintings.

WINSLOW: Yes, I did, and I still do.

NELL: Oh?

WINSLOW: Yes.

NELL: Tell me one good thing about my paintings.

WINSLOW: They're...very nice.

NELL: [*Rising.*] Very nice?...Thanks a lot.

> SHE picks up HER dishes and walks over to the sink.

218

WINSLOW: [*Sitting on stool.*] Remember how hungry we were?

NELL: When?

WINSLOW: The canned peaches. Didn't they taste good?

NELL: You're romanticizing again.

> SHE abruptly dumps HER dishes into the sink.

WINSLOW: Nell?

NELL: What do you want?

WINSLOW: ... Should I ... make another pot of coffee?

NELL: Not for me.

WINSLOW: What's wrong?

NELL: Nothing.

WINSLOW: I think something's wrong.

NELL: I just don't want any coffee now, okay?

WINSLOW: Please say something. We really have no reason to—

NELL: I hate openings. They make my feet hurt.

> SHE starts to leave. WINSLOW meekly touches
> HER arm. SHE stops briefly.

WINSLOW: Wait.

NELL: What?

WINSLOW: Uh...How was your egg?

NELL: [*Triumphantly.*] Perfect.

> SHE leaves. HE begins to tidy the kitchen as:

> LIGHTS DIM TO BLACKOUT.

SCENE TWO: The Deli Show

> A delicatessen. On an easel is a sign: "Portraits by Nell Mutari". A small table and chairs. WINSLOW—on a stepladder—is carefully hanging NELL'S abstract portraits on wires. There are four paintings up so far. NELL is stepping back to see how they look.

WINSLOW: Is that better?

NELL: It's fine.

> On the ladder, WINSLOW takes a sip of something from a Styrofoam cup.

WINSLOW: Are you sure you don't want some of this?

NELL: I told you. I don't drink anything that shade of green. What is it, anyway?

WINSLOW: Parsley tea. It's loaded with chloroplasts, Nell. It has to be green. Any other color and it wouldn't have chloroplasts, and if it didn't have chloroplasts, it wouldn't be—

NELL: I'll pass.

WINSLOW: It will soothe your nerves.

NELL: My nerves are fine, thank you.

WINSLOW: It might not sound good, but it's delicious. It really is.

220

   HE holds the cup down to HER.

NELL: Well ...

   SHE takes a cautious sip. SHE hates it.
   WINSLOW replaces cup on ladder shelf.

WINSLOW: Would you hand me the tag?

   SHE does. HE affixes the price tag. HE takes a
   carpenter's level out of HIS pocket. HE checks
   the picture. It is level. HE moves the level to
   the side, preparing to position the next picture.

NELL: Uh, you really don't have to put them in a straight
line. If you don't want to.

WINSLOW: No problem.

NELL: I mean, it wouldn't hurt if you'd stagger them a little.

WINSLOW: Don't worry; I'll handle it.

NELL: Actually, I think they'd look good sort of...staggered.

WINSLOW: No, they'll look sloppy. It has to be a straight
line.

NELL: A straight line is too...straight, Winslow.

WINSLOW: It's no trouble, really. You deserve the best, and
that's what you're going to get.

   WINSLOW continues to plot the line of pictures:
   HE descends the stepladder, moves it, picks up
   the next picture, climbs ladder. NELL re-
   arranges the easel. SCOTT enters. HE is
   dressed in a stylish, understated shirt, slacks,
   and shoes of the latest fashion. HE holds a
   tray: corned beef sandwich, a large Styrofoam
   cup, and a pickle. SCOTT takes a seat at the

table. HE picks up the pickle and takes a bite. Then the sandwich. HE watches WINSLOW as if it's a TV show. HE glances at the paintings. Then HE regards NELL. HE puts down the sandwich and wipes HIS mouth. When HE speaks HE tends to gesture with HIS hand.)

SCOTT: [*To NELL.*] Fabulous jawbones.

NELL: Pardon me?

SCOTT: [*Pointing to painting.*] And the eyes. Won-der-ful eyes. Won-der-ful. You're...[*Reads sign.*] Nell Mutari?

NELL: Yes.

SCOTT: Scott Lamonte, but you can call me Scottie.

NELL: Hi.

SCOTT: Good stuff, Nell.

NELL: Thanks.

SCOTT: I like it. It's fresh. What do you call it...The sub special?

HE reads from a sign in the delicatessen.

NELL: No. No, that's ... that goes with the sandwich bar.

SCOTT: Oh, that's funny.

NELL: Yes ... Actually, this is just my ... Sidewalk Series.

SCOTT and NELL regard WINSLOW, WHO is busily measuring the paintings, the wire, and the spaces between the paintings.

SCOTT: Sidewalk Series. I like it.

NELL: Thanks.

SCOTT: [*Indicating WINSLOW.*] Who's that, your agent?

NELL: Oh, no. I don't have an agent.

SCOTT: You're kidding.

NELL: No. I ... I haven't needed one.

SCOTT: Well, you do now.

NELL: You think so? Why?

SCOTT: Politics.

NELL: Politics? That's got nothing to do with it.

SCOTT: That's just what I'm talking about. I mean, that you think it doesn't.

NELL: It couldn't.

SCOTT: Oh, but it does. Work like that, you could go anywhere, doll. But you won't.

NELL: You never know. Some people have told me they're good.

SCOTT: Good? They're won-der-ful ...

NELL: Thanks.

SCOTT: ... But that doesn't mean anything.

NELL: Why not?

SCOTT: Could you pass me the horseradish?

SHE does.

NELL: I don't understand.

SCOTT: It's not enough to paint. You've got to get to know the right people.

NELL: I know people.

SCOTT: Yeah?

NELL: I know lots of people.

SCOTT: [*Indicating WINSLOW.*] Yeah. Him, and who else?

NELL: Uhm ... Jack Grisson.

SCOTT: Let me guess. The owner and manager of Grisson's Delicatessen?

NELL: [*Defensively.*] My work stands on its own.

SCOTT: Nell, Nell. You're making the same mistake they all make.

NELL: I am not, because my work is ...

SCOTT: Yes?

NELL: Sincere. I can show you a clipping from the Weekly Advertiser.

> SHE fumbles around in HER wallet trying to find it.

SCOTT: I'll take your word for it.

> HE takes a bite of HIS sandwich, then indicates the paintings.

NELL: Well ...

SCOTT: [*Shaking HIS head.*] Look. You put your heart and soul up there, the most won-der-ful stuff ... But let me tell you something, Nell.

NELL: What?

SCOTT: It doesn't mean a thing. Unfair? Yes. Frustrating? Absolutely. But it's true.

NELL: I don't believe you.

SCOTT: ... See, nobody knows what's good, and everybody pretends to like whatever the right people say they like.

NELL: You're too cynical.

SCOTT: Not cynical; just realistic. I know the business inside and out, and let me tell you something. Nobody has the guts to say what they really think, because nobody has the guts to think for themselves.

NELL: Really?

SCOTT: Uh huh. And you know why?

NELL: It's too risky?

SCOTT: A beautiful woman with brains. I think I'm in heaven. See, the only people with the guts to say what they think are the miserable bastards with nothing to lose.

> WINSLOW takes a moment to admire HIS arrangement.

WINSLOW: I think that's better now, don't you?

NELL: Looks good.

> SCOTT gives WINSLOW "thumbs up". NELL is a little disconcerted.

225

NELL: How about you?

SCOTT: What about me?

NELL: Do you say what you think?

SCOTT: Oh, yeah.

> HE winks. HE takes a sip from HIS Styrofoam
> cup. HE indicates WINSLOW.

NELL: Thought so.

> SCOTT and NELL share a smile.

SCOTT: Why don't you tell him to scatter them a little?
Loosen up a little? I mean ... Is he in control or what? You
know what I'm saying?

> HE and NELL share a snicker.

WINSLOW: [*To NELL.*] How's that?

NELL: Looks good.

> WINSLOW almost loses HIS balance.

WINSLOW: Don't worry; I've got everything under control.

NELL: Be careful.

> SCOTT stifles a snicker and nudges NELL,
> WHO can't help being a little amused at
> WINSLOW'S antics. WINSLOW continues to
> hang the pictures while NELL watches HIM.
> SCOTT continues eating HIS sandwich and
> planning HIS next move.

SCOTT: They've got great sandwiches here.

NELL: Yes. They're so ...

SCOTT: Succulent.

NELL: Oh, my, well, yes. I guess they are.

SCOTT: I'd come here more often, but it's pretty far from my gallery and I can't always get away.

> Beat. NELL nearly chokes HER response.

NELL: Gallery?

SCOTT: Yes. Hard to get away sometimes.

NELL: I ... I know what you mean.

SCOTT: Good sandwiches, though.

NELL: Uh ... How far is it? From your gallery, I mean.

SCOTT: Oh, eight, ten blocks. I'm on Fifty-Seventh Street ... Sometimes you get a cab, and sometimes you don't; know what I mean?

NELL: Right.

SCOTT: Want to taste some really good parsley tea?

> NELL grabs the tea and takes a gulp. SHE still doesn't like it, but this is SCOTT'S tea.

NELL: Uh ... sure ... Thanks ...

SCOTT: Nice shade of green, isn't it? Of course I don't have to tell an artist about color –

NELL: Did you say <u>Fifty-Seventh</u>?

SCOTT: Uh huh. Why?

> HE is pleased with HIMSELF.

NELL: Oh, nothing. It's just that...That's a long walk. When you're in a hurry, I mean.

SCOTT: Yeah, it is. That's why I usually take a cab.

NELL: Oh, right. The cab. They're ... convenient.

SCOTT: The gallery is such a madhouse I had to get away.

NELL: [*Letting it sink in.*] I really can't think of another restaurant where the sandwiches are so, um—

SCOTT: Succulent?

NELL: Right. Succulent.

SCOTT: Yeah, and I just felt like corned beef today. I mean, I'm going crazy in the gallery and all of a sudden I felt like corned beef. You ever had that happen?

NELL: Oh, it ... it happens a lot. I mean, not all the time. But now and then.

SCOTT: Now and then. That's just like with me.

NELL: Things can get crazy.

SCOTT: I hear you ... But I'll tell you something. It's worth every minute, you know what I'm saying?

NELL: I know what you mean.

SCOTT: Hey, want some more tea?

NELL: Sure.

> SHE takes the cup and drinks. This time SHE seems to enjoy it.

SCOTT: Like it?

NELL: [*Another sip.*] Mmm.

SCOTT: [*Reading tag.*] Parsley.

NELL: [*Nodding.*] Parsley. [*Smells.*] Mmm.

> SHE brings the cup to HER lips and takes another long sip. SHE hands the cup to SCOTT, WHO takes a long sip of HIS own. Pause. WINSLOW completes another hanging.

WINSLOW: Nell? Would you take a look at this, and tell me if it's straight?

SCOTT: Tell him it's straight.

NELL: Winslow, it's straight.

WINSLOW: [*Cheerfully.*] Five down, five to go ...

> WINSLOW resumes HIS task, selecting another picture and measuring it carefully.

NELL: He's really very sweet.

> SHE takes another gulp of SCOTT'S tea. SCOTT finishes HIS lunch and rises. NELL does not want HIM to leave just yet. SCOTT reaches into HIS pocket and pulls something out. HE gives it to HER.

SCOTT: Hey. Here's my card. Why don't you bring me some of your work sometime?

NELL: Really?

SCOTT: Sure.

NELL: Why?

SCOTT: I'd like to see it.

NELL: Oh.

SCOTT: Unless you're too busy.

NELL: Uhm ... Sure. Maybe when things slow down a little for me.

SCOTT: Sounds good.

> HE starts to walk toward the door.

NELL: How about tomorrow?

SCOTT: You're on.

NELL: Good.

SCOTT: Hey, I've got an idea. How about lunch?

NELL: L...Lunch?

SCOTT: Are you free?

> HE takes out HIS Palm Pilot.

NELL: Uhm ... I think so. I'll have to check.

> SHE glances at WINSLOW, WHO is thoroughly absorbed in hanging the paintings. SHE glances quickly at an imaginary calendar in HER purse.

SCOTT: If you can't work me in, we can just take a rain check and get together some other time.

NELL: Tomorrow is great. I'll, uhm, work you in.

SCOTT: Fabulous. At the gallery, then? Noonish?

NELL: I'll be there.

SCOTT: And don't forget to bring some of your work.

NELL: O...kay.

> HE leaves. NELL is ecstatic Clutching the card,
> SHE jumps into the air, causing the paintings
> to move a little. But WINSLOW barely notices.
> HE continues to hang Number Six, checking to
> make sure that it is absolutely level.

SCENE THREE: Breakup

> NELL is in the kitchen of WINSLOW'S
> apartment, as in Scene One. SHE is slamming
> the pots, pans, and dishes, looking for
> something. There is a large bottle of wine on the
> table. WINSLOW enters, pleased. In HIS arm
> HE cradles a small parcel.

WINSLOW: Wait 'til you see what I've got.

NELL: [*Rummaging in cabinet.*] Oh boy; I can hardly wait.

WINSLOW: [*Unwrapping parcel.*] You are not going to
believe this ... a nineteen forty Philadelphia!

> HE proudly holds up the tie.

NELL: Uh huh ...

> SHE continues HER search.

WINSLOW: Mint condition. Look at these colors! ... Nell?
What's wrong?

NELL: [*Interrupting.*] ... Where is the corkscrew?

WINSLOW: [*Examining tie.*] Did you check the third drawer
in the back on the left?

> NELL slams the cabinet. SHE opens the third drawer, looks in the back on the left, and pulls out the corkscrew. SHE grabs the wine, places the bottle between HER knees, and proceeds to open it. SHE struggles with the bottle, not paying much attention to WINSLOW'S treasure.

WINSLOW: Look at the detail! You know where I found it?

NELL: The dipsy dumpster.

> SHE pops off the cork. During WINSLOW'S speech below, SHE will respond negatively, shaking HER head, drinking straight from the bottle until WINSLOW finally notices HER behavior and asks if something is wrong. When HE does, SHE does not respond except to take another swig. Finally SHE will slam down the bottle on the table.

WINSLOW: On the street. Can you believe it? ... Someone threw it out ... It was right there on the street with a pile of old shoes and a broken table! ... Is anything wrong? [*No response. SHE takes another swig.*] NELL, what is the matter? [*No response.*] Are you okay? Your blood sugar. Did you forget to have lunch again? ... That's it, isn't it? I'll fix you something to eat.

> Suddenly, still clutching the wine bottle, NELL races ahead of HIM to the refrigerator, and as HE opens it, SHE pulls out a small dish with HER free hand. SHE holds the dish in front of WINSLOW'S face.

NELL: Here.

WINSLOW: What is it? It looks like an egg.

NELL: It is an egg.

WINSLOW: Well, it looks like an egg.

NELL: I said it is an egg.

WINSLOW: I know it's an egg, but—

NELL: It's only half cooked, Winslow. It's a half cooked ice-cold still runny yolk egg, that's what it is. I was going to make an egg salad sandwich with it. It was going to go with some mayonnaise and some pickle and some dill weed and some mustard into an egg salad sandwich.

WINSLOW: Why would you want to make egg salad with a half cooked egg?

NELL: [*Clenched teeth.*] Because I thought it was an already all-cooked egg, that's why.

WINSLOW: [*After a moment.*] Hey, you know what? I'll bet that's the egg—

NELL: You are absolutely right, Winslow. That's the egg I was cooking for you which would have been perfectly done if you would have taken it out when I said to and eaten it. But instead, you had to take it out and leave it out and cook your own with your goddamned egg-timing second hand.

WINSLOW: Nell, it's an egg, for God's sake. It's only an egg.

NELL: It looked terrible. I opened it and it was cold and runny and—

WINSLOW: So you didn't have lunch?

NELL: I'm having it now.

SHE takes a big swig of the wine.

WINSLOW: I'll have a delicious stir fry ready in less than fifteen—

NELL: I don't really want a stir-fry, but thanks anyway.

WINSLOW: You'll change your mind in a couple of minutes when I start sautéing a little chopped fresh garlic and ginger root.

> HE begins to chop vegetables rapidly. NELL lifts HER foot, slips off one of HER shoes, and flings it in WINSLOW'S direction. HE exhibits no response except:

WINSLOW: Why can't you remember to think of your blood sugar?

NELL: I don't know; let me guess.

WINSLOW: Do we have to go through this again?

NELL: Too many things on my mind, maybe?

WINSLOW: You know perfectly well that whenever you let your blood sugar drop, you get upset.

NELL: I am not upset!

WINSLOW: By now you should be familiar enough with the physiologic condition to take the necessary precautions.

NELL: [*Surly.*] I am not a scientist, Winslow. I'm just me.

WINSLOW: [*Taking pan from shelf.*] The worst part is, it's so preventable.

NELL: No, that's not the worst part.

> NELL plops the wine bottle on the table and walks off. WINSLOW hangs the tie where HE can admire it while HE works in the kitchen. HE puts on an apron. HE selects a large onion. HE admires the tie as HE peels the onion. HE does not notice NELL, WHO is preparing to go out.

234

When WINSLOW hears HER opening the door to go, HE calls after HER.

WINSLOW: Fourteen minutes and counting...Nell? I've got dinner all planned.

NELL: Oh, I'm sure you do.

WINSLOW: Where are you going?

NELL: I don't know; Boston, maybe.

WINSLOW: Why?

NELL: [*Calling back.*] To look for my very own Boston '49, why else?

> SHE slams the door and hobbles outside just as SCOTT approaches the building, checking HIS Palm Pilot. At first NELL pretends not to see HIM. Then, when SHE realizes he's recognized HER, SHE pretends to be looking for HER dog.

SCOTT: Nell?

NELL: Oh. Hi.

SCOTT: How are you doing?

NELL: Oh, fine. You doing okay?

SCOTT: I'm great.

NELL: Good.

SCOTT: I thought that sounded like your voice.

NELL: It's me, all right.

SCOTT: Did you say you were looking for a Boston 49?

NELL: Uhm...A dog. My dog. I'm looking for him.

SCOTT: Son of a gun. Just when you think you've heard all the breeds, they come up with another.

NELL: He's a nice dog.

SCOTT: [*Noticing HER feet.*] If he's so nice, why did he run off with your other shoe?

NELL: You saw him?

SCOTT: Not really.

> NELL realizes that SHE is wearing only one shoe. SHE tries to conceal the other foot.

NELL: You didn't see him.

SCOTT: No. But I did see some people—about your portfolio.

NELL: You did?

SCOTT: I never lie to a woman wearing only half her footwear.

NELL: Which people?

SCOTT: The right people, Nell. The big boys.

NELL: What happened? [*Beat.*] Did anything happen?

SCOTT: Miss Mutari, we've got some celebrating to do. Taxi! Taxi!

> HE picks HER up in HIS arms and looks off.

SCENE FOUR: Duet

NELL and WINSLOW stand separately, EACH
addressing the audience.

WINSLOW: It started out small. Ordinary...

NELL: It started out like an ordinary Saturday. I was
working on my senior series: "Rooftop Moods on the Slope",
when I realized I had used up my last empty can. You
know. For paint.

WINSLOW: ...Bottle caps, baseball cards, postage stamps...

NELL: I tried an orange juice bottle but it kept tipping over.

WINSLOW: Then at med. school they wanted everyone to
look like everyone else. So they made us wear a white lab
coat and trousers. And a tie. But I didn't want to look like
everybody else.

NELL: I was mopping it up with newspapers when I saw
this ad about a huge garage sale. I wrote down the address,
and set out after some paint cans.

WINSLOW: I was determined to be...courageous.

NELL: God, I was gutsy.

WINSLOW: In a scientific experiment, there are things held
constant—a while lab coat and trousers—and there are
things which are variable...

NELL: And stubborn. And yes, lucky. That's it. That's how I
found success. It was stubbornness, luck, guts...

WINSLOW: I wore the loudest ties I could find. A
flamboyant, bright blue cocker spaniel. A crimson trout.

NELL: ...And the love of an extraordinary man.

WINSLOW: ...For the first time in my life, I was having fun.

237

ACT II

SCENE ONE: The Big Night

>SCOTT'S apartment. Closet door is open.
>NELL, inside, is tossing ties out on the floor.
>Outside door opens. SCOTT enters.

SCOTT: Nell?

NELL: [*From closet.*] In here.

SCOTT: I thought you'd be at the gallery.

>HE takes off HIS jacket, and tosses it on a
>chair. HE notices something in the pocket. It is
>a black net stocking. HE chuckles, tosses it into
>the wastebasket.

NELL: [*From closet.*] How was your conference?

SCOTT: Okay...Why aren't you at the gallery?

NELL: It's early.

SCOTT: It's not that early. What are you doing in there?

NELL: Cleaning. Look at this mess.

>SHE emerges from closet in underwear and
>slip.

SCOTT: You're not even dressed!

NELL: I can be out the door in five minutes.

SCOTT: I've heard that before.

>NELL tosses another tie on the pile. SCOTT
>checks out the wastebasket, keeping HIS eye on
>NELL.

238

NELL: I can't stand all this clutter.

SCOTT: That's what I love about you.

NELL: My intolerance for old clothes?

> SHE deposits a few old ties in the wastebasket as SCOTT diverts HER attention from the net stocking in the wastebasket:

SCOTT: Look at you, baby. You are a natural. Every screw-up in the Village stays awake nights trying to find a gimmick. But you don't need a gimmick. You've got style without even trying.

> HE runs HIS hand along HER neck and THEY embrace—while HE checks HIS watch.

SCOTT: ...But it is getting late.

NELL: How was lunch?

> SHE starts to put on a simple, elegant cocktail dress.

SCOTT: Lunch? Oh, fine. Everything went great.

> HE rummages in refrigerator. Finds a bagel.

NELL: Did all the clients show up?

> SCOTT searches the refrigerator.

SCOTT: Oh, the usual...Damn.

NELL: What's wrong?

SCOTT: Don't we have any more cream cheese?

NELL: Look behind the lemons.

SCOTT: I did.

> NELL goes over to refrigerator and shows HIM
> where the cream cheese is.

NELL: Oh my goodness. The eggs.

> SCOTT slathers cream cheese on HIS bagel.

SCOTT: What's the matter with them?

NELL: They're almost out of date.

SCOTT: So throw them out.

NELL: I don't want to waste them.

SCOTT: You don't want to waste them? Okay. Let's cancel your opening and stay here and cook eggs all evening. CNN will understand. So will governor what's-his-face.

> HE takes a vicious bite out of HIS cream cheese
> bagel.

NELL: You don't have to yell.

SCOTT: I take you from nowhere to the opening everybody's talking about. I get you media coverage other painters only dream about. I get you buyers with more money than God, and what thanks do I get? You want to cook eggs.

NELL: No. I...I want YOU to cook them.

SCOTT: Oh, well. That's even better.

NELL: Would you? When we get back?

SCOTT: You're kidding.

NELL: It would mean a lot to me.

SCOTT: You're serious?

> NELL nods HER head and bursts into tears.

SCOTT: What'd I say? Jesus, look at you. You're going to wreck your makeup.

> HE dabs at HER eyes and consults HIS watch.

NELL: Don't worry. It's...w...waterproof.

> SHE cries harder.

SCOTT: You want eggs? You got them.

NELL: Really?

SCOTT: Sure. I'll scramble you a batch right after the show, okay?

NELL: S...Scramble?

SCOTT: Soon as we get back, and that's a promise. Now let's get going...

NELL: O...kay...A little lipstick, and I'll be ready.

SCOTT: You're not nervous, are you?

NELL: Just a bit.

> SHE tries to apply HER lipstick. HE takes it
> from HER and puts it on HER lips.

SCOTT: A little here...A little here...Not too much...There. Perfect.

NELL: [*Pulling at HER outfit.*] Are you sure this is okay?

SCOTT: Won-der-ful. Now let's get out of here.

NELL: Wait.

SCOTT: Now what?

NELL: Could you...Could we have them...soft-boiled?

SCOTT: [*Rolling HIS eyes.*] Anything you say, baby. Anything you say.

> HE rushes HER out the door.

SCENE TWO: Alone

> A telephone starts to ring. Lights up on WINSLOW, kneeling next to a chair. There is a telephone and, next to it, a large suitcase, opened, on the floor near the chair. In the suitcase is WINSLOW'S tie collection. HE is taking out the ties one by one, examining each, then draping them over the chair. Finally HE answers the phone:

WINSLOW: Hello? Oh, hi, Mom. I'm fine. How are you?...Good. She's going to be on TV? No, I hadn't heard about it. [*HE crosses HIS fingers, touches HIS forehead, and stamps HIS feet three times.*]...No thanks...No, Mom. I don't have time to come over and watch it on your TV. I just...Yes, but I've got too much work to do...Oh...She said that? When?...Oh. By phone...I don't care what my voice sounds like; I am not disappointed. I just thought she may have dropped in to see you, that's all...Oh, I don't know; maybe for some home cooking...She did?...Simpson's? That's nice...Me? Uhm, soup...Lentil...No, it was delicious, Mom. Yes, everything's fine. I just...Uh huh...Uh huh...I'm doing just fine, so don't worry about a thing...Yes...Okay. You too. Good-bye.

> HE hangs up the phone. HE continues to arrange the ties on the chair. Suddenly HE loosens the tie around HIS neck, rips it off, and

throws it on the floor. HE takes a tie from the chair and crumples it up and throws it on the floor. HE continues to do this. HE sweeps an armful of ties from the chair on to the floor. HE sinks down to the floor on top of the pile of ties as the lights dim to blackout.

SCENE THREE: The Best in Show

> SCOTT'S gallery after the big night. Empty champagne bottles, glasses. Fake plant in pot. It is late. SCOTT, loosening HIS tie, is exuberant. NELL, barefoot, is exhausted.

NELL: Whew. I thought that guy would never leave.

> SCOTT takes off HIS tie and throws it on the floor. HE rolls up HIS sleeves.

SCOTT: That guy can stay as long as he wants.

NELL: Somebody special?

SCOTT: Bart Worthington.

NELL: The Bart Worthington?

SCOTT: I've got his check to prove it.

NELL: He didn't look like a billionaire.

SCOTT: Look at that signature.

> NELL sinks into a chair.

NELL: Bart Worthington. I still can't believe it.

SCOTT: [*Pouring the rest of a champagne bottle into glasses.*] Believe it. And here's one from the VanDeveres.

NELL: Matching purple outfits?

SCOTT: You got it. They only came in for a peek, but they didn't walk out until they'd commissioned your next series. Thanks to *moi.*

NELL: Really?

SCOTT: Sight unseen...How does it taste?

NELL: [*Re: champagne.*] A little stale.

SCOTT: <u>Success</u>, baby. Savor the flavor. How does it feel?

> HE sips the champagne. It is flat. HE empties glasses into the fake plant. HE finds another bottle of champagne, and begins to open it.

NELL: Stupid.

SCOTT: No way.

NELL: Well that's how it feels.

SCOTT: Hey, I know stupid. Stupid walks in here every week, wants me to represent them. Stupid, I know. You? Uh uh.

NELL: Easy, then. I mean, it's so easy. I used to work so hard. You can't believe how I used to struggle, and...and this is so easy.

SCOTT: Let me tell you something. Struggling is supposed to be good for your soul, right?

> HE aims the cork off, pops it, pours champagne into the glasses, gives HER one.

NELL: I guess so.

SCOTT: But <u>not</u> struggling is even better, baby. And best of all? Success. Here's to success.

NELL: Success.

THEY toast, SHE more hesitantly than HE.

SCOTT: Now, how about a couple of steaks at Grisson's? Accepting checks always gives me an appetite.

NELL: You said you'd make scrambled eggs.

SCOTT: Too messy.

NELL: But you promised.

SCOTT: You can't be serious. We've got some celebrating to do!

NELL: You go on. I'm tired.

SCOTT: How can you be tired when I got you a commission from the VanDeveres?

NELL: It's easy.

SHE lies back and holds HER head.

SCOTT: Hey, you're not getting sick on me, are you? You've got the Council luncheon tomorrow, and you're doing an open studio after dinner.

HE feels HER forehead.

NELL: Leave me alone, okay?

SCOTT: Now what?

NELL: Nothing. I just wondered...Why am I doing this?

SCOTT: Uh oh, it's that artistic temperament creeping up.

NELL: I'm serious. Why?

SCOTT: For this. So you could know what it feels like.

NELL: It is?

SCOTT: Absotively and posilutely. All you have to do is sit back and enjoy.

NELL: Oh.

SCOTT: You can do that, can't you?

NELL: I...guess so.

SCOTT: Great. Now how about we go get something to eat? I'm starving. Put on some lipstick and some rouge, and we'll—Now what is it?

NELL: I think I just need to get centered. You go along. I'll lock up.

SCOTT: Sure?

NELL: Sure.

SCOTT: [*Blowing a kiss at HER.*] Okay. Love you.

NELL: Love—[*SCOTT slams door as HE leaves.*]...you.

> Lights dim. NELL goes up to one of the paintings and straightens it. SHE notices something on the floor. It is Scott's tie – very modern, very boring. SHE picks it up and examines it.
>
> Now the lights dim except on one of the paintings, which suggests abstractly the garage sale where SHE had met WINSLOW. The painting grows—as the Christmas tree in the Nutcracker grew—until it becomes real.

SCENE FOUR: How They Met

> Lights up on a garage sale.
>
> WINSLOW, in a white lab coat, slacks, shirt,
> and another very loud tie, stands, several old
> ties on one arm, HIS back to NELL.
>
> SHE is a senior in the College of Art, and has
> taken great care to look like it: dressed all in
> monochrome and smoking something
> unfiltered as SHE searches for containers in
> which to mix HER paints.
>
> NELL and WINSLOW do not see one another.
> EACH is examining the merchandise.
> WINSLOW bends over to examine the contents
> of an old trunk. NELL stoops to pick up a Chef
> Boyardee Ravioli can—family size. THEY bump
> bottoms.

TOGETHER: Excuse me/I'm sorry.

> NELL stands up quickly and is dizzy. SHE
> catches HER balance. Embarrassed, NELL
> moves away to allow WINSLOW to dig through
> the trunk. SHE resumes looking about, but is
> increasingly distracted by WINSLOW'S
> enthusiasm:
>
> HE moves in for a better point of attack, but
> one of the ties on HIS arm catches the rough
> edge of one of NELL'S cans. It takes a moment
> for HIM to notice, but when HE does, HE treats
> the tie like a nearly extinct bird, snared by
> sheer thoughtlessness of a careless hunter.

WINSLOW: My tie!

NELL realizes what has happened, and tries to free the tie. But WINSLOW wants to handle it HIMSELF.

NELL: Oh. Here...

WINSLOW: Be careful...Let me do it. I'll do it.

Tenderly, HE un-snags HIS treasure.

NELL: I'm awfully sorry.

WINSLOW: I don't know why they don't just throw those stupid cans away.

NELL: Some people need them.

WINSLOW: For what? [HE smoothes the scarred tie tissue.] Slitting wrists?

NELL: Holding brushes.

WINSLOW: You...paint?

NELL: Constantly.

WINSLOW: What do you paint?

NELL: Abstract mood patterns. And variations.

WINSLOW: Oh.

NELL: My work represents the conflicts inherent in interpersonal communication.

But WINSLOW is not interested in explanations now. HE glances about until HIS eye catches something.

WINSLOW: Here. Would you take these a minute?

HE hands HER HIS armload of ties. HE takes HER cans, looks about, finds an old rusty wrench. HE squats down, puts one of the cans on its side, pounds the sharp edge with the wrench.

NELL is trying HER best to look cool standing there holding HIS armload of old ties as WINSLOW pounds the cans. SHE is puzzled by HIS white lab jacket.

NELL: [*Cautiously.*] What are you, a dentist?

One of the ties drags perilously close to the ground.

WINSLOW: [*Continuing pounding.*] Resident...Uh, would you try to keep them off the ground?

NELL raises the endangered tie to safety.

NELL: So you're going to be a doctor?

WINSLOW: Pathologist.

NELL: You mean like diseases? [*HE nods.*] I'm afraid I'm too visual for that.

WINSLOW checks smoothness of the pounded can by running HIS finger along the inside edge.

WINSLOW: [*Starting to pound another can.*] Clinical pathology is much more visual than painting. I mean you look through the microscope at patterns and variations. You analyze them to determine what they mean...Through my microscope I see the most beautiful patterns in the world.

NELL: [*Out of cigarettes.*] Really?

WINSLOW: Definitely. You should leave the patterns to nature.

NELL: What about the variations?

WINSLOW: Those too.

NELL: Well, I guess I'll just have to throw away all my brushes.

WINSLOW: Oh, no. I didn't mean that. There's plenty to paint...

NELL: I really would like my cans now, if you don't mind.

WINSLOW: ...Trees. Hills. Rivers. Waterfalls. That's what you should paint.

NELL: [*Fuming by now.*] There's not enough conflict in trees, hills, and waterfalls.

> WINSLOW stops pounding. HE stands, holding wrench. HE tries to remember where HE found the wrench. HE puts it back where it was.

WINSLOW: Notice the difference?

> SHE stoops down and peeks at the pounded cans.

NELL: Yes. Thanks.

> SHE stands too quickly and again loses HER balance. This time WINSLOW catches HER.

WINSLOW: Are you okay?

NELL: It's just my blood sugar.

WINSLOW: Hypoglycemia is not uncommon this time of day.

> HE looks at HIS watch to verify this
> observation.

NELL: I get busy, and I forget to eat.

> WINSLOW reaches into HIS pocket and takes
> out a Snickers bar.

WINSLOW: Here.

NELL: I'm okay.

WINSLOW: Take it. I buy them by the six-pack. [*With some urging, SHE does.*] In no time at all, the glucose will shoot through your pyloric valve and you'll have energy galore.

NELL: Thanks.

> SHE munches the candy. WINSLOW moves a
> tie out of harm's way. Pause. SHE likes
> chocolate. WINSLOW takes HER free hand and
> looks closely at it. SHE responds.

WINSLOW: You know, if you'd just take the time to flatten the sharp ridges on those cans, the way I showed you, you wouldn't have all these little nicks on your—

NELL: What's your name?

> HE looks absently around, then remembers the
> ties. HE takes them from HER arm, one by one.

WINSLOW: Winslow. Yours?

NELL: Nell. But I sign my work with just an "N"... I believe in minimalism. [*WINSLOW looks around, shakes HIS head.*]...What's wrong?

WINSLOW: [*Miserable.*] Oh, nothing.

NELL: Look, it was my fault it got snagged. I'll be glad to pay for—

WINSLOW: It's not that. It's just that I was hoping they'd have a bigger selection.

NELL: There's a big rack of clothes out by the—

WINSLOW: First place I looked.

NELL: Hmm. [*SHE looks around.*]...Did you check those boxes over there?

> SHE indicates a pile of old cartons. WINSLOW follows HER glance. HE tries to get to them as quickly as possible, stumbling over the yard sale items. SHE follows. HE starts to rummage through them without letting the ties drag on the ground.

NELL: Here. I'll hold them.

> NELL takes the ties from HIS arm. HE searches with renewed vigor.

WINSLOW: [*Digging.*] Post World War II ties are not really that uncommon, you know.

NELL: Uh huh.

WINSLOW: You just have to keep at it.

NELL: Uh huh.

WINSLOW: You never give up the search. You've got to keep the hope alive, keep trying, no matter how hopeless it seems, even if you think there's no realistic chance of finding one...

Little by little, NELL is caught up in HIS enthusiasm.

> Soon SHE, too, is rummaging through the stack
> of boxes, holding HIS ties on HER shoulder so
> they won't drag. Suddenly SHE pulls out a
> wide, bright green tie decorated with a huge
> bright pink flamingo. SHE looks at it
> questioningly.

NELL: Here's a funny one...

> WINSLOW looks up briefly, preoccupied with
> HIS search. Then HE double takes. HE stands
> slowly, HIS hands full of clothes dropping to the
> ground. HE walks over to NELL, gazing at the
> outrageous tie. HE reaches out and touches
> the outline of the flamingo as if it were a sacred
> relic.

WINSLOW: It's...It's...

NELL: A flamingo.

WINSLOW: A Boston forty-nine flamingo! Oh, God. I mean,
I've read about them, of course, but...Oh my goodness; it's
in mint condition. Beautiful. It's beautiful!
And...wonderful...You are so wonderful...

> Suddenly, passionately, HE embraces NELL
> and kisses HER. Then HE steps back.

NELL: Wow.

WINSLOW: Oh dear. I...I'm sorry. I shouldn't have...It's just
that...

NELL: No problem.

WINSLOW: See, when all those soldiers came home from
World War II, they were really...really...

NELL: Yes?

WINSLOW: Tired of khaki.

NELL: I see.

WINSLOW: They were happy to be alive, that's what they were. And they wanted to wear ties that said so...Sort of like...like you.

NELL: Me?

WINSLOW: I mean, you're an artist.

NELL: Yes.

WINSLOW: Well, you have an opportunity that no one else has.

NELL: I don't do ties.

WINSLOW: No, I didn't mean that. I meant, well, first of all, you're dealing with living people, people who can feel glad to be alive, just by looking at what you put on a rectangle on a wall.

NELL: I never thought of it like that.

WINSLOW: If I were a painter, I would think of it every time I picked up my brush.

> NELL wants to be angry or at least defensive, but can't SHE is quite taken with the eccentric tie collector. WINSLOW fingers the tie. NELL is beginning to be glad that she found the Boston forty-nine flamingo.

NELL: Do you go out a lot? I mean, to look for ties for your collection.

WINSLOW: Every Saturday unless I'm on call.

NELL: Are you going next Saturday?

WINSLOW: I'm on call.

NELL: Oh.

WINSLOW: But...The Saturday after that, I'm going to the Poconos—unless the weather gets bad. I really don't like to drive in the snow, but it's been so warm this year...See, I wrote to this place. One of those mountain towns. [*SHE nods.*] Only one restaurant, but several antique shops, and, well, I was wondering...I mean, what I mean is...

NELL: One of my landscape assignments is a mountain. I've been putting it off. I mean, if I'm going to paint a mountain it would be a good idea to experience the visual...

WINSLOW: It's beautiful. You should go there sometime. The Poconos.

NELL: Do you go often?

WINSLOW: Not very often. I hate riding all that way alone.

NELL: Oh. Right, I guess it's a pretty long drive.

WINSLOW: Yes, but that's the thing about ties. You really can't leave any stone unturned.

NELL: I guess you never know when you might hit the jackpot.

WINSLOW: Like today.

NELL: [*Suddenly.*] Um...I was wondering...

WINSLOW: I think I know what you're going to ask.

NELL: Oh? And what's your answer?

WINSLOW: No.

NELL: [*Disappointed.*] Oh.

WINSLOW: Everybody always asks me, and nobody expects the answer, but it's true: vintage ties are not expensive at all. In fact, sometimes they are an outright bargain.

NELL: [*Amused.*] Is that the truth?

WINSLOW: I swear it. Look at this one, the gem you found. Look at that price tag.

NELL: A steal.

WINSLOW: [*Exhibiting tag.*] Can you believe it?

NELL: No. I can't.

> End of flashback. Now the lights dim to darkness, and we are once more in the gallery after the show.
>
> NELL has been deeply moved by the memory. With an attitude of finality, SHE searches for something and finally finds it: a phone. SHE is in a hurry to call. There is no answer. SHE hangs up the phone and brushes away a tear.
>
> Suddenly, the lights go out. SHE hears a noise from someone approaching. SHE wipes HER eyes. Alone in the gallery SHE is a little worried. In the darkness, the glowing silhouette of a flamingo appears, gliding slowly forward.

NELL: ...Scott?

> No response. Now SHE is afraid. SHE looks around for a weapon but all SHE can find is the tie, so SHE holds it taut, ready to strangle an attacker. Then, suddenly, the glowing flamingo sinks downward and all but disappears.

WINSLOW'S VOICE: Hello? Anybody here?

> The lights go on. WINSLOW is on HIS hands
> and knees plugging in an extension cord. The
> flamingo is on HIS tie, a particularly large one.
> Next to HIM on the floor is a suitcase.

NELL: Hello, Boston forty-nine flamingo.

WINSLOW: Hello, Nell

NELL: Hello, Winslow.

WINSLOW: Sorry about the lights. I tripped over the cord.

NELL: You should be more careful.

> WINSLOW notices the tie SHE is still clutching.

WINSLOW: What's that?

NELL: Scott's tie. I was about to strangle you.

WINSLOW: That would've been something.

NELL: Yes.

> THEY laugh nervously, then stop. THEY stand
> facing one another.

WINSLOW: ...So.

NELL: So.

WINSLOW: So...How have you been?

NELL: Okay. You?

WINSLOW: Fine.

NELL: How are you doing?

WINSLOW: I'm fine. Everything's just fine.

NELL: Your mom called.

WINSLOW: How is she doing?

NELL: Oh, fine.

WINSLOW: Good.

NELL: I...took her out to dinner.

WINSLOW: I'm sure she liked that...Uh...Where did you go?

NELL: Simpson's.

WINSLOW: Do they still give you so much you have to get a doggy bag?

NELL: Yes.

WINSLOW: Remember every time we went out to Simpson's you'd come home with a doggy bag?

NELL: Yes.

WINSLOW: Do you still like cold flounder for breakfast?

NELL: Yes.

WINSLOW: Because it's not fishy?.

NELL: Because it's just fishy enough...

       Beat.

WINSLOW: Nell...

NELL: We didn't order it, Winslow. Neither of us ordered flounder. I forgot what it was, but I know what it wasn't.

WINSLOW: How's, uh, Scott?

NELL: Scott? Fine. He left. I mean, he was hungry, and—

WINSLOW: How's, uh, your blood sugar?

NELL: It's okay.

WINSLOW: Are you tired?

NELL: No.

WINSLOW: I thought you might be tired.

NELL: Well I'm not.

WINSLOW: I wondered if maybe you'd like to talk.

> Beat.

NELL: I would...But I don't have anything to say.

> HIS hopes dashed by this response, WINSLOW
> turns sharply.

WINSLOW: Oh. Okay, then. Well, I guess I'd better go now.

> HE puts all the feeling HE wants to share with
> HER into swooping HIS suitcase off the floor. It
> snaps open. Ties everywhere. THEY pause a
> moment. THEY start to pick up the ties.

WINSLOW: Me and my damn ties.

> Now NELL stops HIS hand with HERS. SHE
> regards HIM.

NELL: I miss your damn ties, Winslow. I...I miss your
damn ties.

SHE smiles but tears are in HER eyes.

WINSLOW: You do?

> NELL nods. WINSLOW is clearly moved by HER
> response. Out of this interaction comes what
> appears to be a ritual:

> Tenderly, slowly, NELL selects one of HIS ties
> from the floor and places it around WINSLOW'S
> neck. SHE kisses HIM.

> Now WINSLOW picks up a tie and gently lays it
> about NELL'S neck. HE kisses HER. Still
> kneeling on the gallery floor, THEY embrace as
> the lights dim to blackout.

SCENE FIVE: Conclusion

> The tiny kitchenette of WINSLOW'S studio
> apartment in New York. The small table now
> has a cloth and flowers. The paint-spattered
> stool has a matching cushion. The same one-
> burner stove, toaster oven, and beverage
> refrigerator, but now there is also a comfortable
> chair.

> NELL, in bathrobe, sits in the comfortable chair
> reading the paper while WINSLOW, wearing an
> apron over HIS conservative suit, white shirt,
> brown shoes, and another extremely loud tie, is
> breaking eggs into a bowl.

NELL: I wish they had funnies.

WINSLOW: The New York Times?

NELL: Yes. Then they would be complete.

WINSLOW: Funnies are obviously not fit to print.

NELL: More fit than all this gushing.

WINSLOW: Any other artist would be thrilled.

NELL: Eugene O'Neill wouldn't.

WINSLOW: He was a writer, not a painter.

NELL: All the more reason why he would appreciate the truth.

WINSLOW: Just because you don't like your Grand Canyon series doesn't mean it's no good.

NELL: We had fun, though.

WINSLOW: No complaints here. I wonder if those coyotes ever found our Chips Ahoy?

NELL: I doubt it. We'll probably go back in a few years, follow our map, and dig them up.

WINSLOW: Sounds like a plan.

NELL: Unless coyotes know how to open a Ziploc bag.

WINSLOW: Would you like more coffee?

NELL: I'd rather have a little milk.

WINSLOW: Milk? That's a switch.

   WINSLOW pours HER a glass of milk.

NELL: Thanks.

WINSLOW: My pleasure. Good to see you starting off your day with a few amino acids and calcium.

   WINSLOW picks up a loaf of bread and notes
   the label on the bread package. HE selects two

slices of bread, and places them into the toaster oven. HE plops some butter into a frying pan. HE checks HIS watch, picks up a spoon, examines it closely, and takes HIS position at the stove. HE pauses, spoon poised, ready to pour in the eggs.

NELL: Winslow?

WINSLOW: Just a second; I'm timing.

NELL: I thought you were going to scramble them.

WINSLOW: I'm not timing the eggs.

NELL: There's not a whole lot left to time here...The toaster oven times itself.

WINSLOW: I'm timing the butter.

NELL: Nobody times butter.

WINSLOW: I do.

NELL: It's already there. You just drop it into the pan and melt it. You don't time it.

WINSLOW: Yes you do.

NELL: Why?

WINSLOW: So you know when to add the eggs.

NELL: You add the eggs when the butter is melted.

WINSLOW: Nell, butter doesn't just melt.

NELL: Oh? What else does it do?

WINSLOW: It absorbs heat.

NELL: Oh.

WINSLOW: And in doing so, it goes from the solid state to the liquid state.

NELL: Also known as melting.

WINSLOW: But it doesn't stop at that.

NELL: You're right. If you stand there talking instead of cooking, it gets all brown.

WINSLOW: Exactly, because it continues to absorb heat energy.

NELL: I think it's time to add the eggs.

WINSLOW: But I haven't scrambled them yet!

>Exasperated, WINSLOW hurriedly beats the eggs and pours them into the pan, spilling some. HE studies HIS watch: HE could still be timing that important track meet, but this time HE is the runner. NELL puts down the paper and helps HIM scramble the eggs properly. SHE rubs the side of HIS cheek, and the tension melts from HIS face.

NELL: Mmm. Smells delicious.

WINSLOW: There.

>HE seems pleased that the eggs are scrambled in the pan where HE left them. HE admires them. HE finds the necessary materials and lines them up neatly: a dish, clean cutlery, salt, pepper, napkin, toast dish.

NELL: Are you ready?

WINSLOW: Almost. The book said to keep them on a medium flame, and to stir occasionally.

NELL: I'm talking about the news.

> WINSLOW'S watch goes off. HE scoops up the eggshells and places them into the garbage.

WINSLOW: News? I'll listen on the way to work.

NELL: No, my news. I was going to tell you, but you said you were too busy timing.

WINSLOW: Another show?

NELL: Yes, but that's not it.

WINSLOW: A commission?

NELL: Two more, actually, but there's something else.

> WINSLOW directs HIS attention to the eggs.

WINSLOW: Now I'm afraid they'll get overdone.

NELL: You're right. Let's eat.

> Pause as WINSLOW serves up the food.

WINSLOW: You're smiling.

NELL: I was just thinking of the look on your face when you found those Paris fifty-two's.

WINSLOW: That wacky yard sale in Jackson Hole. Unbelievable.

NELL: ...Remember those ice cream cones?

WINSLOW: Do I ever. We should go back there next year.

NELL: We'll see.

WINSLOW: I thought you had a good time.

NELL: I had a wonderful time, and got lots of work done, but...

WINSLOW: Did you think of a name yet?

        NELL is surprised at HIS question.

NELL : What?

WINSLOW: The series you're working on.

NELL: Oh.

WINSLOW: Did you come up with a name for it yet?

NELL: Oh, I've had a few ideas.

WINSLOW: Such as?

NELL: Streptosomething and Staphlosomething.

        NELL puts down HER fork and looks a little ill.

WINSLOW: Has a definite ring to it...You feeling okay?

NELL: Sure.

WINSLOW: You look a little queasy or something.

NELL: I'll be right back.

        SHE hurries out of the room. WINSLOW is
        concerned.

WINSLOW: You okay, Nell? Nell?

NELL: What is it?

WINSLOW: You're not feeling sick, are you? I could make you some lemon and honey tea.

NELL: Will you have some too?

WINSLOW: If you're the one who's sick, why should I have lemon and honey tea?

NELL: So we can toast.

WINSLOW: Oh.

NELL: And I'm not sick.

WINSLOW: Something must be wrong. You're not acting like yourself.

NELL: Maybe it's that nasty artistic temperament creeping up.

WINSLOW: I don't think so. Once you get to know it, it's not really nasty at all.

NELL: And how would you know?

WINSLOW: A little encounter out on the prairie, comes to mind.

> SHE starts to look through the paper again. WINSLOW meekly touches HER arm.

WINSLOW: Wait.

> SHE turns to HIM.

NELL: What is it?

WINSLOW: Uh...How were the eggs?

NELL: [*Affectionately.*] Perfect.

266

WINSLOW: Then why weren't you feeling good?

NELL: A little encounter out on the prairie...

WINSLOW: You mean...?

NELL: Yes. That's what I wanted to toast.

WINSLOW: What?

NELL: To the three of us.

WINSLOW: Three?

NELL: One...two...three.

WINSLOW: You can't count yourself twice.

NELL: I didn't.

WINSLOW: You mean...?

> NELL nods. WINSLOW accepts this calmly at first. Then, as it sinks in, he lets out with a long, loud, most uncharacteristic yelp of joy.

NELL: Come here, you wild, impetuous cowboy.

> WINSLOW's head is spinning as HE begins to set up a mental schedule.

WINSLOW: We...We've got to make plans.

NELL: I am, Winslow. Oh, I am...

> SHE walks toward HIM, grabs HIS arm, pulls HIM to the chair, and kisses HIM.

VOICE OF NELL: The person I wasn't—and the one I am now—said goodbye a long time ago. And it was won...derful.

END

Causa Mortis
or
The Medical Student
By Jacob M. Appel

Jacob M. Appel is a graduate of Brown University, Harvard Law School, Columbia University's College of Physicians and Surgeons, and the graduate program in creative writing at New York University. He is the author of over one hundred short stories, twelve plays, and numerous articles in the field of bioethics.

This play was first staged on November 5, 2009, at the Detroit Repertory Theatre, under the direction of Bruce Millan. The play is dedicated to the memory of Gerald and Darlene Larson.

For rights to this play, please contact: Jacob M. Appel, 140 Claremont Ave #3D, New York, NY 10027.

Characters

Eleanor, a neurology patient (F—50s/60s)
Paige Eleanor's older daughter (F-30s)
Gloria, Eleanor's younger daughter (F-20s/30s)
Robyn, a medical student (F-20s)
The Amnesiac, a quadriplegic (F—20s/30s)
Dr. Gwendolyn Falk, a brain surgeon (F—50s)

Setting:
The neurology ward of private hospital in a major American city. The present.

ACT ONE

SCENE ONE

> Paige and Robyn. A hospital corridor. Robyn
> carries a towering stack of patients' charts.

PAIGE: Let me ask you something, doctor.

ROBYN: I'm *not* a doctor. I'm a medical student.

PAIGE: That's all right. So here's my question—

ROBYN: Honestly, I'm probably not the best person to ask. This is my first day at the hospital....I've only been working here for three hours....

PAIGE: Don't worry. It's an easy question, doctor. Let's say you'd been having debilitating headaches every afternoon for the past six months. Headaches so bad that you thought your brain was on fire. What would you do?

ROBYN: I suppose I'd see a doctor....*which, for the record, I am not.*

PAIGE: So you wouldn't try to work through the pain?

ROBYN: I'm a medical student. They expect me to work until I keel over....

PAIGE: Very well. But let's pretend you aren't a doctor. Let's say—hypothetically speaking—you're a senior marine biologist at the city aquarium. Now would you seek medical attention? Or would you put it off until one day, when you were halfway through feeding the dolphins, you ended up keeling over into a tank of salt water with dozens of schoolchildren looking on?

ROBYN: Oh, no. I wouldn't do that.

PAIGE: I didn't think so. Now tell me this, doctor: If you had a serious and longstanding medical condition, would you tell your daughters, your daughters who love you more than any other human beings on the entire planet? Or would you tell nobody?

ROBYN: Please don't call me *doctor*....My name's Robyn.

PAIGE: Very well, Robyn. You'd tell your daughters, wouldn't you?

ROBYN: I don't have any daughters....

PAIGE: But if you did.

ROBYN: ....I guess I would....

PAIGE: Of course, you would. You've only been a doctor three hours and *already* you know that.

ROBYN: Listen to me. I am a medical student. *NOT* a doctor. We're required by law to make that clear to the patients and their families....It's the very first thing they tell you when they give you your white coat. Honestly, it's the *only* thing that they tell you. That *under absolutely no circumstances* are you allowed to pass yourself off as a physician. Otherwise, you can get expelled—or sued—or you can even go to jail for practicing medicine without a license....So *please* don't keep calling me doctor. Because I'm only a layperson. An ordinary citizen, just like you. There is *nobody* in the world who is less a doctor than I am! [*Robyn loses her grip on the patients' charts and they topple to the ground. Pages fly in all directions.*] Oh God!

> Robyn falls to her knees and begins to sort through the charts, attempting to guess which pages belong to which patients. Paige kneels down alongside her and assists her as best she can.

PAIGE: It's okay. I know you're not a doctor....

273

ROBYN: And I'm never going to become one at this rate.

PAIGE: What should I do with the torn pages?

> She holds up two halves of a ripped page from
> a patient's chart. Robyn takes the scraps from
> her and examines them. Then she stuffs them
> inside her blouse.

PAIGE: It's just that it's so hard to find a real doctor to talk
to around here....

ROBYN: Please don't tell anybody I got the charts mixed
up.

PAIGE: —I suppose I'd have better luck on a golf course—

ROBYN: —Dr. Falk would have my head if she ever found
out.

PAIGE: —Or maybe a carwash....Doctors always drive such
clean cars. Have you noticed that?

ROBYN: [*Breaking into sobs.*] I didn't go to medical school
to play golf....or to drive a shiny car....All I wanted to do
was help people, as old-fashioned as that sounds...and now
I'm going to get expelled on my first day in the hospital....

PAIGE: Oh, honey.....It's not such a big deal, is it? The
pages don't even seem to be *so* mixed up. All of *these* over
here are for the same patient. Sally Brown....and she
sounds like a very sick woman anyway....although I
suppose I shouldn't be reading through her records.....

> Robyn uses the chart pages as tissues: first
> she dabs her eyes, then she blows her nose.

ROBYN: All of these charts are for *different* patients named
Sally Brown. Dr. Falk sent me to get Ms. Brown's files from
medical records...but there were nineteen different patients

named Sally Brown who've been treated in this hospital at one time or another....and I didn't know which one she wanted, so I brought them all....

PAIGE: Damn. This is serious.

ROBYN: You don't know the half of it. Dr. Falk sent a medical student home last year for *slouching*....

> Robyn stuffs additional pages into her blouse until papers are poking out of her clothing from all sides.

PAIGE: Do you know what else is a serious matter?

ROBYN: No. I'm afraid I don't.

PAIGE: My mother's health is a serious matter.

ROBYN: Of course, it is.

PAIGE: *You* know that. *I* know that. The only person who doesn't appear to understand that is my mother. Has anybody told you *why* my mother's head hurts?

> Robyn gathers the charts and stands up. Several pages fall out of her blouse. She tucks them into her pants.

ROBYN: Who is your mother again?

PAIGE: Eleanor Powell. Room 125, Bed 2. Do you know why Eleanor Powell's head hurts?

ROBYN: Honestly, I don't.

PAIGE: My mother has a wrist watch lodged inside her skull.

ROBYN: A wrist watch?

PAIGE: A *man's* wrist watch....

ROBYN: I didn't know that was possible. Last year, they showed us slides of a drunk musician who tried to swallow a clarinet on a dare. You could see all the tiny gauges on the X-ray of his stomach.

PAIGE: Well, my mother didn't swallow anything....My mother had a benign brain tumor removed as a teenager....while she was at boarding school in Switzerland....and it appears one of the Swiss surgeons accidentally left his watch inside her cranium....

ROBYN: That *does* sound painful.

PAIGE: So much for Swiss precision.

ROBYN: At least it wasn't a cuckoo clock.

PAIGE: Although who can be certain it was even an accident? Maybe the surgeon did it *intentionally.*

ROBYN: Or a clarinet. Can you imagine having a clarinet lodged in your skull?

PAIGE: All sorts of crazy people become doctors. You'd have to be rather crazy to spend your life cutting open other people's skulls, if you ask me....

ROBYN: But I guess nobody brings a clarinet into an operating room.

PAIGE: Are you listening to me?   My mother has a forty-year-old timepiece trapped inside her head. I'll bet they didn't teach you about that in medical school....

ROBYN: I'm not done with medical school yet.

PAIGE: The bottom line is that my mother has been keeping this a secret. She found out about the watch in the 1970s, when they installed metal detectors at the airports....But since it didn't cause her any discomfort her, she didn't bother to tell anybody....

ROBYN: Maybe you should be telling this to someone with a medical degree....

PAIGE: It's easier to tell you know and wait for you to graduate....Besides, it's not very complicated: After minding its business all these years, the watch has started encroaching on things inside my mother's head. Important things: Arteries, ventricles, gray matter.

ROBYN: Those are important.

PAIGE: So I'm told. If she doesn't have surgery soon, the watch may cut off the blood supply to her cerebral cortex— and I'm sure you understand what that means....

ROBYN: It doesn't sound very promising.

PAIGE: Preciscly, Robyn. It doesn't sound very promising....Needless to say, when Mom collapsed, my sister and I consulted the leading neurologists in the country and they all recommended the same surgeon. I'm sure you've heard of him: Dr. Hiram T. Luxby.

ROBYN: You mean the Dr. Luxby who—

PAIGE: I swear that man's résumé weighed more than I do. Harvard Medical School, surgical residency at Johns Hopkins in Baltimore, a fellowship at the Mayo Clinic, specializing in the removal of foreign objects from within the cranium. The ideal candidate for the job....So we sent Dr. Luxby my mother's X-rays....He was so intrigued by her case that he flew in from Heidelberg four days later to perform the procedure.....and then he dropped dead.

SCENE TWO

> Hospital room 125. Eleanor and the Amnesiac, in adjacent beds.

277

ELEANOR: Right there in the operating room....One minute he was holding the scalpel and the next he was what the doctors call R.A.R.T.

AMNESIAC: R.A.R.T?

ELEANOR: Rapidly Assuming Room Temperature....Not that I actually saw him collapse, you understand. I was still under anesthesia. But I knew I was in trouble when I woke up and the bandages were on my chest, not my head....During his heart attack, Dr. Luxby fell on the scalpel....

AMNESIAC: That's just awful....

ELEANOR: So then my daughters brought in another surgeon, Dr. Lawrence Spatnick, who was Luxby's protégé at Harvard. He's such a decent, likeable young man, this Dr. Spatnick—nothing at all like a surgeon. He even plays the harp in a chamber quartet....I'll confess I was hoping that I'd wake up from the surgery and he'd be having coffee with Paige. She's my single daughter, the one there's still hope for....Gloria threw herself away on a....Oh, I can't bear to say it....

AMNESIAC: It can't be *that* bad, can it?

ELEANOR: A professional grave robber....

AMNESIAC: I'm sorry.

ELEANOR: The man was a real life body-snatcher. He'd slink around cemeteries, waiting for the mourners to leave, and then he'd shovel out the corpses, strip them of their valuables, and sell the bodies to medical schools in California. You can't imagine how mortifying it was for Gloria to give back all that jewelry....

AMNESIAC: At least she found out while she was young....She'll have a second change with someone else....

278

ELEANOR: She's *still* with him!

AMNESIAC: At least there's hope for your other daughter and Dr. Spatnick.

ELEANOR: Unfortunately, there isn't. Instead of waking up from surgery with a future son-in-law who doesn't pinch wedding bands from cadavers, I found myself in the recovery room with another chest wound. That poor man, Dr. Spatnick...surrounded by all those doctors and all that equipment...and nobody could do anything for him.

AMNESIAC: Another heart attack?

ELEANOR: So you understand why I won't let them try again. It's not only that I've killed two leading neurosurgeons in the prime of their careers, but you have to consider all of the future patients whose lives they might have gone on to save....I could be indirectly responsible for hundreds of deaths....even thousands....

AMNESIAC: I hadn't thought of that.

ELEANOR: So that's *my* story, honey. I won't let them operate and my daughters won't agree to take me home without the operation....And what about you? What's your name?

AMNESIAC: I don't know.

ELEANOR: For real?

AMNESIAC: I wish I did know. All they can tell me is that a road crew found me at the side of the interstate with a bullet in my neck and another lodged in my brain. So I could have been the victim of a carjacking or a drive-by shooting. Or someone close to me—maybe even my own husband—might have abandoned me for dead....You can't imagine how horrific this is! My own husband might have tried to murder me, and I don't even remember whether I'm married.

ELEANOR: So you honestly don't know who you are...?

AMNESIAC: [*Suddenly angry.*] I know exactly who I am. You heard the doctors this morning. I'm Jane Doe. Quadriplegia with Retrograde Amnesia.

ELEANOR: I never cared for the name Jane....You look more like an Amanda. I think I'm going to call you Amanda, if that's all right. Until you remember who you are.

AMNESIAC: And what if I *never* remember?

ELEANOR: Then at least you'll have a name that suits you....Now, quick! It's nearly four o'clock. Pretend you're in a coma.

AMNESIAC: I don't understand.

ELEANOR: Just trust me, Amanda. The new medical student is coming.

> Robyn enters, carrying a clipboard, and approaches Eleanor's bed. Eleanor and the Amnesiac play dead.

ROBYN: Sorry to disturb you, Mrs. Powell. Would you mind if I asked you a few questions? [*Robyn attempts to rouse Eleanor. Eleanor does not move.*] Mrs. Powell? Do you know where you are, Mrs. Powell...? [*Eleanor says nothing.*] You're in a hospital, Mrs. Powell. Please wake up. I only have a few questions and then I'll let you go back to sleep. I promise. [*Eleanor remains silent.*] Do you know who the President is, Mrs. Powell? Try to answer me....[*The room remains silent. Robyn grows desperate.*] So I read your chart, Mrs. Powell. And *yesterday*, you were oriented to time and place and knew the name of the President. Nothing has changed since then, has it? [*Eleanor continues to play dead. Robyn writes on her clipboard.*] "Oriented to time and place....Knows the name of the President. Patient reports that she is well, without any complaints, but sleepy during the afternoon."

> Robyn attempts to place her stethoscope on Eleanor's chest, but Eleanor rolls over without warning. Then Robyn attempts to take Eleanor's pulse, but Eleanor yanks her hand away. Finally, Robyn removes her reflex hammer from the pocket of her white lab coat and taps Eleanor's knee. Eleanor's leg does not move. Robyn hits her harder. Still no response. As a last measure, Robyn swings down her reflex hammer and pounds Eleanor on the kneecap. Eleanor "reflexively" kicks Robyn in the stomach, still without "waking." When Robyn regains her composure, she writes on the clipboard as she speaks:

ROBYN: "Powell, Eleanor. Heart sounds normal. Regular rate and rhythm. Lungs clear. Abdomen non-tender. Reflexes moderately brisk....." [*Robyn crosses out these last words.*] "Reflexes significantly brisk."

> Robyn approaches the Amnesiac's bed. The Amnesiac follows Eleanor's example and pretends to be sleeping. Robyn is unable to rouse her.

ROBYN: How about you, Ms. Doe? Do you know where *you* are? [*The Amnesiac says nothing.*] Fine, be that way. [*Robyn writes on her clipboard.*] "Oriented to time and place....Knows the name of the President. Patient reports that she is well, without any complaints, but sleepy during the afternoon." [*Robyn takes her reflex hammer out of her white coat, then changes her mind and returns it to her pocket.*] "Doe, Jane. Heart sounds normal. Regular rate and rhythm. Lungs clear. Abdomen non-tender. Reflexes moderately brisk....." [*Robyn exits. Eleanor opens her eyes.*]

ELEANOR: All clear, Amanda.

The Amnesiac opens her eyes.

AMNESIAC: What was *that* about?

ELEANOR: We get a new medical student every two weeks. They're supposed to practice taking histories and physicals on us....but if you pretend you're in a coma, eventually they give up and find a different patient.

AMNESIAC: You know a lot about this place.

ELEANOR: I've been here sixty-six days. Shared this room with nine different women. When you've been here sixty-six days, you'll know an awful lot too.

AMNESIAC: I don't want to be here at all.

ELEANOR: Better than a nursing home.

AMNESIAC: If I knew who my family was, at least I could ask them to kill me.....

ELEANOR: You don't mean that.

AMNESIAC: I mean every word of it, goddamit.

ELEANOR: Oh, honey....

AMNESIAC: Ever since last night, I've been lying here, thinking of all the things I'll never be able to do....Dancing and ice-skating and holding my own children. There might already be children out there somewhere, waiting for me to come home....

ELEANOR: You can borrow my daughters anytime you want.

AMNESIAC: You know what I wish for, Eleanor. I wish *I* could perform the surgery on you—and keel over right there on the operating table....But the best thing I can hope for now is that one night you'll cross over to this side of the room and cover my face with a pillow.

ELEANOR: Don't talk nonsense.

AMNESIAC: That's what I want, Eleanor....I'll go to sleep one night and you'll make it so I don't wake up....

SCENE THREE

Paige and Dr. Falk. Dr. Falk's office.

DR. FALK: Your mother's case is really quite marvelous—from a medical standpoint, that is. In my fifteen years as chief of neurosurgery, I've seen wedding rings, I've seen clamps, I've seen Latex gloves ....but I've done an extensive search of the relevant literature and I couldn't find any watches. Mrs. Powell is a genuine first. One of the students should get a great original paper out of her.

PAIGE: But do you think you can remove it safely?

DR. FALK: Remove what?

PAIGE: *The watch.* The watch in my mother's brain!

DR. FALK: Are you familiar with the case of Phineas Gage, Ms. Powell?

PAIGE: I'm afraid I'm not.

DR. FALK: Phineas Gage was a twenty-five year old railroad foreman from Cavendish, Vermont, who had an iron spike driven through his head during a blasting accident. The spike pierced his maxilla, sliced through both lobes of his anterior cortex, and popped out the other side of his cranium. Fortunately for Gage, the spike missed his sagittal sinus and he survived another twelve years.

PAIGE: What does this have to do with my mother?

DR. FALK: Before this blasting accident, Phineas Gage was a mild-mannered, church-going family man....*After* the accident, he cursed like a sailor, took to fighting in bars, and propositioned any woman he encountered between the ages of fifteen and fifty. Somehow, that spike must have knocked out his inhibition control center.

PAIGE: So you're saying that my mother's going to end up a bar-fighting sex fiend?

DR. FALK: Oh, not at all. Quite the opposite, Ms. Powell. What's remarkable about your mother's case is how few cognitive symptoms she has. Except for the motor difficulties with her extremities, and her balance, and her headaches, of course, and her blind spells—other than those specific complaints, she is, neurologically speaking, quite intact.

PAIGE: Aren't you forgetting that this watch could clot off her brain and kill her at any moment?

DR. FALK: There is that, yes. Quite unfortunate. But I was thinking of the case from more of a scientific vantage point than a personal one.

PAIGE: If you don't mind, Dr. Falk, *I'd* like to talk about the personal aspects of the case....

DR. FALK: Very well. Talk.

PAIGE: When are you planning to take the watch out of my mother's skull?

DR. FALK: Oh, I'm not.

PAIGE: You're not?

DR. FALK: She hasn't consented, Ms. Powell. I can't go cutting open your mother's head without her permission.

PAIGE: Why the hell can't you?

DR. FALK: The law is rather clear on that point.

PAIGE: Laws are meant to be broken. I'm a lawyer. I know what I'm talking about.....Why don't you let me consent for her? She is *my* mother.

DR. FALK: Be reasonable. Your mother is a competent adult. She's capable of making her own decisions....
PAIGE: She's not thinking clearly. How is she supposed to think clearly with a watch cutting off the blood supply to her brain?

DR. FALK: I understand what you're going through. When my own mother turned ninety, she decided that she didn't want to be on dialysis anymore, and there was no convincing her otherwise....

PAIGE: My mother's not ninety, she's fifty-six. And she's mad as a hatter.

DR. FALK: I'll be candid with you, Ms. Powell. I'm not sure how much longer your mother can remain in the hospital under these circumstances. This isn't a hotel. If she doesn't want the operation, it's honestly time to think about taking her home...or finding a facility that can look after her for the long-term....

PAIGE: You mean you want to ship her off to a nursing home while we wait for her brain to shrivel up.
DR. FALK: I'm sorry that you have to go through this, Ms. Powell—

PAIGE: My mother is convinced that she's responsible for the deaths of Dr. Luxby and Dr. Spatnick and that she's going to murder you if you try to operate on her....She's delusional, Dr. Falk.

DR. FALK: Possibly.

PAIGE: What do you mean: "Possibly"?

DR. FALK: I don't actually believe she killed Hiram or Larry, but it *is* a mystery. Are you aware of the difference between Christian Scientists and Jehovah's Witnesses in regard to their views of medical assistance, Ms. Powell?

PAIGE: What on earth are you talking about?

DR. FALK: I'm trying to explain the limits of modern medicine....Christian Scientists believe that prayer cures illness. So, for example, if they come down with bacterial pneumonia, they refuse treatment with penicillin and place their faith in God. In other words, they doubt the *efficacy* of antibiotics. That, from a medical standpoint, is a delusion. As a surgeon, I can't say whether prayer helps to cure disease—I imagine it very well might—but I am quite confident that antibiotics are effective in treating bacterial infections.

PAIGE: My mother's not a Christian Scientist. She's a Unitarian. If she believes in a god at all, it's not a god who can *do* much of anything.

DR. FALK: Please, let me finish. Jehovah's Witnesses, in contrast, turn down blood transfusions because they believe that accepting another person's blood leads to eternal damnation. They acknowledge that turning down donor blood may kill them....but they care more about their salvation. In other words, they don't doubt the *efficacy* of medical intervention, merely its *morality*. I may not agree with Jehovah's Witnesses on this, but I can't say they're delusional. There is no scientific consensus on the subject of eternal damnation....

PAIGE: Can you please get to the point, doctor...?

DR. FALK: What I'm telling you is that I cannot be *certain* your mother, in some tangential way, isn't responsible for the deaths of Dr. Luxby and Dr. Spatnick. Maybe the unique pattern in the irises of her eyes provokes seizures in genetically predisposed individuals, and this, in turn, leads to cardiac arrhythmias....Who can say? For years, the medical community mistakenly prescribed bed rest for heart attacks and, as a result, thousands of people died from deep vein thromboses. We used to believe ulcers were caused by worrying, and now we think they're the product of infectious agents....So until we understand why two of the world's leading neurosurgeons collapsed while the same patient was on the table, I can't say you mother is truly delusional. For the present, she's more like a Jehovah's Witness than a Christian Scientist....

PAIGE: Are you out of your mind? It was a coincidence. Bad luck.

DR. FALK: Most likely....

PAIGE: People drop dead all the time....

DR. FALK: I'm not disagreeing with you. People *do* drop dead all of the time.

PAIGE: You're afraid, aren't you! You're *hoping* my mother won't consent to the operation, because you think she might kill *you* too.....

DR. FALK: I'm going to have to excuse myself, Ms. Powell. I have patients to see....[*Dr. Falk walks toward the door.*] You're welcome to stay here and compose yourself for as long as you need....But please be sure to pull the door shut behind you....

PAIGE: You goddam coward! I swear you're going to saw open my mother's skull, even if it's the last thing you ever do!

SCENE FOUR

> Hospital room 125. Gloria and Eleanor. Gloria sits beside Eleanor's bed with a notepad.

ELEANOR: Are you sure you're getting all of this down, dear?

GLORIA: I told you I'm getting it all down. Why can't you ever give me the benefit of the doubt?

ELEANOR: Because I'm your mother. I love you far too much to have any confidence in you....Now can you please read the guest list back to me?

GLORIA: Okay, but first, there's something I want to tell you.

ELEANOR: What?

GLORIA: I just want you to know how happy I am—and how happy Phil will be—that you've decided to go through with the operation.

ELEANOR: Why will Phil be so happy? It's one less body that he can ship to California.

GLORIA: That's cruel and uncalled for. Phil never did anything to you.

ELEANOR: He never had a chance.

GLORIA: It was all a misunderstanding. I've already explained this you to a thousand times: Phil had to admit to those things in court or the judge wouldn't have accepted his plea deal. It was a matter of serving two years or risking twenty....

ELEANOR: Believe what you'd like, dear. But I want the high-end coffin with the Kryptonite lock.

GLORIA: I'm too happy right now to let you upset me....So when is the operation?

ELEANOR: There isn't going to be an operation.

GLORIA: I don't understand....What about the party? I thought this party was to celebrate your recovery after you went through with the surgery.

ELEANOR: There isn't going to be a party either.

GLORIA: But the guest list?

ELEANOR: That's the guest list for my funeral, dear.

GLORIA: You lied to me!

ELEANOR: Otherwise you wouldn't have written out that list....Now read it back to me, please....

GLORIA: I will not. [*Gloria tears the list in half.*] Plan your own damn funeral. I don't want any part of this.

ELEANOR: You're starting to sound like your sister. "You'll do *this.*" "I won't have any part of *that.*" Now be a dear and read that list back to me. There should be some tape in my purse.

GLORIA: I don't understand what's wrong with you. You have a wonderful job and a loving family....and as soon as Phil gets out of prison, you'll have grandchildren... Four of them....Two boys and two girls...

ELEANOR: I wanted three boys and only one girl....That way I won't have to divide your grandmother's jewelry....

GLORIA: I don't understand why you want to die all of a sudden.

ELEANOR: I don't *want* to die, honey. But I'm sure Dr. Luxby and Dr. Spatnick didn't either....

GLORIA: You can't blame yourself like that. Do you think I blame myself for not working harder at the beauty parlor so Phil didn't have to do business with certain people...?

ELEANOR: You mean mobsters?

GLORIA: Please have the operation. For your future grandchildren.

ELEANOR: I can't. Every time I consider signing the forms, I find myself thinking about Dr. Luxby's grandchildren....and Dr. Spatnick's elderly mother in New Hampshire....I had Paige clip their obituaries out of the *Times* for me....

GLORIA: That's morbid.

ELEANOR: I don't think it's a coincidence that it's a wrist watch that's going to kill me.....It's a very feminine way to go....So much of my life has been about timing....menstruation, ovulation, menopause....counting up, counting down....Men just go from one end of life to the other—like sperm. But for a woman it's a constant cycle, an ebb and a flow.....

GLORIA: You're thinking way too much.

ELEANOR: Did you realize that women who share the same hospital rooms end up synchronizing their menstrual cycles....? That's the way it is with us girls. We may not get along with each other on the surface, but deep down we share a certain solidarity. We're all sisters in blood.

GLORIA: Paige isn't going to let you get away with this.

ELEANOR: With what? Dying? Anyway, it's not as though I'm deciding between dying or *not* dying. It's more a matter of timing....You girls must have realized that I'd have to die eventually...
.
GLORIA: I don't see how you can be so blasé about this.

ELEANOR: That's because you're twenty-five and I'm fifty-six. When my mother died, I thought the sun was going to come crashing into the earth in a fiery Armageddon...but it didn't. We went to the funeral and said our farewells and the next morning they still delivered the newspaper, and the trains still ran, and the world carried on with its business as it always had. And when your father had his unfortunate incident with the polar bear, I could barely get out of bed for a year. You remember. So maybe I'm all suffered out, and now I've developed an immunity....There was a time, you know, when I would have been willing to sacrifice ten thousand brain surgeons—to bankrupt the entire health care system—if it could earn me a few extra hours of life....and somehow I've lost that. Not my will to live—but my will to live *at any expense*....Besides, if I wasn't so blasé about dying, I wouldn't be able to go through with it.

GLORIA: Maybe somebody poisoned those doctors and is trying to pin the blame on you....I saw that once on a made-for-television movie....

ELEANOR: Life is so much like a made-for-television movie, isn't it?....Now will you be a dear and go over that list with me before my roommate gets back from her CT-scan.

> Gloria retrieves the tape from Eleanor's purse reluctantly, patches up the list, and begins reading names...

GLORIA: Arnold & Patti Powell....Cousin Freddie...Dr. Serspkinski....Annie Beck and Emma Beck....

ELEANOR: —You and Paige don't have to make all these calls yourself, of course.... The easiest approach would be to set up a telephone tree....like on snow days at the aquarium....

SCENE FIVE

> Dr. Falk's Office. Dr. Falk and Robyn.

DR. FALK: [*Looking up from a stack of charts.*] You're Robyn, right?

ROBYN: Yes, Dr. Falk. Robyn Pastarnack with a "ck" at the end.

DR. FALK: With a "ck" at the end? You don't say. And how long have you been working here in the hospital, Ms. Robyn Pastarnack with a "ck" at the end?

ROBYN: Seven hours, Dr. Falk.

DR. FALK: Do you know how long I've been working in this hospital, Robyn?

ROBYN: No, Dr. Falk.

DR. FALK: Six hundred years.

ROBYN: [*Uncertain.*] Really, Dr. Falk?

DR. FALK: No, not really....But it feels that way sometimes.

ROBYN: Yes, Dr. Falk.

DR. FALK: I've actually only been here thirty years....What do you think of that?

ROBYN: Thirty years is a long time.

DR. FALK: Damn right, thirty years is a long time. And do you know how many mistakes I've made in those thirty years, Robyn?

ROBYN: No, Dr. Falk.

DR. FALK: Guess.

ROBYN: I couldn't, really....

DR. FALK: [*More forcefully.*] Guess a number.

ROBYN: Two or three.

DR. FALK: Thousands....

ROBYN: I'm sorry.

DR. FALK: Don't be sorry. Mistakes come with the territory. You have to crack eggs to make omelets, and you have to crack skulls to scoop out tumors. The unfortunate truth of the matter is that if you don't kill a patient now and again, you're not doing your job well. You show me a neurosurgeon afraid of taking risks and I'll show you a body trail as long as the Erie Canal....I've severed the wrong arteries, I've punctured the wrong chambers, I've even left a gauze pad inside a patient's tentorium...But I've never been sued. Not once. Do you know why?

ROBYN: Because people are afraid of you?

DR. FALK: Because I always admit when I'm wrong. I never try to cover anything up. Do you understand what I'm saying, Robyn with a "ck"?

ROBYN: Don't lie to the patients, Dr. Falk?

DR. FALK : Screw the patients. Don't lie to *me*....

ROBYN: I'm not sure—

DR. FALK: Of course, you're not sure. You don't have any idea at all. According to your report, the patient in room 104 is oriented to time and place....The patient in room 104 is brain dead, Robyn. They're keeping him on life support until this evening so they can harvest his organs.

ROBYN: I must have been confused.

DR. FALK: And Mrs. Powell in room 125 can't possibly have shown you that she was oriented to time and place or have told you the name of the president. She pretended she was in a coma. How do I know that? Because she's been pretending she's in a coma for sixty-six days, every time I send in a fresh medical student to examine her.

ROBYN: I'm sorry, Dr. Falk. It won't happen again

DR. FALK: You bet it won't happen again. There are only two ways you're going to make it through this clerkship, Robyn with a "ck". Do you know what they are?

ROBYN: No, Dr. Falk.

DR. FALK: Either you can work your ass off twenty-four hours a day until you know your patients so well that you can predict three days in advance when their noses are going to itch—until you forget that there's a world outside this hospital building—or you can grow a penis and a pair of testicles and start screwing the nurses in the linen closets.

ROBYN: Dr. Falk?

DR. FALK: I was the first female surgeon on the faculty here. On *my* first day as a medical resident in the hospital, the senior surgeon looked through my progress notes on the patients...and then dropped his pants and urinated on them....That's the way it is for women in surgery. If you do a great job, your patients appreciate you and your male colleagues tolerate you. But if you screw up—and believe me, you *will* screw up—it's going to be because you can't urinate standing up. Am I making myself clear?

ROBYN: You're saying that there's a double standard.

DR. FALK: There's only one standard around here. Excellence.

ROBYN: Yes, Dr. Falk.

DR. FALK: You've managed to make more mistakes in seven hours that I have in six hundred years. Now go back

294

and get *thorough* histories and physicals from your patients.

ROBYN: Yes, Dr. Falk.

> Robyn backs toward the door.

DR. FALK: And don't slouch. People pay thousands of dollars for health insurance in this country. They're entitled to physicians with good posture.

SCENE SIX

> Hospital room 125. Eleanor and the Amnesiac.

ELEANOR: How was your CT-scan?

AMNESIAC: Awful. The lab technician kept asking me questions about my medical history....Have I ever had cancer? Do I have a drug problem? I don't even know if I have a drug problem....[*Sobbing.*]....I keep talking about myself, don't I? How are *you*?

ELEANOR: I spent the afternoon planning my funeral....

AMNESIAC: I'm sorry.

ELEANOR: Don't be. It's not nearly as difficult as you might think. Much easier than planning a wedding...and there's no obligation to invite anybody you don't like....

AMNESIAC: I'm not sure I'd care what happens to me after I'm dead....But for your sake, Eleanor, I do hope the funeral lives up to your expectations.

ELEANOR: We make a pretty pair, don't we? All gloom and death.

AMNESIAC: I'm not gloomy. I'm jealous. It's not fair that you're going to die and I'm going to be stuck like this....

ELEANOR: Who said anything about life being fair?

AMNESIAC: You've got to help me!

ELEANOR: [*Ignoring the Amnesiac's plea.*] My late husband and I saw this play one time called *The Replacement*, about a middle-aged mother who finds out that she's dying, so she recruits a lonely, childless woman to stand in for her and to raise her children. Like in *The Sound of Music*, only the first Mrs. Von Trapp is still alive. So the "replacement" moves in with the family for a month-long trial run—to learn the ropes of the household. The only problem is that this "replacement" proves to be so much more effective as a wife and mother than the first woman, that the original woman wants to fire her—but by then she's already insinuated herself into their household and it's too late....At least *my* husband is dead and *my* daughters are grown. Nobody's going to replace me and show me up.

AMNESIAC: I'm begging you....

ELEANOR: I can't, Amanda....I've killed two innocent people already.

AMNESIAC: Look at me. Ask yourself: Would you want to live in my condition?

ELEANOR: I don't know....

AMNESIAC: Would you want to keep going if your daughters walked into this room and you didn't know who they were...?

ELEANOR: Don't torture yourself, dear—

AMNESIAC: Or if I told you that you'd never see them again, because you'd have no way of finding them.... You wouldn't even know they existed....

ELEANOR: Don't do this....

AMNESIAC: [*Increasingly upset.*] What if somebody would replace you! Somebody would take over your job and raise your children and make love to your husband and you'd be a pale shadow receding into memory! Don't torture myself, Eleanor?! Every waking minute is torture for me, Eleanor. And you're the only person in the world who can help me, because you're the only person in this world other than the doctors who even knows I exist.

ELEANOR: ....Okay, I'll do it.

AMNESIAC: I'm not asking so much. You don't even have to warn me. Just take a pillow one night when I'm sleeping and press it over my face.

ELEANOR: You have my word. Now let's not talk about it.

      A long pause.

AMNESIAC: Thank you.

SCENE SEVEN

      Hospital room 125. History and Physical, Take Two.

      Robyn enters, carrying her clipboard. Eleanor and the Amnesiac play dead. Robyn approaches Eleanor's bed.

ROBYN: I'm sorry to bother you again, Mrs. Powell, but you really have to wake up this time. [*Eleanor does not move.*] I'm not leaving this room until you answer my questions....All you have to do is tell me where you are, and what day of the week it is, and the name of the President of the United States, and I promise I'll leave you alone....[*Eleanor still does not move. Robyn paces the room, her anxiety increasing. She pauses before the Amnesiac.*] How about you? Are you willing to talk? [*The Amnesiac does not move.*] Goddamit. I didn't spend four years of college memorizing molecular formulas so that a pair of crazy sick people could get in the way of my becoming a doctor. Now one of you had better say something or I swear to God I'll inject myself with an overdose of insulin, or morphine, or toner from the photocopier, and I'll do it right here in the middle of your room so that this will become an active crime scene, and the police will be in here asking you questions, day and night, never giving you a moment's peace. Now this is your last goddam chance: Who is the President of the United States?

ELEANOR: [*Eleanor speaks without opening her eyes.*] Harry Truman.

ROBYN: That's better. Now we're getting somewhere. [*Robyn writes on her clipboard.*] "Patient Powell identifies U.S. President as Harry Truman."

AMNESIAC: Lyndon Johnson

ROBYN: [*Robyn continues to write on her clipboard.*] "Patient Doe identifies U.S. President as Lyndon Johnson"

ELEANOR: Gerald Ford.

ROBYN: You already said Truman. Do you want to change your answer?

AMNESIAC: Herbert Hoover.

ELEANOR: Dwight Eisenhower.

ROBYN: Stop! Please stop!

AMNESIAC: Richard Nixon

ELEANOR: Teddy Roosevelt

AMNESIAC: Woodrow Wilson

ELEANOR: Abraham Lincoln.

ROBYN: Why are you doing this to me?

ELEANOR: James Garfield.

AMNESIAC: James Buchanan

ELEANOR: Grover Cleveland.

AMNESIAC: Grover Cleveland. Again.

ROBYN: [*On the verge of tears.*] You two are the worst patients ever! [*Robyn runs from the room.*]

ELEANOR: Well done. I knew I was going to like you...

AMNESIAC: How very strange. I can remember James Buchanan and Woodrow Wilson, but not my own name....You don't think we were too hard on that girl, do you?

ELEANOR: Don't go soft on me, Amanda. It's us against them. Once you let the medical students get the upper hand, they'll spend all day long in here asking you to count backwards by nines. You might as well sign up to be a laboratory rat....But I have a bad feeling about this new girl....I can't tell whether she's extremely clever or extremely naïve, but we'd best be careful....

AMNESIAC: She's not really going to kill herself in our room, is she?

ELEANOR: I don't think so, but that's the problem with medical students.   They seem so calm and detached and then, every so often, one of them jumps out a window.

SCENE EIGHT

Paige and Gloria. The Family Waiting Room.

Paige opens the window and pokes her head out. She takes a deep breath.

PAIGE: I'd almost forgotten.

GLORIA: Forgotten what?

PAIGE: That there's a world out there.   That there are people who don't spend all of their time arguing with doctors and insurance companies....

GLORIA: I wish I could be more helpful. Are you sure there isn't anything I can do?

PAIGE: It's generous of you to offer....but, quite frankly, no.

GLORIA: Because you're afraid I'll mess up.

PAIGE: I didn't say that.

GLORIA: But you're thinking it....

PAIGE: I'm not the one who deposited her Publishers Clearinghouse check in the automated teller machine and ended up being banned from the bank....

GLORIA : It was an honest mistake.

PAIGE: Like when you tried to convince mom that women didn't have to pay income taxes because the tax laws dated from before women gained the right to vote.

GLORIA: It made sense at the time. No taxation without representation. I read about it in a magazine.

PAIGE: You and your magazines, I swear....Look at it this way. You're an artist—aren't you always telling me that styling hair is as much an art form as painting or sculpting? Well, at times like this, the best thing an artist can do is stay out of the way....

300

GLORIA: Don't patronize me, Paige.

PAIGE: I'm sorry....I just keep thinking about how quickly everything has changed. It seems like only a few years ago that I was shouting for help because I thought the shadows in my bedroom were pirates, and Mom would come running to tuck me in....

GLORIA: You used to scare *me* too. I'd hear you shouting about pirates and I'd also start crying....

PAIGE: And all those times I called her at the aquarium when I needed help with my biology homework, or when I maxed out my credit cards at college, or when I went to visit Tommy Phelps at Cornell and my car rolled down that embankment into the gorge....She always managed to fix things....

GLORIA: You're talking about Mom in the past tense....You're scaring me....

PAIGE: I'm scaring myself. Part of Mom is already in the past tense....Do you ever have the desire to lean out the window and scream for help? Not for anything in particular—just help with everything. With life.

GLORIA: All the time.

PAIGE: That's how I feel right now....Only I won't. Because nobody is going to help....I phoned nineteen neurosurgeons today, but the minute they heard Mom's name, they wanted nothing to do with her. One of them even said that he'd like to help, but that he has his own wife and children to think of....They're all as crazy as Mom is.

GLORIA: You don't think she could be right, do you? I saw a television movie once where this woman killed men by sleeping with them. Every time she took a new lover, he had a heart attack....

PAIGE: *No, I don't think she's right!* I think she's cuckoo....We have to stick together on this. Promise me you won't take Mom's side.

GLORIA: I'm not taking Mom's side—

PAIGE: Promise! Promise or I swear I'll hold you accountable for whatever happens.

GLORIA: Okay....I promise.

PAIGE: Good. Mom hasn't killed anyone and I won't have people suggesting otherwise.

SCENE NINE

>Hospital room 125. Night. The Amnesiac is sleeping.

>Eleanor climbs out bed, takes hold of her pillow, and inches across the room with the help of her walker. She arrives at the Amnesiac's bed, lift's the pillow above her head in preparation to suffocate the Amnesiac—and she loses her balance. She shouts for help and the stage goes dark.

SCENE TEN

>Hospital room 125. Eleanor and Paige. Eleanor has a bandage wrapped around her head.

PAIGE: What were you thinking? You could have died.

ELEANOR: There's no reason to make a federal case out of this. I'm fine.

PAIGE: You're *not* fine. If you were fine, you wouldn't have a six-inch gash in your scalp.

302

ELEANOR: Don't blow this out of proportion, Paige. I fainted. People faint all the time. In your grandmother's day, it was considered fashionable.

PAIGE: When I heard Dr. Falk's voice on the telephone last night, my first thought was that you *had* died....

ELEANOR: And what if I had? I'd be dead. And that would be that....Why do you have to take everything so seriously? I can still remember that morning I came downstairs to the kitchen—you couldn't have been more than ten years old—and there you were, reading the obituaries and sobbing because a bunch of strangers had died. Meanwhile, Gloria's a glorified hairdresser married to a common criminal and she's as content as a pig in mud....Anyway, the bottom line is that I'm still alive. So let's have some breakfast.

PAIGE: How difficult is it to call the nurse if you want to get up?

ELEANOR: I didn't want to call the nurse. I was conducting personal business.

PAIGE: Couldn't it have waited until the morning? I would have helped you.

ELEANOR: I'm not so sure.

PAIGE: I'll make you a deal. If you promise not to go traipsing about the hospital alone at night, I'll be glad to help you with any personal business you might have.

ELEANOR: Promise?

PAIGE: Promise. Now what was so personal that you couldn't ask the nurse for help?

ELEANOR: You know my roommate, Amanda? The paralyzed girl with amnesia.

PAIGE: It's so awful, isn't it?

ELEANOR: My roommate asked me to adjust her pillows. She can't do it on her own, you understand.

PAIGE: That's all?

ELEANOR: More or less....She was hoping I might adjust one of the pillows over her face and push down on it as hard as I can....

PAIGE: You don't mean...?

ELEANOR: She can't do it on her own.

PAIGE: But that's....For the love of God, Mom, I don't understand you. You're going to let yourself have a stroke because you're afraid of killing your surgeon, but you're willing to suffocate an innocent woman in cold blood.

ELEANOR: She *wants* me to....But I can't do it on my own either. I don't have the strength.

PAIGE: Thank heavens for small blessings.

ELEANOR: You've got to help me, honey....It's the only way.

PAIGE: Are you out of your mind?

ELEANOR: One night, while she's sleeping...You can hide in the bathroom after visiting hours end....

PAIGE: This is insane. Neither of us is going to kill anybody.

ELEANOR: If you do this for me, I'll go through with the operation.

PAIGE: [*A long pause. Paige is dumbfounded.*] I can't....I'd kill someone to defend you....I swear I would....but not like

304

this...[*Eleanor realizes that Paige will not help, so she feigns laughter.*] Hold on. This is another one of your games, isn't it?

ELEANOR: You really do take things too seriously, Paige. You know what I was doing when I fell down? I was going to the vending machine in the corridor for a candy bar...Did you really think I'd kill that poor sweet girl?

PAIGE: I don't know what to think anymore.

ELEANOR: Maybe you should have a wrist watch implanted. It seems to have a calming effect.

SCENE ELEVEN

> Dr. Falk's office. Robyn and Dr. Falk. Dr. Falk is seated at her desk, reading a hospital chart. She looks up when Robyn enters.

ROBYN: You wanted to see me, Dr. Falk?

DR. FALK: Robyn with a "ck," right? So I have a case for you to write up....

ROBYN: Yes, doctor?

DR. FALK: A truly remarkable case...It's our patient Sally Brown.

ROBYN: Sally Brown?

DR. FALK: Surely, you remember. I sent you to retrieve her old records earlier this week....Well I was reading through them over breakfast, and I discovered the most unusual phenomenon. It turns out that Miss Brown had a radical hysterectomy last year at the age of eighty-six....and that five months later, if the chart is to be believed, she gave birth to quadruplets....Do you have any idea how that might have happened?

ROBYN: Look, I can explain...I tripped and....Mrs. Powell's daughter....and I don't know....

> Robyn starts sobbing.

DR. FALK: This is unacceptable. You are going to kill somebody....

ROBYN: Give me another chance....I worked so hard to get here....

DR. FALK: Do you know what the airplane pilot said to the control tower after she confused her flight plans and took off from the wrong runway?

ROBYN: I don't know...

DR. FALK: Nothing. She was dead.

ROBYN: You're going to have me expelled, aren't you?

DR. FALK: I'm not sure what I'm going to do....What I suggest, young lady, is that you think long and hard about the damage you might have caused with your carelessness...and then you do something to convince me you're not a one woman menace to the public health. Got it?

ROBYN: Yes, Dr. Falk.

DR. FALK: And stop slouching, for God's sake. You're a medical student, not an orangutan. If you're not going to read your textbooks, at least go balance one on your head.

SCENE TWELVE

> Hospital room 125. Eleanor and Gloria, while the Amnesiac sleeps.

ELEANOR: Gloria, dear, how would you feel about doing a small favor for your sick mother?

GLORIA: I'm not making any more lists.

ELEANOR: No more lists. I swear.

GLORIA: Because if Paige ever finds out I made that list for you, she's going to plan *my* funeral...

ELEANOR: I'm done planning funerals. One is enough for me....What I need your help with is much easier than all that....[*Eleanor whispers her request in Gloria's ear.*] If you'll do this for me, I'll go through with the operation.

GLORIA: You're serious, aren't you?

ELEANOR: Phil can even have the body....

GLORIA: [*On the verge of hysterics.*] Paige is right. You really have gone mad!

ELEANOR: Calm down. You'll wake up Amanda.

GLORIA: I have to find Paige. *She'll* know how to handle this....[*Gloria runs toward the door, then stops.*] You're not going to do anything...to her...while I'm gone, are you?

ELEANOR: Not a thing. I swear. But I might club the day nurse over the head with my bed pan when she's not looking....

GLORIA: Oh, Mom!

> Gloria runs out of the room. The amnesiac
> wakes up.

AMNESIAC: What was that all about?

ELEANOR: I read somewhere that the Ancient Spartans believed children were a form of property. You could buy them, sell them, trade them. And they had to do anything that you asked them to do, because they were your children. Such a simple philosophy...makes you wonder why we bother with all those self-righteous Athenians... Socrates, Aristotle....when the Spartans already had the key to happiness all figured out.

AMNESIAC: I was sleeping.

ELEANOR: I'm sorry if we woke you.

AMNESIAC: I was *sleeping*, Eleanor....You haven't forgotten, have you?

ELEANOR: I gave you my word, Amanda. Consider yourself dead.

SCENE THIRTEEN

ROBYN: [*To the Audience.*] It's nothing like I expected. I thought medicine was all about helping people...going from room to room with good cheer and a bag of pills....Nobody warned me about the people who don't want good cheer.... The angry, tired, abusive people who come seeking free food and shelter, seeking narcotics, trying to squeeze the breasts of the medical student while she's taking their temperature, sliding their lecherous fingers inside her white coat while she's drawing blood....Nobody told me about the caverns of paperwork, in duplicate, in triplicate, about the notes that nobody ever reads documenting examinations that didn't need to take place....Nobody told me about the waiting time in the emergency room, about the patients on gurneys in hallways, for hours, for days, about the ninety-five year old widows groaning on gurneys and the hospital staff walking by them, indifferent, telling themselves, she's not my patient, she's not my responsibility. Sometimes I think that if God spent Christmas Eve in a hospital emergency room instead of church, He'd take his mighty, wrathful Old Testament arm and obliterate us all!...

SCENE FOURTEEN

Hospital room 125. Robyn and Eleanor.

ELEANOR: You're back.

ROBYN: You're not comatose.

ELEANOR: Touché.

ROBYN: Where's your roommate?

ELEANOR: She went for a jog.

ROBYN: Excuse me?

ELEANOR: She's having an MRI.

ROBYN: Look, Mrs. Powell...I'm not sure what I've done to upset you, but I'm hoping we can start over again, because I really need your help.

ELEANOR: Then we're in the same boat. Because I need *your* help.

ROBYN: Here's the thing, Mrs. Powell. I have to do something to convince my supervisor, Dr. Falk, that I'm not utterly incompetent. Something big. Like curing cancer or performing a brain transplant—only I'm not capable of anything like that. But I thought maybe I could convince you to let Dr. Falk take that watch out of your head, and that might count as something impressive.... I'm begging you—

ELEANOR: Sure. I'll do it.

ROBYN: You will?

ELEANOR: Of course, I will.

ROBYN: Thank you!

ELEANOR: But on one condition.

ROBYN: Anything....I'll give you free medical care for life....I'll come home with you and clean your garage— [*Eleanor whispers her request in Robyn's ear.*]

ROBYN: I can't do that.

ELEANOR: I'm afraid you don't have a choice, young lady.

ROBYN: I can't....I won't.

ELEANOR: But you will. Otherwise, I'll complain to Dr. Falk that you're the worst medical student I've ever had....Which, at this hospital, is saying quite a lot.

ROBYN: Please don't put me in this situation, Mrs. Powell. It's not fair.

ELEANOR: Whoever said life was fair, my dear? My husband was mauled to death by a polar bear at the age of forty-seven. Was *that* fair? The world is full of babies born without eyes, and families massacred by rabid wolves, and pianos that fall out of windows onto busloads of unsuspecting schoolchildren. Life is, at its essence, highly unfair. Unjust. Unreasonable. If life were fair, we wouldn't need hospitals. If life were fair, we wouldn't need medical students.

ROBYN: Why are you doing this *to me*?

ELEANOR: Nobody made you go to medical school. You could have been a lawyer or a flight attendant or one of those young women who wear black skirts and hand out napkins at art shows....But you chose to become a medical student, and fate or chance or the divine hand of a wrathful god put you in the wrong place at the wrong time, and right now I need your help....So go tell Dr. Falk that she can cut my skull open tomorrow. And while I'm in the operating room, you'll sneak back in here with a some morphine and an extra-soft pillow. Got it? Let's get all the killing and dying over with as quickly as possible....

SCENE FIFTEEN

> Dr. Falk's Office. Dr. Falk is adjusting her
> diplomas. Robyn enters, glowing with
> excitement.

ROBYN: So I did it! I convinced her.

DR. FALK: What are you talking about?

ROBYN: I convinced Mrs. Powell in room 125 to let you remove the watch from her brain?

DR. FALK: How in the world did you do that?

ROBYN: I told her how talented a surgeon you were....

DR. FALK: And she agreed?

ROBYN: She wants it done as quickly as possible....tomorrow, if you're willing....

DR. FALK: Jesus Christ. I can't believe you did that.

ROBYN: I had to redeem myself somehow....

DR. FALK: [*After a long, reflective pause.*] You've done well. We might make a passable physician of you yet.

ROBYN: Thank you, Dr. Falk....Does this mean you're not going to have me expelled?

DR. FALK: I was never going to have you expelled. I'm not nearly that powerful....I'll tell you a secret....Even if you killed someone, they probably wouldn't throw you out of medical school. It would take too much effort—and the inertia is already on your side. You'd probably have to kill someone *intentionally* to get thrown out of medical school....

ROBYN: Thank you, Dr. Falk.

DR. FALK: Now get out of here before I change my mind and report you to the dean....

ROBYN: Yes, Dr. Falk.

> Robyn exits. Dr. Falk paces her office nervously.

DR. FALK: [*To herself.*] Am I afraid? Of course, I'm not afraid.....I'm *terrified.* And I have to do it, don't I? There's really no two ways about it....[*She sits down at her desk, her face in her hands.*] Oh, God. I don't want to die....

ACT TWO

SCENE SIXTEEN

> Dr. Falk's Office. Dr. Falk and Paige. Dr. Falk is seated at her desk. She appears to be dead. Paige knocks on the door and then enters.

PAIGE: Dr. Falk....[*Paige approaches Dr. Falk's body.*] Dr. Falk? Are you all right?

> Paige nudges Dr. Falk's body. No response. She pushes harder. Dr. Falk's body responds at though she is dead.

PAIGE: Oh my God! You're dead!....Now we're never going to find a surgeon....[*She pushes Dr. Falk's body harder.*] Don't be dead. Please don't be dead.

> Paige hits Dr. Falk in the shoulder as hard as she can. Dr. Falk jolts upright.

DR. FALK: Enough already. You could hurt someone.

PAIGE: I thought you were dead.

DR. FALK: Well, I'm not.

PAIGE: But you weren't....I mean....

DR. FALK: I was *pretending* to be dead, Ms. Powell.

PAIGE: Oh. I can come back later....

DR. FALK: No need. Have you ever pretended to be dead, Ms. Powell?

PAIGE: Not since I was a little girl. I used to read the obituaries every morning....and there were days when I'd pretend that I found my name and that I didn't have to go to school....

DR. FALK: You should try again sometime. From a medical standpoint, I highly encourage it. People spend far more of their time dead than alive. It can't hurt to practice.

PAIGE: I suppose not.

DR. FALK: You don't think it's *that* bad, do you? Being dead?

PAIGE: Actually, I think it's awful.

DR. FALK: I was afraid you'd say that. I also think it's awful.

PAIGE: Not existing.

DR. FALK: Not being able to speak, or think, or read the morning paper....

PAIGE: Not knowing what's happened to your loved ones....whether they've found romance or had children...whether they're safe....

DR. FALK: Not knowing if we've cured cancer....if we've transplanted brain tissue....

PAIGE: Rotting....

DR. FALK: Decaying....

PAIGE: Nothing....

DR. FALK: Nothing....[*A long, tragic pause.*] So can we keep the watch?

PAIGE: Excuse me?

DR. FALK: If I take out the watch in your mother's skull, can the surgery department keep it? I thought it might make a promising souvenir for our display case....

PAIGE: You can't be serious?

DR. FALK: I've been searching the internet and there's an abdominal surgeon from Belfast, Maine, who claims that he once removed a clock from the stomach of a retired dentist. You could apparently hear the device ticking if you placed your ear against the patient's umbilicus. Dr. Ingram emailed me a photo of the timepiece.... one of those small travel clocks from the days before digital watches....So I've arranged for my secretary to send him photos of the ticker in your mother's brain....a bit of surgical one-upsmanship. And then I thought an exhibit on your mother's case might be a valuable legacy to leave the department....So you don't mind if we keep the watch, do you?

PAIGE: Only if she survives.

DR. FALK: I'm not sure I follow.

PAIGE: If my mother lives, you keep the watch. If she dies, we bury it with her.

DR. FALK: But what good will that do?

PAIGE: It will give you an added incentive to cut carefully.

DR. FALK: I *always* cut carefully.

PAIGE: Then you have nothing to worry about....Now when exactly are you planning to operate?

DR. FALK: As soon as I get my affairs in order.

PAIGE: Every day that goes by is another day that my mother might die....She's got a time bomb ticking in her head, for God's sake!

DR. FALK: [*Standing and walking toward the door, visibly upset.*] This isn't a fast food restaurant, Ms. Powell. I'll cut when I'm good and ready to cut.....

SCENE SEVENTEEN

> Hospital room 125. Eleanor and the Amnesiac. They have exchanged beds.

AMNESIAC: It feels so odd being on this side of the room....

ELEANOR: One summer, we relocated the artificial island in the seal tank and the fur seals suffered a collective mental breakdown. Barking like hounds, slapping the keepers with their flippers.

AMNESIAC: It's amazing how easily you can get attached to a small corner in a hospital room—even to a prison cell, I imagine—if you don't have anything else.

ELEANOR: I didn't understand those seals until my husband died. Suddenly, I had this giant bed all to myself....

AMNESIAC: Can we trade places again?

ELEANOR: Tomorrow morning, dear....Thank you for being such a sport. I've shared this room with eight other women, and none of them was willing to switch beds....

AMNESIAC: I suppose they were worried they'd get the wrong medication.

ELEANOR: In this hospital, they'd be more likely to get the *right* medication by mistake....But that wasn't what they objected to. They just didn't understand that the nursing students are not our friends....That you need to go out of your way to confuse them—to scare them off like crows—or they'll keep coming back forever ....Oh, this is so exciting.

AMNESIAC: Are you sure someone's going to come?

ELEANOR: It's Wednesday afternoon. We get a new nursing student *every* Wednesday afternoon.... They're as bad as the medical students.....Worse! They're honest.

AMNESIAC: I don't know if I'm up to this.

ELEANOR: Of course you are, dear. Now let's practice. How are you feeling today, Mrs. Powell?

AMNESIAC: Not so bad....Except I'm having a touch of nausea...and I am coughing up some blood now and then....oh, and I keep having these sudden bouts of blindness....and deafness....and yesterday my tongue and my toes turned blue simultaneously....and I'm afraid my tuberculosis may be flaring up again....and I keep hearing voices....I'm not sure what language they're speaking....for some reason I think it might be Norwegian....I don't actually speak Norwegian, you understand, so I can't be certain....but their tone sounds hostile...as though they were urging me to set my mattress on fire....and then last night I had this awful dream in which I was a patient in a hospital, and one of the nursing students asked me how I was feeling, so I wrapped by hands around her throat and I strangled her....[*To Eleanor.*] How was that?

ELEANOR: Brilliant. But when you mention the tuberculosis, make sure you cough at her.

SCENE EIGHTEEN

Paige and Gloria. The Family Waiting Room.

PAIGE: Hospital. It's a strange word, isn't it?

GLORIA: What do you mean?

PAIGE: Just the way it sounds. *Hosp-it-al.* There's nothing in the sound of it that tells you people are suffering and dying inside.

GLORIA: You're thinking too much.

PAIGE: Hospitals could actually be fun places—if not for all the sick people. Where else do you cross paths with men and women from all backgrounds and walks of life? Only airports and hospitals. Even in cemeteries they divide you up by religion.

GLORIA: Now *that's* a strange word. Cemetery. *Cem-et-er-y.* Every time I hear it, it reminds me how much I miss Phil....

PAIGE: Do you remember when we were in high school and they had "Backwards Day" during the final week of the year, and the teachers traded places with the top students? Well, I think they should do that at the hospital. Once in a while, they should have the doctors trade places with the best patients....

GLORIA: I'm not an idiot, you know. I'm fully aware of what Phil was doing at those cemeteries....Just because I'm a loyal wife, and I *pretend* I don't know, doesn't make me an idiot.

PAIGE: Nobody thinks you're an idiot.

GLORIA: And just because you're a high-powered lawyer and Mom has a Ph.D. in marine biology doesn't give you two the right to look down on me. Cutting hair is as much a form of art as composing symphonies.

PAIGE: Nobody said otherwise.

GLORIA: But you *think* it. I know you do. You think that just because you spend all of your time in an oak-paneled office full of artificial fruit and plastic flowers, pushing papers clockwise and counterclockwise, it makes you better than me. Well, you're not, Paige Powell. I'm a highly skilled professional who brings piece of mind to thousands of desperate women. I don't merely cut hair. I'm a hair surgeon. Hell, I'm practically a doctor.

PAIGE: I do love you, Gloria. But honestly, *now* you sound like an idiot....

       Dr. Falk enters.

DR. FALK: Ms. Powell. I'm glad I caught you.

PAIGE: This is my sister, Gloria....She's also a surgeon.

DR. FALK: Good to meet you, doctor. What's your specialty?

GLORIA: Hair.

DR. FALK: I see....

PAIGE: Any word about my mother?

DR. FALK: She's on the schedule for tomorrow.

PAIGE: You mean she's actually agreed to go through with it?

DR. FALK: So it seems.

GLORIA: Thank you, doctor. Phil will be so relieved....

DR. FALK: Don't thank me. Thank the medical student....On second thought, please *don't* thank her. It might go to her head.

SCENE NINETEEN

>Hospital room 125. Night. Eleanor and the Amnesiac are asleep. Robyn enters, carrying a pillow. She tiptoes to the bed in which Eleanor is now resting, believing that it contains the Amnesiac. However, the audience recognizes Eleanor—possible through distinctive slippers or even distinctive feet. Robyn appears anguished. She raises the pillow over her head and squeezes her eyes shut.

ROBYN: Get all the killing and dying over with as quickly as possible....

>Robyn begins to lower the pillow over Eleanor's face. At the last moment, she drops the pillow and flees the room. Eleanor awakens with a start. She notices the pillow.

ELEANOR: An extra pillow....I must remember to leave it out for that medical student....

SCENE TWENTY

>The Operation.   Dr. Falk and Robyn enter in surgical scrubs.

DR. FALK: Now don't forget. It's a skull. Not a person. If you think of it as part of a live human being, you won't be able to saw through it.

ROBYN: Yes, Dr. Falk.

DR. FALK: I do have one more thing to ask of you, Robin with a "ck." A personal favor...

319

ROBYN: Yes, Dr. Falk. Anything.

DR. FALK: Well, I imagine you've studied CPR and basic lifesaving skills in medical school...And in the *unlikely* event that something should happen to me during the procedure....I mean, if I were to keel over and stop breathing....I would find it immeasurably comforting and reassuring to know that you'd be staying as far away from my body as possible....

ROBYN: Yes, Dr. Falk.

DR. FALK: Thank you. You've taken a weight off my mind....Now let's cut!

> The operation is performed behind a screen. We see a body wheeled behind the screen from one direction, then Dr. Falk and Robyn entering from the other. We witness the operation taking place in silhouettes possibly with incongruous music, such as a John Phillip Souza march or the Battle Hymn of the Republic. Then we hear a blood-curdling scream. Robyn staggers out from behind the screen.

ROBYN: She's dead!

SCENE TWENTY-ONE

> The Family Waiting Room. Paige and Gloria. Dr. Falk enters, covered in blood.

GLORIA: Is it over?

DR. FALK: Yes, it's over. But it didn't go as well as I would have liked.

PAIGE: She's all right, isn't she? I mean: She's alive? [*Dr. Falk says nothing. She appears dazed.*] Oh my god! She's dead! You killed my mother!

320

> Paige attempts to strangle Dr. Falk. Gloria
> restrains her.

GLORIA: Please forgive her. She's in shock.

DR. FALK: It's all right. Really....[*Dr. Falk composes
herself.*] It started off like any other procedure. The
nurses draped the patient before I entered the operating
room, and I pretended that the body in front of me was
already dead. Just a cadaver's skull. Not a living human
being....That's the only way to get through it. So I was
cutting along, not so different from carving a turkey or a
ham...although brains tend to be a bit more
tender....maybe a bit like venison....But then—without any
warning—the patient had a massive allergic reaction to the
anesthesia, and her blood vessels all dilated
simultaneously...and then I really was just mucking about
inside a cadaver's skull.

PAIGE: That doesn't make any sense. Mom's had surgery
countless times before. How did she suddenly become
allergic to the anesthesia?

DR. FALK: That's the worst part. From the hospital's
point-of-view, at least. It wasn't your mother.

GLORIA: I don't understand.

DR. FALK: They brought in the wrong patient. Something
about changing beds during the night. It's really quite
unconscionable....

PAIGE: So Mom is still alive?

DR. FALK: I'm afraid she is....

PAIGE: She's alive! Thank God!

> Paige and Gloria hug and dance around the
> room.

DR. FALK: I'm not sure what you're both so festive about....The patient may not have been your mother, but she's still dead....which means we'll have to report the episode to the state....and it was that poor amnesiac girl too. We don't even have someone to claim the body.....

GLORIA: I should go call Phil....To tell him that Mom survived the operation.

PAIGE: But there's still a watch in her brain....When do you intend to try again, Dr. Falk?

DR. FALK: That's just the thing. I did some reflecting while I was scooping through that poor girl's brain and I don't think I do intend to try again. I think you should find yourself another surgeon....In all fairness, I'm far too talented a physician to throw my skills away on one patient, no matter how intriguing a case she may be....

PAIGE: But you're our only hope....

DR. FALK: I'm sorry.

PAIGE: You're a coward!

DR. FALK: Yes, Ms. Powell. I'm a coward. I can live with that.

PAIGE: But what about your moral duty as a physician? Your Hippocratic Oath?

DR. FALK: Quite frankly, I've had it up to here with my Hippocratic Oath....I'll have you know that I haven't turned down a case in thirty-one years. I've operated on child killers, war criminals, even the cretin who divorced my sister. I've skipped birthdays, college reunions, free vacations in the Caribbean on the tab of the pharmaceutical industry.....I've also skipped marriage and childbirth and carpooling and college applications and just about everything that normal women enjoy between the ages of twenty-five and sixty. And I've skipped it all in order to save the lives of total strangers. So don't you go lecturing me on my Hippocratic Oath! I'm truly sorry about your mother, but not sorry enough that I'm willing to skip old age for her sake....Now if you'll excuse me—Ms. Powell, Dr. Powell—I'm going to go have my car washed and then I'm going to learn how to play golf.

Dr. Falk exits.

PAIGE: [*On the verge of tears.*] Oh, God. Now what do we do?

GLORIA: Did you see all that anger, Paige? All that frustration? That's what comes from a lifetime of second-rate haircuts....

SCENE TWENTY-TWO

Hospital room 125. Eleanor and Robyn.

ELEANOR: I'm sorry, but we had a bargain—and you didn't uphold your end.

ROBYN: Please, Mrs. Powell. I didn't have a chance.

ELEANOR: And that seems unfair to you, doesn't it?

ROBYN: I know exactly what you're going to say, Mrs. Powell. *Life* is unfair....But that doesn't mean you can't go out of your way to make it a little bit fairer....You got what *you* wanted, didn't you? She's dead.

ELEANOR: Something of a windfall, isn't it?

ROBYN: I'm begging you. If Dr. Falk finds out you won't consent to the operation, she's going to blame me. She's already blaming me for sawing open the wrong patient....

ELEANOR: You're as good a person to blame as any. Don't you look before you cut?

ROBYN: I was afraid to....Honestly, blood makes me a little bit queasy....

ELEANOR: And you want to be a doctor?

ROBYN: I have a confession to make....

ELEANOR: I'm not a priest.

ROBYN: Please listen to me, Mrs. Powell....I've never wanted to be a *real* doctor....I want to be a...psychiatrist....If it were up to me, I wouldn't set foot in the operating room again.

ELEANOR: Then let's make a deal. From now on, we'll both stay out of the operating room.

ROBYN: I don't have a choice. Surgery is a required course....and I really might not pass it if you decide to back out on our agreement. Dr. Falk has already cleared away a space for your watch in the department's display case. If she can't operate on you, she's liable to spontaneously combust.

ELEANOR: She's a very talented surgeon, isn't she?

ROBYN: The best in the world....that is, now that Dr. Luxby and Dr. Spatnick are no longer operating.

ELEANOR: I was afraid you'd say that....I am not going to murder the best neurosurgeon in the world.

ROBYN: But she *wants* to take the risk....

ELEANOR: That's because she's not thinking clearly....How many physicians really understand the risks of the procedures they're performing? Not too many, if you ask me....I'm sorry, but sometimes patients have to make decisions for their doctors....

ROBYN: You really are the most unreasonable person I've ever met....

ELEANOR: Thank you.

ROBYN: Please don't tell anyone I want to be a psychiatrist. Especially Dr. Falk. There's a rumor that she barbecues psychiatrists for breakfast.

ELEANOR: Your secret is safe with me, dear. Now go do me a favor and find my nitwit daughters....I'm going home today, with or without their permission. I don't have it in me to educate any more medical students....

SCENE TWENTY-THREE

> Dr. Falk's office. Gloria and Dr. Falk. Dr. Falk is seated at her desk, wearing an old-fashioned barber's gown. Gloria cuts and styles the surgeon's hair.

DR. FALK: I do appreciate this, but I'm still not going to change my mind.

GLORIA: Lean forward, please.

DR. FALK: Though I am sorry that I lost my temper with your sister. Please apologize to her for me.

GLORIA: Lean back again.

DR. FALK: I don't know what came over me....I suppose I just felt very mortal all of a sudden. I trained with Larry Spatnick, you know....and I did an elective with Hiram Luxby as a medical student. They were cut from the same cloth. Many people don't realize this but behind their gruff, detached, arrogant exteriors....were two of the meanest sons-of-bitches I ever met in my life....

GLORIA: Hold still....

DR. FALK: But it's still hard to believe they're dead....That means I'm at the top of the field...All alone...which, from a mortality perspective, means I'm next in line.

> Gloria stops cutting and passes Dr. Falk a hand mirror. Dr. Falk's hairstyle is now quite fashionable.

GLORIA: Voila! Now you have nothing to be ashamed of....

DR. FALK: Was it really *that* bad?

GLORIA: You'd never believe how much anger you can store in your hair. Don't you feel better now?

DR. FALK: Yes. Surprisingly, I feel much better.

GLORIA: Good. Now you can perform Mom's surgery.

DR. FALK: But I already told you, I won't do that.

GLORIA: [*Raising her voice, still holding the scissors.*] Like hell you won't.

> She brandishes the blade of the scissors at Dr. Falk's throat.

DR. FALK: Please calm down. I'm sure we can work something out.

GLORIA: Did you know that I've given more than fifty thousand haircuts...?

DR. FALK: You must be worn out....You'll take a vacation and you'll feel better....

GLORIA: How many operations have you performed?

DR. FALK: I honestly don't know....

GLORIA: Fifty thousand?

DR. FALK: Not that many....

GLORIA: You know what the difference is between hair stylists and other surgeons? You don't need anesthesia to have your hair cut, so people talk to their hair stylists....

DR. FALK: I suppose they do.

GLORIA: They talk and talk and talk....about the great injustices of their lives....about how their sister-in-law didn't thank them properly for cooking the Christmas dinner....about how their son's eighth grade teacher didn't grade his essay fairly....about how hard it is to live in a world with taxes and jury duty and homeless people begging for change....They talk about *themselves*....Do you know why they talk about themselves?

DR. FALK: Because that's what they know about?

GLORIA: Because they're selfish. Because they think the world revolves around them....And do you know what I do? I listen. Day after day, year after years, fifty thousand times, eighth grade teacher after eighth grade teacher, I listen to these wealthy, beautiful women complaining about how life has given them the short end of the stick. And sometimes, when one of these women says something particularly objectionable, I want to jab my scissors into the flesh of their artificially-tightened necks. But I never do. Do you know why?

DR. FALK: Because you're a reasonable person.

GLORIA: Because I'm a kind person. A good human being....

> She snips the scissors open and shut quickly at Dr. Falk's neck.

DR. FALK: I can tell you're a good human being....Now please put down that scissors....

GLORIA: I may be a good, decent, kind-hearted woman—
but I'm not an angel....Everybody has a breaking
point....Even hair stylists!

DR. FALK: Think clearly, Ms. Powell. What good will you
accomplish by hurting me?

GLORIA: I'm not going to hurt you. I'm not even going to
have Phil's colleagues taking your for a swim in cinderblock
boots. All I'm going to do is phone the state medical board
and tell them you *intentionally* operated on the wrong
woman....

DR. FALK: But that's crazy! They won't believe you....

GLORIA: They will when I explain that you planned to sell
the body to my husband's former associates....My family
has a lot of credibility when it comes to trading in
cadavers....And you might win your case in the long run,
but that could be months, years....Think of the publicity.
That's the wonderful thing about a reputation. It's easy to
get one and it's easy to lose one....

DR. FALK: It was an honest mistake, for heaven's sake.
Have you no decency?

GLORIA: I've used up all my decency....And I'm tired of
letting people like you and Paige and mother make all the
decisions around here. I am taking control of the
situation....on behalf of all the ordinary people in the
world—the hair cutters, the cab drivers, the men and
women who read gas meters, and paint street lines, and
deliver bottled water. We have a right to make decisions
too, dammit—even where our own healthcare is concerned.
So you're going to cut my mother's head open this
afternoon, and you're going to take that watch out, and
you're going to make sure she lives to be one hundred
twenty, whether she wants to or not. Am I making myself
clear?

DR. FALK: Indeed you are.

GLORIA: Good. Now would you like me to do your nails?

SCENE TWENTY-FOUR

Hospital room 125. Eleanor and Dr. Falk.

ELEANOR: Who are you?

DR. FALK: I'm Dr. Falk.

ELEANOR: Oh, Dr. Falk. I didn't recognize you.

DR. FALK: Your daughter styled my hair.

ELEANOR: You hardly look like a doctor anymore.

DR. FALK: I'm sure you're already aware of the mix-up this morning....

ELEANOR: I knew something was wrong when I woke up without any stab wounds.

DR. FALK: In any case, I wanted to reassure you that this unfortunate incident was an extremely rare occurrence and that it will have no impact on your own care.

ELEANOR: Of course, it won't. I'm going home as soon as I have my lunch.

DR. FALK: Actually, you're not getting lunch today. We're operating this afternoon.

ELEANOR: I've changed my mind....I'm not having the surgery..

DR. FALK: Let's not go through all of this again, Mrs. Powell.....*You* know you're going to have the surgery and *I* know you're going to have the surgery, so what's the point of hemming and hawing about it, when at the end of the day we both know that you're going to stay in the hospital and let me remove the watch?

ELEANOR: I don't think I like your tone....Dr. Luxby and Dr. Spatnick both had lovely bedside manners....

DR. FALK: Some good it did them.

ELEANOR: Are you insinuating something by that?

DR. FALK: Nothing at all.

ELEANOR: If you're going to accuse me of things, I'm going to skip lunch and walk out that door....

DR. FALK: Go ahead.

ELEANOR: I will. When I'm good and ready.

       Eleanor folds her arms across her chest. She does not get up.

DR. FALK: You'll *never* be ready. Who do you think you are to play tricks on the nursing students and foul up the operating room schedule? I've been putting up with your games for sixty-six days and now I've done playing. You're lucky I don't lobotomize you while I'm taking out that watch.

ELEANOR: Nobody has a right to talk to me like that. I don't care how good a surgeon you are....You're a very nasty person, Dr. Falk....I feel for your children....

DR. FALK: [*Defensively.*] I don't have any children, thank-you-very-much. I'll have you know that a woman can lead a perfectly meaningful, fulfilling life without being a wife or a mother. This is not a one-size fits all world, Mrs. Powell.

ELEANOR: You have no children?

DR. FALK: And no regrets.

330

ELEANOR: And your parents? You don't happen to have an elderly mother living in New Hampshire?

DR. FALK: My parents are both long gone. My sister too....I have my work.   And when I retire, I'll have a rewarding career to look back upon. How many women of my generation can say that?

ELEANOR: All work and no play can make Jane an insufferable bitch.

DR. FALK: Excuse me! I'm a doctor. You can't speak to a doctor like that!

ELEANOR: You know what: Go ahead and do the surgery. See if I care....Quite frankly, I'm not going to shed any tears over a woman like you.

DR. FALK: Is that a threat?

ELEANOR: All I'm saying is that I have a track record in the operating room.

DR. FALK: So do I, Mrs. Powell. So do I.

SCENE TWENTY-FIVE

> The Operation, Take Two. The second operation is performed behind a screen. We see a body wheeled behind the screen from one direction, then Dr. Falk and Robyn entering from the other. We again witness the operation taking place in silhouettes, this time more exaggerated, possibly accompanied by incongruous music such as Ella Fitzgerald or Billie Holliday. The music should build to a crescendo. At its conclusion, Robyn staggers from behind the curtain, bloody and dazed. Robyn attempts to address the audience, but no words come out of her mouth. After several

attempts at speech, punctuated by desperate gestures, she passed out cold.

SCENE TWENTY-SIX

Hospital room 125.   Eleanor with Paige and Gloria. The other bed remains empty.

PAIGE: Wake up, Mom. It's all over.

Eleanor opens her eyes and sits up.

ELEANOR: Did I kill her?

PAIGE: You're fine. Dr. Falk is fine. Everybody is fine.

ELEANOR: Dammit. I thought I might go three-for-three.

GLORIA: You're as good as new, Mom. Better. Phil will be so pleased.

ELEANOR: I miss Amanda.

PAIGE: Who?

ELEANOR: That sweet girl the two of you refused to kill.

PAIGE: Her name was Amanda?

ELEANOR: No, her name was Sally. Sally Brown....You can learn a lot listening to people talk in their sleep....But I thought Amanda suited her better.

PAIGE: I can't believe you. You knew who that woman was and you didn't tell her? She could have gone back to her family....

ELEANOR: She didn't want to. Trust me....Even if half of what she said in her sleep was true, she never wanted to see them again....

PAIGE: So you played God with her life?

ELEANOR: Don't be so judgmental. Sometimes playing God is the right thing to do.

GLORIA: Let's not fight. Please.

ELEANOR: Quick. It's four o'clock. Pretend I'm dead.

> Eleanor closes her eyes as though she's in a coma. Gloria does the same.

PAIGE: What are you doing? [*Eleanor does not respond.*] Gloria, what the hell is going on?

GLORIA: If the medical student thinks we're in a coma, she won't bother us. [*Gloria returns to her feigned coma.*]

PAIGE: The two of you are truly impossible. Don't you ever think that it might be *useful* to have the medical student ask you some questions? For instance, to find out whether you need any medical help....She's a very nice girl, that medical student. Totally clueless, but sweet as sweet can be....[*A long pause.*] Dammit, mother. Wake-up! You are *not* in a coma. [*A longer pause.*]

> Eleanor opens her eyes and looks at her watch.

ELEANOR: She's late. How do you like that?.....I hope I didn't scare her off.

SCENE TWENTY-SEVEN

> Dr. Falk's Office. Dr. Falk and Robyn.

ROBYN: You wanted to see me, Dr. Falk?

DR. FALK: Relax. You're not in trouble. Not yet, at least. But I do have a serious question to ask you: Are you sure you want to be a doctor?

ROBYN: Yes....I mean I think so....I mean I really don't know anymore.....

DR. FALK: That's progress. At least, you're honest....You can always become a nurse.

ROBYN: I'm guess I'm just very confused.

DR. FALK: Me too. I'm *still* not sure I want to be a doctor and I've been practicing surgery for six hundred years....

ROBYN: Are you serious?

DR. FALK: I'm *always* serious. Haven't you figured that out yet? But the patients keep showing up, so I keep on cutting.....

ROBYN: [*A long pause.*] Is that what you wanted to tell me, Dr. Falk.

DR. FALK: More or less. Oh, and I have something for you. Courtesy of Mrs. Powell. [*Dr. Falk hands Robyn the watch.*] I've even had it engraved.

ROBYN: To Robyn with the "ck".

DR. FALK: Don't leave it inside anybody's skull....at least not until I retire.

ROBYN: Wow. Thank you....But I thought you were going to put it on display?

DR. FALK: No room anymore. Dr. Navare removed fifty quarters from a psychiatric patient's stomach last night. One for each of the fifty states—the woman had been collecting them for nearly ten years....

ROBYN: I swear I'll treasure this....I'll take it with me everywhere, Dr. Falk, even when I'm old like you.

DR. FALK: I hope you will.... But call me Gwendolyn from now on.... Just not in front of the patients.

ROBYN: Thank you, Dr. Falk. I mean Gwendolyn.

DR. FALK: Now get back to work before I come to my senses and have you expelled....I'll meet you at the nurse's station in half an hour.

ROBYN: Yes, Dr. Falk. Right away, Dr. Falk.

> Robyn retreats toward the door. Dr. Falk looks at her wrists and calls after Robyn in alarm.

DR. FALK: Robyn. Have you seen *my* watch?

ROBYN: Not since we were in the operating room....

DR. FALK: Good God! You don't think—

ROBYN: [*Concerned, but still clueless.*] Are you alarmed, Gwen?

DR. FALK: Never mind. I'm sure it will turn up somewhere eventually....

> Robyn exit. Dr. Falk, to the audience.

DR. FALK: I thought I'd be lost without my watch, but it actually feels rather liberating....It gives you the illusion that you have all the time in the world.

Small Things

By Cary Pepper

Cary Pepper has had plays produced throughout the United States and in Europe. His work is included in *Best American Short Plays 2005–2006* (*Small Things*), and *Best American Short Plays 2007–2008* (*House of the Holy Moment*). Cary is a member of the Dramatists Guild, and a founding member of the San Francisco Bay Area playwrights group ThroughLine.

Small Things won the Tennessee Williams/New Orleans Literary Festival 2006 One Act Play Contest, the 2004 Robert R. Lehan Playwriting Award for One Act Plays (Westfield State College), and was presented at the 2004 Gettysburg College World Premiere One-Act Festival.

Characters:
Hoyt, (50's) tall; deliberate; tired.
Drew, (19) clean-cut; well-scrubbed; innocent; sincere; gives the impression of being almost fragile.

Setting:
Hoyt's apartment.
Stage Right, a couch, in front of which is a coffee table.
Stage Left, an easy chair.

Hoyt sits on the couch, cleaning a revolver. The doorbell rings. Hoyt glances at the door, but doesn't move. The bell rings again. Hoyt thinks...then tucks the pistol under a couch cushion, goes to the door, and opens it. In the doorway is Drew, who has started to walk away. When Hoyt opens the door, he stops. Drew is clean-cut and well scrubbed. He wears a suit and tie, neither of which looks natural on him. He carries a briefcase, which also seems out of place: it should be carried by an accountant or a businessman twice his age.

DREW: Oh. I didn't think anyone was home.

HOYT: No one is.

DREW: Uh, I represent the Assembly of Hubristic Evangelicals. We...

HOYT: The what?

DREW: The Assembly of Hubristic Evangelicals. Have you experienced the one true god?

HOYT: Not lately.

DREW: Well, if you'll give me just a few minutes, I'll tell you how you can experience the one true god.

HOYT: Right now?

DREW: There's no more perfect time to experience the one true god than the moment he comes to you.

HOYT: Has he come to me?

DREW: He will, if you open yourself to his love and his power.

HOYT: Right now?

DREW: There's no more perfect time to experience the one true god than the moment he comes to you. May I counsel with you?

HOYT: Now?

DREW: There's no more perfect time to...

HOYT: Experience the one true god. Got it.
To tell you the truth...

DREW: There is only one truth. That of the one true god.

        Hoyt gazes at Drew.

DREW: That truth will save you. [*Hoyt's gaze becomes a stare.*] And when...you...experience... [*Something in Hoyt's stare causes Drew to hesitate...*] this...experience... [*then falter...*] it...strikes...you...dumb... [*then stop.*] ...with awe.

        Hoyt continues to stare... Drew stands
        there...dumbstruck with awe... Several Beats.

HOYT: Oh, this...is...perfect.

DREW: Well... Sorry to have....

        He turns to go.

HOYT: Come in.

DREW: What?

HOYT: Come in.

DREW: Really?

HOYT: Yes. I want to be struck dumb with awe.

        Hoyt steps back. Drew enters uncertainly.

341

DREW: Thank you. For allowing me to....

HOYT: Sit down.

        Drew starts for the couch.

HOYT: Not there.

DREW: Sorry.

        Hoyt motions toward the chair.

HOYT: Here. Sit there.

> Drew sits in the chair. Hoyt sits on the couch.
> His hand automatically goes to the cushion, on
> top of where he put the pistol. Drew seems to
> be thrown, uncertain of himself. Beat.

HOYT: So... Strike me.

DREW: Excuse me?

HOYT: Strike me dumb with awe.

DREW: Oh... There is only one true god.

HOYT: Is there?

DREW: Yes. And he...

HOYT: And you know who he is.

DREW: Yes. He's the...

HOYT: When you say you know who he is... You mean
you, personally? Or the entire Assembly of Hubristic
Evangelicals?

DREW: Oh, yes. All of us. For we have...

HOYT: How old are you?

DREW: Nineteen. Well, I'll be nineteen in two days.

HOYT: Aren't you a little young for this?

DREW: We all do it. Everyone in the assembly does a year of missionary work when they turn eighteen.

HOYT: You're nineteen.

DREW: Yes.

HOYT: So...you're...extra evangelical?

DREW: I'm finishing my year of missionary service. Today's my last day.

HOYT: And how does that make you feel?

DREW: Relieved! Uh...To experience the one true god...

HOYT: What's his name?

DREW: Who?

HOYT: The one true god.

DREW: His names are many. His spirit is omnipresent... His power is omnipotent... His love is...

HOYT: But what do you call him?

DREW: Who?

HOYT: The one true god.

DREW: ....God.

HOYT: That's it? God?

DREW: Those who know the one true god need no other name. His spirit and power dwell within us. His essence flows through us like an endless stream of eternal sustenance. His glory...

HOYT: But he has no name.

DREW: Who?

HOYT: God.

DREW: Once you experience the one true god, he is within you, and you within him. Only the uninitiated need an earthly name for him. For they have not felt his power and glory.

HOYT: And you want to...initiate me?

DREW: Only the Initiated can experience the one true god.

HOYT: So, the rest of us can't?

DREW: Until you're Initiated, you have no true concept of god.

HOYT: What about <u>my</u> religion?

DREW: There is only one true faith.

HOYT: Yours.

DREW: Only the Initiated know the true path. Only the Initiated see the true light.

HOYT: So the rest of us are just stumbling around in darkness.

DREW: Only the Initiated experience the true sublimity of knowing the one true god.

HOYT: OK. How do we do this?

DREW: What?

HOYT: How do I get to see the true light?

DREW: You become Initiated.

HOYT: Right. How do I do that?

DREW: What?

HOYT: Get initiated.

DREW: You join the Assembly of Hubristic Evangelicals.

HOYT: How do I do that?

DREW: What?

HOYT: Join the club. Become a hubristic evangelical. I want to see the true light. I want to experience the one true god.

DREW: Oh... I have some pamphlets here... These explain, pretty much...

> Drew takes pamphlets out of his briefcase and puts them on the table. Hoyt picks up the pamphlets and reads their titles.

HOYT: "The One True Path to the One True God".... "The One True God and You"... "Being Hubristic"... "Be God and Be Good"....

DREW: [*Handing over another pamphlet.*] And this pamphlet will tell you about our bible.... The One True Book. We combined the old and new testaments, took out the parts that are wrong, and revealed the one true message of the one true god. You'll get your own bible when you're Initiated.

345

HOYT: Yeah, let's do that.

DREW: What?

HOYT: Get initiated.

DREW: Well, if you come to a meeting, you can speak to a...

HOYT: No, I want to do it now.

DREW: What?

HOYT: Get initiated. I want you to initiate me.

DREW: Now?

HOYT: There's no more perfect time.

DREW: Here?

HOYT: There's no more perfect place.

DREW: No! I can't do that.

HOYT: Why not?

DREW: Uh...I only came to give you some literature.

HOYT: That's it?

DREW: Yeah. That's all we do in our missionary work.

HOYT: Well I want more.

DREW: Well come to a meeting.

HOYT: I don't want to wait for a meeting. I want to be initiated now. And I want you to do it.

DREW: I've never done that!

HOYT: No one's ever asked you to?

DREW: No one's ever let me in!

HOYT: You've been doing this for a year and no one's let you in?

DREW: No!

HOYT: That must be frustrating.

DREW: It totally sucks!

HOYT: Well, you've hit the jackpot this time. You're going all the way, son. Initiate me.

DREW: Uh... Why don't you read the pamphlets. And then you can...

HOYT: I'll read the pamphlets later. Just go ahead and do...whatever needs to be done.

DREW: I can't.

HOYT: Why not?

DREW: Um...uh...I'm not an elder.

HOYT: But you've been initiated, right?

DREW: Yeah. When I was, like, seven.

HOYT: OK. Do to me, what they did to you.

DREW: I can't!

HOYT: Why not? What'd they do to you?

347

DREW: They...had me stand before the Assembly... and...they...Gestured over me...and they...Questioned me... and I answered rightly...and they... Gestured over me some more.

HOYT: That's it?

DREW: That was it.

HOYT: Did you feel initiated?

DREW: Yeah.

HOYT: Did you feel different?

DREW: Yeah! I was Initiated!

HOYT: Did you know the one true path?

DREW: I was Initiated!

HOYT: Did you know the one true god?

DREW: We all did! We were all Initiated!

HOYT: Did you see the true light?

DREW: Well...no. They said that would come later. All the older people said they saw it.

HOYT: What did you feel?

DREW: When?

HOYT: When you were initiated.

DREW: Feel? I'd been initiated!

HOYT: Did you feel happy?

DREW: Yeah!

HOYT: Did you feel special?

DREW: YEAH!

HOYT: Did you feel at peace?

DREW: I was seven.

HOYT: Right. OK... So. Just do to me what they did to you.

DREW: I can't.

HOYT: Why not?

DREW: I shouldn't.

HOYT: Why not?

DREW: It wouldn't be right.

HOYT: Why not?

DREW: I'd rather not say.

HOYT: I won't tell anyone.

DREW: No. I'd rather not.

HOYT: C'mon. It's just you and me. And I'm about to become one of you. You've done your job well. You've got a convert. Your first one. They'll love you for this.

DREW: They'll hate me.

HOYT: No they won't.

DREW: They already hate me.

HOYT: Would that be the one true hate?

DREW: Might as well be.

HOYT: Do they believe in hate?

DREW: Not officially.

HOYT: Well, they sound like everyone else on that one. So... Convert me! Initiate me!

DREW: It wouldn't be right.

HOYT: [*He will not be denied.*] Why?

DREW: Because I'm leaving the Assembly.

 HOYT: Something you haven't mentioned?

DREW: Could I...have a glass of water? Or something?

HOYT: Sure. Would you prefer water? Or something?

DREW: No...water will be fine, thanks.

> Hoyt goes into the kitchen. Drew sits looking at the floor, deflated. Hoyt returns with a glass of water and gives it to Drew.

DREW: Thanks.

> He gulps down all the water.

HOYT: We're a little thirsty.

DREW: I guess.

HOYT: Want some more?

DREW: No, thanks.

HOYT: So... Why are you leaving?

DREW: I'd rather not say.

HOYT: It's a little late for that.

DREW: What do you mean?

HOYT: You started this.

DREW: What?

HOYT: The forced intimacy.

DREW: I don't know what you're...

HOYT: You ring my bell...you interrupt what I'm doing... you come into my house...and you immediately question my religious beliefs. Then you challenge my beliefs... invalidate them... And try to impose your beliefs on me.

DREW: I... I never thought of it that way.

HOYT: What did you think you were doing?

DREW: Spreading the one true word.

HOYT: Why do you want to do that?

DREW: They tell us to.

HOYT: So you just go out and do it?

DREW: We all do.

HOYT: What makes you think I want to hear about your religion?

DREW: It's the one true faith.

HOYT: For you. Maybe I've got my own faith.

351

DREW: Ours is the one true religion.

HOYT: How do you know mine isn't the one true religion?

DREW: There can be only one true religion.

HOYT: Well maybe it's mine!

DREW: It can't be.

HOYT: Why not?

DREW: Because it's mine.

HOYT: How do you know that?

DREW: The one true book tells us it is.

HOYT: Who wrote this book?

DREW: The one true prophet.

HOYT: This is one hot belief system, huh?

DREW: It's the one true religion.

HOYT: So why are you quitting?

DREW: I'd rather not say.

HOYT: And I say you owe it to me.

DREW: I do? Why?

HOYT: Because you've not only imposed all this on me, but you've caught me at a very...vulnerable time. I was doing fine before you walked in here. No, I wasn't doing fine at all. In fact you caught me a real low point. And you ring my bell, and I open my door, and what you do you offer me? Salvation! And what did that do? It made me hopeful. By doing that, you interfered with the natural order of my misery. In that misery, I'd found answers. But then there you were, and suddenly there were other answers. That took me out of my place and brought me to another. Yours. Now you're telling me this place is a sham. But where does that leave me? Disturbed, desperate, and in despair... Which I was before. But now it's your fault. So I tell you I want to know...I need to know... What's wrong with your one true religion? And it's important that you tell me. More important than you know. And...I think you want to. [*He waits...Drew is silent...*] Why are you leaving the assembly?

DREW: I'm gay.

HOYT: So?

DREW: So...in their eyes...I'm an abomination.

HOYT: The assembly you've given a year of your life to... The religion you've given your heart and soul to... Considers you an abomination.

DREW: Yes.

HOYT: Because you're gay.

DREW: Yes.

HOYT: Bummer.

      Beat.

DREW: Can I use your bathroom?

HOYT: Down the hall.

      Drew leaves. Hoyt retrieves the pistol from under the cushion and thoughtfully rubs it with a cloth. The sound of Drew returning... Hoyt puts the pistol back under the cushion.

HOYT: So... The one true faith for all humankind...hates some people. Because they don't love the people they're supposed to.

DREW: I guess you could put it that way.

HOYT: Why? A sin of Onan thing? A don't-disturb-the-natural-order thing? Or are you just a generic abomination?

DREW: Uh...the last one, I think.

HOYT: And how do they know this?

DREW: It's in the one true book.

HOYT: How can you be part of this thing?

DREW: I can't. That's why I'm quitting.

HOYT: Then how can you go out there and ask other people to be part of it?

DREW: It's what we're brought up to do. You're taught to want to do it. You look forward to it. You don't even think about it.

HOYT: So what happened?

DREW: I started thinking about it.... I started thinking! All these years, I'm getting the message, this is the one true religion. But I'm also getting another message: I'm no good. At first I accept that, because I think maybe I am no good. Like, I've got....this affliction...or this...bad gene...or a disease. Maybe it's a Test. And I'm always being told that if you have enough faith any test can be met. So if you're sinful...or you have sinful thoughts...or do bad things... You have to have more faith...pray harder...go to more meetings...work harder for the Assembly... And it'll be OK. But the older I get, I begin to realize...I'm not hurting anybody. I don't kill. I don't steal. I don't wish anyone

354

evil. I don't lie. Except about one thing, and I only do that because of them. But, except for that, as far as I can tell, I don't sin at all. But...according to them, I'm bad. And I begin to think, "What is wrong with me?" And I realize.... Nothing. So why do they say I'm bad? I begin to ask more questions... And they tell me, have more faith. It's in the one true book. It's the will of the one true god. But those answers don't work for me any more. And I'm just beginning to really question everything, when it's time to begin my year of mission work.

HOYT: So off you went?

DREW: I was still working things out. And also, I'd made a commitment to do it. It felt wrong not to honor my commitment.

HOYT: So, on a scale of one to ten, ten being the worst, where was the missionary work?

DREW: Twenty-Seven!
They tell you you're doing something important. Spreading the one true word. Bringing people to the one true god.... So why was it, that every time someone opened the door, as soon as they realized why I was there, what I wanted, there was That Look on their face? They tell you it's because people don't know how much they need help. Everyone's walking around in darkness, unable to see the one true light, so when you come to the door, they think you're just another one of those other groups that does missionary work. And they react that way out of their own ignorance. So it's all the more important that you keep doing it, because people really need to hear about the one true faith. So, OK...that makes sense. But not for very long. Because you keep seeing That Look. And no one wants to hear what you have to say. And everyone is always Doing Something when you ring the bell. And I begin to think... Is this really helping anyone? Or is it just bothering people?

Six months into it, I decide it's just bothering people. I mean, if people really needed help...wouldn't they be out getting it? Wouldn't they be somewhere, talking to someone, instead of sitting around the house, as if they were hoping someone would ring the bell and save them? Or, if they are home, maybe they're on the phone, talking to someone who can help them. And I come along and interrupt them! So I'm stopping them from getting help! So the whole thing just isn't working for me at all. It just doesn't mean anything.

Unless... Unless you happen to ring someone's bell just when they're in the middle of a crisis. And you happen to be the exact person they need, because what you have to say, helps them. If that happens... If you come along just at the right moment, and you make a difference in someone's life...then it means something.

HOYT: Well, you've hit the jackpot.

DREW: And for a while that works. It keeps me going. Until I realize that I'm terrified it <u>might</u> happen. Because... I'm 18! I don't know anything! How can I help anyone! "But you're not supposed to know," I tell myself... It's the one true religion that has the answers. The one true god, and his one true book. So just tell them about that, and it'll be OK.

Except, according to Them...that religion...that book... I'm no good. So I'm their messenger, spreading the one true word, but, according to that word, I'm...what?... The one true evil? And everything starts to fall apart. I'm walking around in a daze. I'm the one who needs help, and even I'm not turning to the one true faith! So now when I ring bells, I'm glad no one's home. And I'm hoping that anyone who is, won't let me in. And somehow, I get through my year.

Today's my last day of service.... It ends at five o'clock. With any luck, yours is the last bell I have to ring. And what do you mean I've hit the jackpot?

HOYT: You know that crisis you were talking about?

DREW: Yeah?

HOYT: I'm having it.

DREW: What....kind...of...crisis?

HOYT: What's the difference? Call it a crisis of faith...
sanity...finances...stability... Doesn't matter. Not any
more. You rang the bell. I opened the door. You said you
had answers. I let you in.

DREW: But I don't have any answers.

HOYT: Afraid you're going to have to do better than that,
son.

DREW: But I can't help you.

HOYT: Well then, we're both in a pickle.

> He reaches under the cushion and takes out
> the revolver.

DREW: Oh...Shit...!

> Hoyt calmly resumes cleaning the gun.

DREW: Is that...loaded?

HOYT: Clean a loaded gun? I considered it... But it's too
chancy. You've got to be more precise than that for
something like this.

DREW: Something like...what?

HOYT: Don't go stupid on me, son.

DREW: You're saying you're going to use that...on yourself?
But why...

HOYT: Like I said...

DREW: ...clean it first? I mean, why bother?

HOYT: You do something, do it right. Neat. Clean. And... I figured it'd be a...cooling-off period. See what happens between the time I start cleaning it and when I finish. See if anything came along to make me change my mind. And you know what happened? You rang the bell.

DREW: Yeah, but that's because no one else in the building was home. Or maybe they were, but they didn't answer. I mean, if anyone else answered the door, or maybe even let me in, I wouldn't be here now.

HOYT: But you are.

DREW: But that doesn't mean what you think it does. It doesn't mean anything.

HOYT: You said you had the answer.

DREW: But I don't!

HOYT: The one true answer.

DREW: There is no one true answer!!

HOYT: Then we're both in trouble.

DREW: We?? You said you were going to...

HOYT: I've got no life... You've got no religion.

DREW: So you're not gonna...

HOYT: Sure I am. There's a bullet here with my name on it.

DREW: I mean...me.

HOYT: Why would I do that?

DREW: People do all sorts of crazy things.

HOYT: Like ring doorbells of people they don't know?

DREW: You...seem so calm for someone who's about to...do that.

HOYT: How do you want me to be?

DREW: I don't know.

HOYT: Should I shout? Jump up and down? Wave my arms about? Say crazy things?

DREW: I don't know, but...

HOYT: [*Studying the gun.*] I never was much of a screamer. Even when I got hurt as a kid. I never cried. Just wondered why the world hurt me, and marveled at how quickly things can change so much.

DREW: But this is so beyond that.

HOYT: Maybe not as much as you think. And don't mistake calmness for lack of resolve. I am going to do this.

DREW: Why? What happened, that you think this is the answer?

HOYT: Oh... Everything.

DREW: Like...what?

HOYT: You really wanna know?

DREW: If you want to tell me. And if you don't...

HOYT: Kind of hoping I do, terrified I will?

DREW: No. Well, yeah, I guess.

HOYT: Relax, son. I'm not gonna. You're off the hook.

DREW: No... Y'know what? I asked. I really do want to know.

      Beat.

HOYT: Like I said... Everything. Lost my job...lost all my money...I'm not eligible for unemployment...can't pay my rent... I'm gonna lose my apartment at the end of the month... Got nowhere to go. Nowhere to live. No one to live with... And no will to keep going. I guess I'm just real, real, real, real tired. So...fuck it.

DREW: That's it? That's why you're going to kill yourself?? Well that's pretty stupid!

HOYT: Watch the insults, son. I've got a gun here.

DREW: No, I mean, really. You can get a job. Some job, somewhere. You can get another place to live. You can start over. I mean, out of all the reasons to kill yourself... that's...really lame!

HOYT: Shows you how tired I am.

DREW: Well you know what? That sucks!

HOYT: Yeah, it's a sin.

DREW: It's... It's lazy! That's what it is!

HOYT: Lazy? Look at how much effort I'm putting into this.

DREW: No, you stop putting in any effort at all! You're just quitting!

HOYT: I'm a bad person.

DREW: And... It is a sin.

HOYT: Well, maybe I need more religion. I asked for yours. You didn't give it to me.

DREW: Wait... If I Initiate you... Will that change your mind?

HOYT: You said you can't.

DREW: Well what if I did?

HOYT: But you can't.

DREW: But what if I did!? Would that make a difference?

      Beat.

HOYT: But you can't.

DREW: ...Why not??

HOYT: You're not an elder.

DREW: Yeah, but I'm leaving, so there's an opening. You can take my place.

HOYT: Yeah... I've seen how much good it's done you.

DREW: Maybe it'll be better for you.

HOYT: The religion that says hate people just because of who they are?

DREW: The religion that says no matter how bad things get, there's always hope.

HOYT: Not good enough. And I don't think I like this religion.

DREW: Well, neither do I! But all the religions say that. That's what religion's for! To give us hope!

HOYT: And sometimes it just doesn't. Come to think of it, I've never been all that religious.

DREW: So why'd you let me in?

HOYT: You rang the bell, said you had the answer.

DREW: No! I ring your bell, I tell you I have the one true word...someone like you slams the door in my face in three seconds.

HOYT: Now how do you know that?

DREW: You had That Look. As soon as I opened my mouth. I even started to walk away. You called me back and said to come in. Why'd you do that? I say it was so I could talk you out of it.

HOYT: I say you're wrong.

DREW: I say you're lying. You wanted to be talked out of it. You don't really want to do this.

> Beat.

HOYT: Know why I let you in? To talk me <u>in</u> to it. To show me it really was the way to go.

DREW: What??

HOYT: Here I am...getting ready to stop it all. And...

DREW: And cleaning your gun to see if anything would happen that would stop it!

HOYT: ...And the doorbell rings. And there you are. Someone offering religion. And I think, well, isn't this perfect. Isn't this a sign? Let's see what this one's got to say. And when he says absolutely nothing that makes any difference... That's the sign. There really is no reason not to do this. That's what I was thinking. That's why I let you in.

DREW: And... I haven't given you a reason...have I?

HOYT: You're kidding, right?

DREW: Well...how about, maybe you just shouldn't do it.

HOYT: Maybe??

DREW: OK, you just shouldn't do it.

HOYT: Is that your religion talking?

DREW: No, it's me talking. It's got nothing to do with religion. I just think you shouldn't do it.

    Beat.

HOYT: You're a good kid. But this isn't working.

    He gives the gun a last wipe, reaches under the table, and comes up with a box of bullets.

HOYT: And I think it's about that time.

    He loads the gun, slowly — almost thoughtfully — putting each bullet into the cylinder. Drew watches his every move. After three bullets, Hoyt spins the cylinder and stops.

DREW: So...you're saying...there's nothing I can say...to make you change your mind.

HOYT: I think we've established that.

> Hoyt resumes slowly loading the gun. Drew watches... Finally, the gun is loaded. Hoyt closes the cylinder and spins it.

DREW: Y'know what? You're right.

HOYT: I know.

DREW: Yeah... OK. If that's what you need to do, go ahead.

> Hoyt gazes at Drew.

HOYT: Reverse psychology? You stop trying to talk me out of it, I'll decide not to?

DREW: Huh? Oh...no. I mean it. I have been trying to talk you out of it. But it's your right. And who am I to talk you out of something you need so badly? You're even willing to kill for it.

I mean, we don't even know each other, and I'm trying to stop you. But if this is what you need to do... It's who you are... And saying don't do it, I'm trying to stop you from being who you are. Which is exactly what they're doing to me.

So...if this really is what you need... I should just shut the fuck up.

HOYT: I guess you should.

DREW: Just one more thing?

HOYT: Which would be what?

DREW: ....Wait until I'm gone. Please. I don't want to....

HOYT: When are you going?

DREW: ...I guess I should go now?

HOYT: I guess you should.

> Beat. Drew stands and heads for the door.
> Hoyt sits back on the couch and studies the
> gun. Drew gets to the door, stops, turns...

DREW: I did it. Tried it... A couple of years ago, it got so terrible... I knew who I was... And they were telling me that was bad. And I believed them... I couldn't live with it any more. I decided to use pills, and I lay down with a bottle, and put it on my chest and stared at it. And nothing happened. No one rang the bell. So I took the pills. And I'm lying there, waiting for them to kick in... And...a song gets into my head.

And I can't get it out. I can't stop thinking this song. And it's got words, and sometimes just the music's in my head, and sometimes it's the words, too. And it's...the theme song from *The Beverly Hillbillies*.

And no matter what I do, what else I think of...it won't go away! And I start thinking... How fucking stupid is this??? My last fully conscious moments, and this is the best I can do?? What – is – wrong – with – me?

At first, that did it. I mean, talk about signs. If this is the best you can do with your last moments... Absolutely, pull the trigger, kick the chair out from under you, pour the bottle down your throat. But then I start to laugh... And... I don't know exactly what happened next... I lost consciousness or something. But not from the pills. But, next thing I know, I'm laughing. I mean, really, really, really laughing. Like, when you're laughing with everything you've got... You're laughing so much it hurts... It completely, totally, fills you. You <u>are</u> laughter.

And... I didn't want to die any more.

And... that's when the pills kicked in.

I started to go all hazy, and I knew that if I didn't get off the bed, soon, it'd be too late. But... I didn't want to die any more.

> Beat.

HOYT: Nice story.

DREW: Yeah... Well...

> He turns to go.

HOYT: Hey, kid.

> He stops, turns.

DREW: Yeah?

HOYT: Congratulations.

DREW: Why?

HOYT: You're out of the assembly.

DREW: I am?

HOYT: You said today was your last day. If you meant it...

DREW: I did. I really did!

HOYT: Well... It's 5:30. You've been out for half an hour.

DREW: Yeah.

HOYT: You're a free man.

DREW: [*Softly.*] Yeah!

> Hoyt spins the cylinder of the gun... Looks at
> it... Then opens the cylinder and shakes the
> bullets out.

DREW: You're...not...gonna....

HOYT: No.

DREW: Why not?

HOYT: Now you want me to justify <u>not</u> doing it?

DREW: No! Sorry. I was just curious. Forget it. I'm sorry.
That was stupid. I don't know what I was thinking.

HOYT: It was something you said.

DREW: No way!

HOYT: Don't argue with me. I still have the gun.

DREW: But all that one-true-faith crap....

HOYT: It wasn't crap.

DREW: You're saying it means something?

HOYT: Oh, geez, of course not! I'm saying it wasn't one-
true-anything crap. You weren't in it when you said it.

DREW: So what'd I say?

HOYT: I think I'd like to keep that for myself.

DREW: You're not gonna tell me?

HOYT: Son... Did you do all that for me, or for you?

DREW: For you.

HOYT: Then your job's done. Walk away.

DREW: Yeah... OK.

He turns...

HOYT: No, wait a minute. You're entitled to know.

DREW: [*Turns back.*] OK.

HOYT: You lying there, full of pills...with the theme song from *The Beverly Hillbillies* stuck in your head.

He laughs.

DREW: [*Singing.*] Come and listen to a story 'bout a man name Jed, A poor mountaineer, barely kept his family fed, Then one day he was shootin' at some food...

HOYT: Son — Don't sing that song.

DREW: Sorry. But...what? You were afraid it would happen to you?

HOYT: No, that wasn't it.

DREW: Then...?

HOYT: It was, you told me the story. You weren't doing it for them... You weren't doing it for you. I don't think you were even doing it for me. You weren't doing anything. You were just telling a story. You were just with me.

DREW: Someone else could have...

HOYT: Someone else? A priest? A rabbi? A shrink? They would have been doing a job. And spouting doctrine. You were just there. You were just...you.

DREW: Yeah... The walking freak show.

HOYT: Hey... I had a gun here, and you didn't run away. Most people's first words would've been, "Don't shoot me." Yours were, "Are you gonna use that on yourself?"

DREW: Actually, I think they were, "Is that loaded?"

HOYT: Yeah, but you weren't thinking about saving your ass.

DREW: Uh, yeah... I was.

HOYT: OK, of course you were. But once you saw you were safe, you didn't haul ass first chance you had. You stayed. You grappled. You tried to help.

DREW: I'm not...

HOYT: Son, you're not an abomination. Get used to it.

> Beat.

DREW: ...So you're saying now it's not so bad?

HOYT: Oh, it's just as bad. But now it's...open-ended. Not a closed box with no way out. That what I needed to know. I'm not even sure why it mattered, but it did.

DREW: All I did was tell you a story.

HOYT: Sometimes that's all it takes.

DREW: That's not what They'd say.

HOYT: Son, you're not one of 'em any more. Get used to it.

DREW: But, just a story?

HOYT: It's the small things. For some people it's big things, but what I needed right then was something small.

DREW: I don't think I know what you're talking about.

HOYT: For you, it was a song. For me, it was someone telling a story.

Sometimes it is doctrine. Could be a look on someone's face...graffiti in a bathroom... A book...a painting. A pizza. Doesn't matter what it is, as long as it gets you to the next moment.

DREW: You sound like you have the answer.

HOYT: I do. The one true answer.

DREW: What??

HOYT: Now, how stupid was that?

DREW: But you just said that was the answer.

HOYT: For me. For this moment. And you know what?

DREW: What?

HOYT: The moment's gone.
You gonna be all right?

DREW: Am I gonna be all right? You're the one with gun! You're the one who's so tired!

HOYT: You're the one who's about to walk away from the last eighteen years of your life.

DREW: I've got a feeling the next eighteen years are going to be a lot better than the last eighteen! But you still have no job, no money.

HOYT: I've still got choices. I picked this one to get out of making other decisions I didn't want to make. Now that I've given this up, I think I can live with some of those others. I'll be all right.

DREW: So...I...did it.

HOYT: What?

370

DREW: Saved someone.

HOYT: Yeah. You. Not them... Not the one true religion.
You.

DREW: [*Smiles.*] Yeah....Me.

END.

The Sweet Abyss

By Jon Tuttle

Jon Tuttle is Playwright-in-Residence at Trustus Theatre in
Columbia, SC, and Professor of English at Francis Marion
University. His other published plays include *Holy Ghost, Drift,
The White Problem, The Hammerstone, Sonata for Armadillos,
Terminal Café*, and *A Fish Story*; his collections include *The
Trustus Plays* and *Two South Carolina Plays*. Jon and his wife
Cheryl live in Florence, SC, and are the proud parents of Staci,
Jill and Josh and the delighted grandparents of Noah.

The Sweet Abyss premiered at the Trustus Theatre in Columbia,
South Carolina, on August 14, 2009. It was directed by Dewey
Scott-Wiley. Cast and crew were as follows:

Cass:Elena Martinez-Vidal
Dori/Caroline:Elisabeth Gray Heard
Roger/David/
Father Daniel/Elias: Joe Morales
Izzy: Holly

Artistic Director:Jim Thigpen
Managing Director:Kay Thigpen
Technical Director:Larry McMullen
Assistant Technical Director:Brandon McIver
Graphic Artist/Prod. Manager:Chad Henderson
Set and Light Design:Chet Longley
Costumer/Makeup:Robin Gottlieb
Props Master:Nate Herring
Stage Manager:Jane Hearn
Assistant Stage Manager:Liz Brownlee
Sound Board Operator:Tyler Jones
Videographer/Photographer:Jason Stellman

Acknowledgments:
Whatever one might make of it, the work of Rita Reynolds, Temple
Grandin and Elizabeth Severino was important to the writing of
this play. Thanks also to my brother Jeff, who gets it, and to my
wife Cheryl, who gets me.

To obtain stock and amateur performance rights contact the
author's agent, Marta Praeger, at the Robert Freedman Dramatic
Agency, Inc., at (212) 840-5760 or 1501 Broadway, Suite 2310,
New York, NY 10036.

Characters:
CASS, 40's. Desperately pretty, maybe.
DORI, her daughter, 20ish. Fragile, sort of goth, a little heavy, probably.
ROGER, middle-aged.
IZZY, a cat. Yes. A live cat, preferably very mellow. The script refers to him as white with blue eyes, but he can be any color.

The following can be doubled by the actors playing Dori and Roger:

DAVID, middle-aged, quirky, opaque.
FATHER DANIEL, any age.
CAROLINE, middle-aged, earthy, flowy, genteel.
ELIAS, older, blind, perhaps wheelchair-bound.

Setting:
The present, in the American south, primarily a lower middle-class home suggested by a couch and a table, with one exit to the kitchen, another to the bedrooms. Other venues—a hospital room, a veterinarian's office, a farmhouse porch—are minimally suggested.

The passing of time—hours, days or weeks—is indicated in the script by quick shifts or changes in lighting. These may also be accompanied by tableaux—the actors freezing for just a moment—and/or a sound cue, for instance a single note on the piano.

> The house and I are all he remembers.
> Next month how will he guess that it is winter
> And not just entropy, the universe
> Plunging at last into its cold decline?
> I cannot think of him without a pang.
>
> "The Happy Cat"
> Randall Jarrell

ACT ONE

SCENE ONE

> At rise: Area lighting up on Cass, lying on a hospital
> gurney, covered by a sheet. She's in her 40's and
> attractive—but too made-up for this occasion. She
> lies on her side, facing us, groggy. A doctor, Roger,
> enters wearing a white lab coat and pulling on latex
> gloves. He passes in front, stops, then bends to
> look at her.

ROGER: ...Well. Hello there. You're not supposed to be
awake.

CASS: ...I know.

ROGER: Hasn't she started the drip?

CASS: ...Yes.

ROGER: Well don't fight it. You can't win, and you'll only
give yourself a hangover. I'm Roger Bush. I'll be your
spelunker today. And you are... [*He consults a clipboard:*]
Cassandra.... Cassandra.... Hey! I know you! You work at
uh, at at at, uh, Fujiyama! The uh, yeah! With the, with
the, and the—. [*He means a kimono and a wig.*] You're a
geisha!

CASS: [*Pleasantly, sort of.*] A hostess.

ROGER: Hostess, sure! I've seen you there! My wife and
I go there all the time! Well, my ex-wife. My FUTURE ex-
wife. Actually we haven't been there in a while. We finalize
in fifty-three days. But: back in the saddle, right? You
make a great Japanese gal.

CASS: Uh-huh.

ROGER: Severe cramping, nausea, constipation and
explosive diarrhea: that's no fun. We get this a lot in

women your age. Usually it's something simple, like impacted feces, but in your case, it might just be a pearl.

He has lifted the sheet to look at her.

CASS: I—

ROGER: Colonoscopy joke. Got a million of 'em. "Louisiana tag—looks like this one swam up from the gulf." In my line of work, you've got to keep your sense of humor. What does your husband do?

CASS: ...My husb...?

ROGER: Will he be taking you home? ...Cassandra. ...Cassandra? [*The lights change: time has passed. Roger removes his gloves.*] ...Cassandra?

CASS [*Groggy.*] ...Hmm?

ROGER: We're all done.

CASS: ...We are?

ROGER: Had a dead gerbil clogging up your pyloric sphincter.

CASS: A—!

ROGER: You had two polyps—and your GI tract looks like a mine shaft. I'll bet you take a buncha laxatives.

CASS: Um, pol...poly...?

ROGER: Polyps. Fleshy outgrowths that attach themselves to the epithelium, like tumors. And frankly, I don't like the color. You'll want to stay off your feet for the rest of the day, get plenty of fluids, and for God's sake lay off the Ex-Lax. You'll end up with osteomalacia.

> Roger has removed her sheet; Cass wears
> clothes underneath—a sexy outfit, in fact, or
> something too young for her.   He hands her a
> foil pill sampler and escorts her from the table.

ROGER: And here. If the pain gets too bad, take one of these. Who's taking you home?

CASS: Oste...?

ROGER: Osteomalacia. Your bones get spongy, you gotta use a walker. But I don't want you to worry. Is your husband taking you home?

CASS: ...Umm. Dori.

ROGER: Dori. Is that your daughter?

CASS: How can I be done?

ROGER: Will she be taking care of you?

CASS: DORI.

ROGER: ...Oh. Sooo...you don't have a husband?

CASS: My husband?

ROGER: Yes.

CASS: [*Trying to recall.*] ...No, he...he left. ...He's gone.

ROGER: Okay then! Well! Lovely meeting you! I'll call in a few days with that lab report. Maybe I'll come see you at work! How about that? Ho-ho-hokay! And now: once more into the breach, dear friends.

> Roger waves/salutes and is gone. The lights
> narrow around Cass, who stands dazed, in a
> void. Beat.

CASS: ...Tumors?

DORI: [*Off, from the darkness.*] ...Mama? ...Mama?

> The lights return and Dori enters. She's 20ish, kind of goth, maybe a little heavy and wearing a garish crucifix. She'll collect Cass and steady her.

DORI: ...Mama? ...Are you coming?

CASS: ...Oh. Dori. How did I...how long was I in there? ...Dori?

DORI: Hm?

CASS: I asked you a question.

DORI: No you didn't.

CASS: I asked you how long I was in there.

DORI: Over an hour. And no you didn't.

CASS: ...What a strange feeling. Like...like when a record skips, and you think..."I missed part of the song," but...you didn't. Or, or there was no song. It was just a, like a...a HOLE. Do you know what I mean? ...Dori? ...DORI?

> The lights change: they are now in their home— a couch with a table in front of it. On the table is a plate covered with foil. This plate will remain on the table and yield a variety of dessert items.

DORI: WHAT?

CASS: Would you please listen?

DORI: To what?

CASS: I was trying to tell you. It's as if everything was... was gone. Or it never existed to begin with, but then everything was the same except for that...that HOLE. How did we get home?

DORI: How do you think we got home?

CASS: I feel like I'm drunk. Get me a Mountain Dew.

Dori places Cass on the couch.

DORI: Here. I made us some brownies.

CASS: You know I can't eat those. Where's Izzy. –Izzy?

Dori sees the foil sampler—and takes it.

DORI: What are these?

CASS: I don't know, he gave them to me.

DORI: Who.

CASS: That doctor. –Izzy?

DORI: Vicodin?

CASS: I think he was hitting on me.

DORI: You always think they're hitting on you.

CASS: I need a Mountain Dew!

DORI: We're all out of Mountain Dew!

CASS: Look under my bed.

DORI: I did already.

CASS: Over the washing machine. Behind the bug spray. And find Izzy. I want Izzy.

> Dori exits to the kitchen. Pause. Cass takes a brownie, eats it, gets her bearings—and realizes:

CASS: ...Holy....   Oh my God.   –Dori? Come in here.

> Dori returns with a bottle of Mountain Dew.

DORI: What?

CASS: ...Dori. Listen to me.   ...You need to brace yourself.

DORI: ...For what.

CASS: ...I'm going to die.

DORI: [*Softly, and horrified.*] ...You are?

CASS: Yes. [*Cass opens the bottle and takes a big chug.*] ...I'm pretty sure.

DORI: ...When?

CASS: ...I don't know.

DORI: Of what?

CASS: ...Cancer.

DORI: ...You have cancer?

CASS: Yes.   ...Well. Tumors.

DORI: ...He said this.

CASS: ...Yes.

DORI: Well...tumors aren't cancer, Mama.

CASS: Tumors ARE cancer. Your Grandpa Walt had a tumor in his neck and look what happened to him. Or Aunt Ruth, she was full of tumors. It runs in our family.

DORI: Daddy had a tumor and he didn't die.

CASS: What?

DORI: Daddy. His tumor. Remember?

CASS: We don't talk about your father.

DORI: But he did. He had that thing, on his arm, he said it looked like Jesus—

CASS: He had a melanoma. A melanoma is not a tumor.

DORI: But that's cancer. He wanted to have it framed and charge people to come see it.

CASS: You imagine these things.

DORI: No, I remember! He—

CASS: Well FORGET it! I told you: I don't want to hear about him. Now go find Izzy.

> Dori exits to bedrooms. Cass eats another brownie and swills her Mountain Dew. Then, to herself:

CASS: ...Oh my God. [*Beat. She registers amazement— or terror.*] ...What if...what if that's what.... —What if that's what it feels like? You know? To be dead. I mean, I was just knocked out, but...I was still alive, but I, I—you know? ...Or, or, or: what if I'm dead now? Like, like I died on the table? Like in that Bruce Willis movie? Everything's so blurry. Maybe I'm in a box already, and nobody told me.

> Dori returns with a cat—Izzy—and hands him to Cass.

DORI: He was in your closet.

CASS: Izzy! Why are you hiding? Why are you hiding?

DORI: He threw up in your red pumps.

CASS: Go get me some ice.

DORI: We don't have any ice.

CASS: Then go buy some.

DORI: I don't have any money.

CASS: Look in my kimono.

DORI: I did. You're broke.

CASS: Then go make some! Jesus, Dori! Do I have to do everything?

> Dori huffs and exits to the kitchen. Cass cuddles up with Izzy...and who knows what will happen in this moment? It's live theatre—with a cat. Perhaps she'll sing a few lilting bars of "You Are My Sunshine" or produce a pipe cleaner from between the cushions and tantalize Izzy with it.

CASS: ...Hello, Izzy. Hello, punkin. What're you doing in my closet? You're always right here on the couch. I need you right here on the couch. Uh-huh. Uh-huh. With me. That's right. Look what I've got. Uh-huh. Oh! Oh! You want it? You want that, don't you. Hmm? Can't have it. Can't have it.

> And so on. The moment continues blissfully, the actor improvising as necessary, the lights settling in around them to create a sense of timelessness. Finally, offstage, a phone starts

ringing. The lights change back, and Dori
returns with a phone.

DORI: Mama?

CASS: ...Hmm?

DORI: ...It's him.

CASS: Who?

DORI: Him. Him. The butt doctor.

CASS: ...God. I'm not ready for this. Take a—.

DORI: [*Into the phone.*] She can't come to the phone right
now. Can I take a message? ...Uh huh. ...Just a minute.
–He says because of privacy something he has to—

CASS: Give it to me.

Cass steels herself and takes the phone. Dori
eavesdrops. Elsewhere, special up on Roger, on
his phone.

CASS: –Hello?

ROGER: Cassandra? Roger Bush. Great news! You've got
irritable bowels.

CASS: What?

ROGER: Both polyps were benign.

CASS: Polyps?

ROGER: IBS is a common reaction to bacterial infection
and irregular levels of seratonin in the gastrointestinal tract
and can lead to complications like Crohn's disease. But I
don't want you to worry. I'm going to prescribe some

Lotronex, you'll want to minimize your glutens, and I'd really like to see you again, as soon as possible.

CASS: [*Interspersed.*] —Wait. —Wait. –I...I need to ask you something.

ROGER: Terrific! How's Thursday?

CASS: Thursday?

ROGER: Say sixish. I have your address. You wouldn't happen to own a Hibachi, would you?

CASS: A what?

ROGER: That's all right! I've got a wok. I make a mean vegetable mushu! How's that sound?

CASS: Um...okay.

ROGER: Terrific! See you then!

> Special out on Roger as he hangs up. Cass takes another brownie and chews, troubled. Beat.

DORI: ...Well?

CASS: ...He's coming over.

DORI: Oh no.

CASS: No, I'm...I'm not dying. ...We're having dinner.

DORI: ...Dinner? With him?

CASS: On Thursday.

DORI: What, like a, like a date?

CASS: I knew he was hitting on me!

DORI: But...

CASS: Huh!

DORI: Can he do that? I mean, he's a doctor, aren't there like rules or, or—

CASS: Who cares? He's a DOCTOR.

> Cass stuffs the rest of the brownie into her mouth and washes it down with Mountain Dew.

CASS: ...You have to stop making this stuff.

DORI: What about Richard?

CASS: Richard?

DORI: Won't he get mad?

CASS: I think we can forget about Richard.

DORI: What happened?

CASS: Please, Dori.

DORI: I like Richard.

CASS: Well he didn't like you.

DORI: Yes he did, he told me. He was always smiling at me or, or—

CASS: NO, he DIDN'T. And neither did Ronald or Allen or, or Bruce or what's his name, the fat one. None of them did anything like that, and none of them liked you. [*Pause. Dori is perplexed, hurt. Cass sighs.*] ...I'm sorry.

DORI: Why are you so mean?

CASS: Look, Dori. Richard was nice, but he was on a pension and he smelled like ham. This is a DOCTOR. We have to make this work.

DORI: He said he liked me.

CASS: Swear to God, Dori, you know exactly what I'm talking—

DORI: I don't swear to God.

CASS: I don't know how much longer I can do this! I can't keep the weight off, we're a month behind on our rent, the Camry needs tires, and now I have, I have polyps or—

DORI: Okay, okay, I swear, whatever!

CASS: ...Good. Now: you need to cut my hair. Nothing drastic, just the ends. And I need to borrow some eyeliner. I can't have him see me like this.

DORI: Like THIS?

CASS: And look at this dump. This is all YOUR stuff.

DORI: He stuck a telescope up—

CASS: Hide all these clothes. Put the dishes under the sink and run the vacuum. There's hair everywhere. Why is there hair everywhere?

DORI: You're pulling it out of him!

CASS: Look at it! It's just coming right out.

DORI: Would you calm down?

> Dori takes Izzy from Cass, and the lights change: it's another evening. Cass starts primping.

CASS: You need to make a dessert. No. Yes. Something lo-cal, but yummy, like—

DORI: Cherry compote.

CASS: No, God no. What about that, that mousse thing, with the layers, or no! Those, those—

DORI: Truffles.

CASS: Yes! Good! But small. And, oh: that coffee, that hazelnut that Ronald brought—

DORI: Allen. No, the fat guy.

CASS: [*Simultaneously.*] —the fat guy, yeah. And apple juice, we'll need some apple juice.

DORI: For dinner?

CASS: Just in case he.... [*Dori "tsks!" judgmentally.*] Don't make that noise. Just make it and then...go to your room. And stay there!

DORI: It's my house too.

CASS: No it's not. I don't want him to see you. [*Dori scoffs.*] Stop making those noises!

DORI: What am I supposed to do?

CASS: Smoke dope and sell your tits on eBay.

DORI: It's incense! And I don't—

CASS: [*Suddenly screaming.*] Just stay in your room! Just stay in your room! Would you please just—!

Cass is seized by a stomach pain. Beat.

DORI: ...Bad one? ...Maybe you should cancel.

CASS: You never cancel on the first date, Dori.

DORI: Want your Ex-Lax?

CASS: Yes. No! I can't eat that. What else have I got?

DORI: Vicodin.

CASS: I have Vicodin?

DORI: He gave you some.

> A doorbell rings. Cass snaps her fingers and holds out her palm; Dori gives her a pill. Cass quickly swallows it, huffs a few times and pulls herself together.

CASS: ...Too much lipstick?

DORI: Way.

CASS: Damn right.

> Cass pushes her boobs up and struts off to the bedrooms. Dori holds Izzy. The lights change; time passes.
>
> From offstage, we hear the sounds of protracted lovemaking: a squeaking bed, groans— especially Roger's. Dori listens, at first intrigued...then frustrated... then maddened. She looks at the pills her hand, thinks, takes one, washes it down with the Mountain Dew, sits and cuddles with Izzy.
>
> Beat. The lights change: it's the next morning. Roger enters from the bedrooms in a crisp white undershirt and shorts and a prominent wristwatch, drinking coffee. He stops when he sees Dori, who immediately stands and backs

away. This is a different Dori; she's very woozy
and seems nervous, scared.

ROGER: Oh. Hey. Sorry! You must be...Lori, right?

DORI: ...Hi. Um. ...Hello.

ROGER: ...You all right?

DORI: ...Uh-huh. Hi.

ROGER: And who is that?

DORI: ...This is...my cat.

ROGER: Oh. Well. So you...live here, then?

DORI: Dori.

ROGER: What?

DORI: D-O-R-I.

> Now, oddly, Dori effects an English accent. She
> becomes juvenile, dramatic, pouty,
> inappropriate—and is still woozy.

DORI: ...I was named after a small boat.

ROGER: No kidding.

DORI: A type of flat-bottomed fishing vessel in which I was
conceived. Accidentally. One drunken afternoon.

ROGER: ...Well. Good thing they didn't name you Dinghy,
eh?

DORI: [*Doesn't get it.*] ...Would you like a truffle, Richard?

ROGER: No thanks. And it's Roger.

DORI: What?

ROGER: Roger.

DORI: What's Roger?

ROGER: I'm Roger. You called me Richard.

DORI: Oh. Um. Sorry. ...Would you like a truffle, Richard?

> Cass enters from the bedroom in a kimono and cock-eyed geisha wig. It's been a long night. She effects a charming southern accent.

CASS: [*To Dori, sweetly but not.*] ...Well. You're up early.

DORI: [*No accent now.*] Izzy wanted out. Then he wanted in.

CASS: Thank you sweetie. Why don't you take him to your room.

DORI: What are you going to do?

CASS: [*For Roger, mostly.*] I thought I might poach some eggs for us.

ROGER: Actually....

DORI: I like poached eggs.

ROGER: I'm just having coffee, thanks.

DORI: I need some coffee.

CASS: [*Meaningfully.*] Dori, dear? ...Hmm?

> Beat. Then Dori exits to the bedroom, carrying Izzy. Cass gives Roger a peck.

391

CASS: ...I'm sorry. I should have told you about her.

ROGER: That explains the smell, anyway.

CASS: Well, she's going through a bit of a rough patch. This is just temporary, until she gets on her feet.

ROGER: I meant the cat. The house reeks of urine.

CASS: ...Oh, no, that's...that's incense.

ROGER: I know what urine smells like.

CASS: Would you care for a truffle?

ROGER: Way too rich. A woman your age, you shouldn't eat that stuff. You'll get a diverticulum.

CASS: Oh.

ROGER: A diverticulum is a pouch or a sac bulging out from your intestinal wall, like a bubble on a hose. Cooked vegetables, whole grain rice, lots of fiber. And somebody drank a whole case of Mountain Dew.

CASS: That Dori.

ROGER: She'll regret it when she's older and peeing in three directions. ...You were incredible.

> He has approached her and now
> nuzzles/fondles her.

CASS: Oooo, so were you. I've never DONE anything like that.

ROGER: Really.

CASS: I'm afraid I don't have much...experience.

ROGER: Did you like it?

CASS: You're soooo strong.

ROGER: [*As they make out.*] You have the most incredible body...I've ever seen...on a woman your age.   Mmmm....
...Mmmm.

> Finally, Cass sneaks a look at his wristwatch.

CASS: ...Oh my, look how late we slept.

ROGER: Better get my clothes.

CASS: Well...if you must.

> Cass exits to the bedroom. Roger sips his coffee, steps forward and looks out a downstage 'window,' filled with a sense of triumph.
>
> Lights change: it's another morning. Dori enters from the kitchen, woozy again.

DORI: Oh. I'm sorry. I'll—

ROGER: Dori!   Good morning!   I haven't seen you for a few weeks.

DORI: Oh. No. I.... [*Again with the English accent:*] ...Mummy hides me in the attic.

ROGER: Ha!   Right.   Are you not feeling well?

DORI: ...It's my medication.

ROGER: Oh? Which one?

DORI: ...Um. Most of them. So you and Mummy are an item now.

ROGER: Well, let's just say I saw something in her I admired.

DORI: Care for an éclair?

ROGER: Colonoscopy joke.

DORI: What?

ROGER: "I saw something in her I admired."

DORI: [*No clue.*] …Care for an éclair?

ROGER: No thanks. And you shouldn't eat so much sugar.

DORI: Oh, I have to, actually. It's comfort food. For all the…discomfort.

ROGER: Which discomfort.

DORI: All of it. …Go ahead. Try one. You'll see.

> She offers the plate. Roger hesitates—but then takes one and eats. Dori takes a bite. It's a very sensuous bite. She luxuriates in it. He watches her; she's in her own world.

DORI: …They're delicious, aren't they.

ROGER: …Mm-mm.

DORI: Don't you feel better?

ROGER: …Mmm!

> Dori finishes hers, popping the last bit in her mouth and licking her fingers.

DORI: Mmmm!   …Well. Um. Goodbye then, Ronald.

> Dori wanders off to the kitchen as Cass returns from the bedroom, still in her kimono, with Roger's neatly-folded clothes and a lint brush.

CASS: [*Accent intact.*] Izzy slept on them. I'm so sorry.

ROGER: They're covered in hair.

CASS: If I lock him in the bathroom he just cries all night. But this'll come right off, I promise. I'm so sorry. I can have it dry-cleaned.

> He begins dressing while she lint-brushes his clothes.

ROGER: No time for that.

CASS: He's not used to sharing our bed.

ROGER: Yes uh...may I um...may I ask you a question?

CASS: Of course.

ROGER: Are you seeing someone else?

CASS: What? No. Of course not!

ROGER: ...So who's Richard?

CASS: ...Richard.

ROGER: Or Ronald.

CASS: ...Ronald. [*She sighs.*] ...I need to tell you something. There's something I need to tell you. ...Dori has...she has some...difficulties. As you may have noticed.

ROGER: She's stoned out of her gourd.

CASS: I know. And a few weeks ago, I found her... exposing herself on Facebook.

ROGER: No kidding.

CASS: I don't understand, Roger. She was such a sweet little girl, such a gentle child, but...there was always...something...different about her, or...wrong with....

ROGER: Hey.

CASS: That's why her father ran off. She doesn't know that. In the meantime I keep waiting for her to show up, my REAL daughter, the one with a...a ponytail and a boyfriend and...tennis bracelets or something but...I don't think she ever will.

ROGER: You should take her to a psychologist.

CASS: I did. It was a nightmare. He was this tall Englishman, and Dori fell in love with him. I mean she THREW herself at him, she was eight years old, and she fawned over him like Elvis. We had to stop going.

ROGER: That's what they call transference. He was taking the place of her father.

CASS: But she was afraid of her father. He screamed at her. He...he would....

ROGER: What.

CASS: ...She says he...did things to her.

ROGER: What things.

CASS: Who knows, I don't know. But after that it was one guy after another: the cable guy, the carpet cleaner, and some...fantasy person named Mr. Little. She'd talk to him, I mean all the time, like he was right here with us. I used to have to set a place for Mr. Little.

ROGER: An invisible friend. A coping mechanism for poor social skills.

CASS: Yeah well, one day Mr. Little was decapitated by the FedEx guy. What do they call that? When a child chops the head off her invisible friend? She cried so much I let her stay home from school. Last year, she had...an incident, and now she's going through this...stupid... religious phase. Sometimes I feel like...running away too.

She has a twinge in her gut.

ROGER: ...You okay?

CASS: I'm having a.

ROGER: Where.

CASS: Here.

ROGER: Does this hurt?

CASS: Ooooh!

ROGER: ...C'mere. C'mere. [*He hugs her, consoles her.*] ...Do you know what you need?

CASS: What.

ROGER: I know what you need.

CASS: What.

ROGER: ...You need an esophago-gastro-duo-endoscopy.

CASS: A—?

ROGER: I snake a hose down your throat, take a gander at your duodenum. Ten bucks says a peptic ulcer.

CASS: A—?

ROGER: A mucosal erosion caused by heliobacter pylori.

397

CASS: I—

ROGER: A hole in your gut. Usually they're benign, so I don't want you to worry. Call my office. They'll set it up.

> Now dressed, he gives her a peck and a pat and starts off.

CASS: Roger?

ROGER: Hm?

CASS: ...Thank you. For. You know.

ROGER: That's all right, babe. Let me know if you need any more.

> He exits to the kitchen. Cass straightens, smiles.

> Lights change: time passes. Dori comes storming in from the bedroom holding a broken rosary.

DORI: You smashed my rosary!

CASS: [*Accent off.*] Hmm?

DORI: You did this on purpose!

CASS: Did what.

DORI: You SMASHED my rosary!

DORI: It was on your floor.

DORI: It wasn't on my FLOOR, it was on my ALTAR! These are SACRED BEADS!

CASS: So we'll go to Hobby Lobby.

DORI: You can't get these at...HOBBY LOBBY! These are religious ARTIFACTS! YOU CAN'T GET RELIGIOUS ARTIFACTS at HOBBY LOBBY! Father Daniel gave these to me PERSONALLY!

CASS: You're not even Catholic, Dori, you're Methodist.

DORI: I am no Methodist! Methodists are WHORES!

CASS: Excuse me?

DORI: I can't live like you! I have a SOUL! I'm a deeply spiritual PERSON! I need my life to MEAN something!

> Dori runs off to the bedroom, hyperventilating.
> Beat.

CASS: ...Oh, give me a break. ...Give me a break!

> Lights change: it's another evening. Roger
> enters from the kitchen carrying a small gift
> box or bag. He removes his tie and will
> continue to strip down.

ROGER: Technically, she makes a good point. Being a Catholic requires much more commitment than being a Protestant. The Catechism provides a much better sense of structure than they sell at vacation bible school. You never hear the term Baptist Intellectual.

CASS: [*Accent on.*] But she's not a Catholic. She's not anything. She just tries them on like shoes.

ROGER: Want me to talk to her?

CASS: Huh!

ROGER: I have a natural rapport with kids. They see me as an authority figure.

CASS: No, I don't want her talking to YOU. God knows what she'll say. [*From behind, he presents her with the gift box.*] ...What's this?

ROGER: Something every good girl should have.

> She opens the box and withdraws a feathery
> hat thingy and a skimpy, glittery costume.

CASS: ...Oh, my. What is it?

ROGER: Showgirl outfit. Real thing, too. Cost me a fortune.

CASS: [*Accent off.*] ...Ooooh...Roger. You shouldn't have.

ROGER: Like it?

CASS: You spend too much on me.

ROGER: Three polyps and a perianal cyst.

CASS: What?

ROGER: Our little secret.

CASS: What is.

ROGER: A little game we play with the insurance companies. Lab gets a kickback, nobody's the wiser.

CASS: I don't know what you mean.

ROGER: That's okay.

CASS: You mean you...you lie to your patients?

ROGER: Noooo! Well, yes. It's a dividend I pay myself, considering what I do for a living.

CASS: ...Oh. Well.

ROGER: Gonna try it on?

CASS: ...Now?

ROGER: You can wear it while you cook.

CASS: But...Dori's—

ROGER: She's not here.

CASS: She's...! Wh-where did—?

ROGER: I gave her fifty bucks, told her to go out and have a good time.

CASS: But...no! She's not...she can't—

ROGER: She'll be fine! Come on. ...Come ON. I'll help you!

> Down to his underwear or thereabout, Roger coaxes her back to the bedroom. She takes the outfit and the box but leaves the feathery thing on the couch.
>
> The lights change: time passes. From offstage, we hear the sounds of love making again. Dori enters from the kitchen, dragging a very large, wooden crucifix—complete with a grotesque, suffering Christ—and listens. Suddenly we hear Roger yell—

ROGER: ...Jesus Christ! Jesus Christ!

> —and he sweeps back in from the bedroom and starts getting dressed. Cass follows in her kimono and holding Izzy.

CASS: Roger, please, you're being silly.

ROGER: He was watching me. I can't do it with him watching me. It's like he's JUDGING me.

CASS: I put him on the floor.

ROGER: Where he sat...GLOPPING himself with his. [*Cass is trying not to laugh.*] You know what? Just forget it. Forget it.

CASS: Oh, come on! Come back to bed!

ROGER: Do you see what he's done to your drapes? Or your couch? You let him destroy everything and then you ask ME for MONEY.

DORI: What's going on?

CASS: What the hell is that?

DORI: Can we hang it in my room?

ROGER: Your whole house smells like ammonia.

DORI: That's the cat.

CASS: Would you PLEASE take that, that—

DORI: I think he's sick. He's walking funny. Like his legs give out.

> Dori props the crucifix up somewhere.

ROGER: I don't like animals, Cass, I'm sorry. They're filthy, they spread diseases, and it's unhealthy when people form attachments to them.

CASS: You're not leaving.

ROGER: The evening is ruined. Thank you very much.

> Beat. Cass gets misty. Her accent comes back.

CASS: ...All right. I understand.

ROGER: ...Well don't cry.

CASS: [*Pathetically submissive.*] No, you're right. You're always right about these things. We'll take him to the vet in the morning. And from now on, we'll lock him in the bathroom. And we're going to mop and vacuum and polish everything. So that it will be clean. For you. When you're here again.

ROGER: ...Well all right.

CASS: So you'll...be here again?

ROGER: ...We'll see.

> Cass exits somberly to the bedroom with Izzy. Roger finishes getting dressed. Dori suddenly grabs her gut.

DORI: ...Oooooo!

ROGER: What is it?

DORI: ...My...my stomach.

ROGER: Probably all that crap you eat.

DORI: No. It always does this...when I'm upset.

ROGER: Are you upset?

> Dori shakes her head no.

ROGER: ...Come here.

DORI: ...I'm not supposed to.

ROGER: I'm a doctor. ...Just relax. ...Can you feel this?

> He probes her gut gently through the following.

DORI: Oooo. ....Mmm.

ROGER: ... What are you upset about.   Hm?

DORI: ...I can't say.

ROGER: You can trust me.

DORI: I'm really not supposed to.

ROGER: ...I think you're just pretending, Dori. I don't think your stomach hurts. I think you're just looking for a reason to tell me something.   And that's okay. ...You can tell me.

DORI: ...Please don't fight with her.

ROGER: We're not fighting. That's just how adults talk to each other.

DORI: [*Flinching.*] Oooo!

ROGER: ...Why? Does it...remind you of someone? [*Dori nods. He probes a bit more deeply.*] ...Who? ...Who does it remind you of?   It's alright.

DORI: ...Him. Before he.

ROGER: ...Him who. Your father? Before he what?

> Dori pulls away, and then changes to her
> British persona and chirps:

DORI: Why are you getting divorced?

ROGER: Hey.

DORI: Catholics can't get divorced. Once we're married we're married forever.

ROGER: All right. I'll tell you mine if you tell me yours.

DORI: ...Okay.

ROGER: ...I don't know why. She...I don't really know.

DORI: [*Accent off.*] ...I'm sorry.

ROGER: Your turn.

DORI: ...All right. [*Accent on.*] ...He...he...he made a big pile of wood. And then he...covered it with leaves and pinecones and old newspapers. And...and he put a lawn chair on top and poured gasoline all over himself and...sat down and...lit a cigar.

ROGER: ...Very funny.

DORI: Actually, he drank one bottle of antifreeze and six bottles of beer, taped himself to a lawn chair and sat there foaming at the mouth until his liver collapsed.

ROGER: Your mother says he ran away. She says he abandoned you, and that you're very, very sad inside.

DORI: ...Well she would, wouldn't she. That's how she copes. She's a very fragile person. She needs me to take care of her.

ROGER: You should try to make some friends, Dori, maybe join the Rotary or something.

DORI: Oh, I have lots of friends. On Facebook. I have hundreds of friends and admirers. They come to see me every day. ...Would you like to be my friend?

ROGER: Probably not a good idea.

DORI: Why not? Don't you like me?

ROGER: You know, there's a good little community college right up the—

DORI: [*Accent off.*] I know. I went there last year. I had to quit.

ROGER: What for.

DORI: [*Accent on.*] I got knocked up.

ROGER: Right.

DORI: So I had to come home.

ROGER: So where's the kid.

DORI: She made me...give him away.

ROGER: Adoption.

DORI: Whatever.

ROGER: Best thing, probably.

DORI [*Accent off.*] I don't think so. Not a day goes by I don't think about him. And he doesn't even know I'm here, I'll bet. That's the worst thing. He doesn't know I'm thinking about him, all the time. [*She moves to the downstage window. She is far away.*] ...Or maybe he does. Maybe there's this thing, like with mothers and children, this magnetic field or something, he can sense I'm here, just like I know he's there. Somewhere. [*An uncomfortable pause. Then she snaps back, accent on:*] ...I think I might get implants!

ROGER: What?

DORI: My tits fell, after my baby was born. Wanna see?

ROGER: Do I—?

DORI: You're a doctor. I can show you, can't I?

ROGER: Dori, I'm trying—

DORI: Do you want to see them or not?

> She's about to lift her shirt. He looks toward the bedroom.

ROGER: ...Okay.

> Beat. She thinks—and then:

DORI: ...I can't.

> Dori runs off to the kitchen. Roger now puts on thick glasses and a blue lab coat and as the lights change crosses to a metal table where Cass—now dressed, of course—awaits with Izzy. He is now David, a rather quirky veterinarian, and this is his office.

DAVID: ...Yes. Well. Diabetes. I'll have to run a curve. But...diabetes, probably.

CASS: That's like...too much sugar.

DAVID: Too little. He's starving.

CASS: I feed him everyday.

DAVID: His body can't metabolize it.

CASS: Oh. So...a curve. What's that?

DAVID: Blood tests. To monitor his glucose. He'll have to stay overnight.

CASS: ...Diabetes is like...you...you take the shots.

DAVID: Insulin.

407

CASS: So...can't you just—

DAVID: The wrong dose could kill him. I have to run a curve.

CASS: ...I don't know how to ask this.

DAVID: One hundred and forty dollars.

CASS: ...And...and then you, you, you give him a shot.

ROGER: Four to six units, twice a day. Depending.

CASS: Twice a day?

DAVID: Depending. You'll need syringes, a box of 31-gauge needles and a glucometer. [*Pause. She tries to calculate that.*] ...For everything...maybe seventy, eighty dollars a month.

CASS: ...What happens if we. What if...

DAVID: Liver disease, ketoacidosis, any number of secondary infections.

CASS: ...How long.

DAVID: [*Sadly.*] ...Not very.

CASS: ...Isn't there something else? Some other....

        She looks at him. He considers, then sighs.

DAVID: ...Wait here.

        David exits, leaving Cass with Izzy.

CASS: ...Oh Izzy. ...Izzy. ...What are we going to do?

The moment lingers. Then she crosses back to her home and the lights change. Dori enters from the kitchen. She'll take a cookie from the plate and offer one to Cass.

DORI: Hey. What's that bag in the kitchen?

CASS: ...Hm?

DORI: That big bag of catfood.

CASS: It's for Izzy.

DORI: Duh.

CASS: He's diabetic. It's some special low-carb or something. That vet was bizarre. Get that away from me.

Dori notices the feather thing on the couch.

DORI: What's this?

CASS: ...A gift.

DORI: From the vet? Was he cute?

Cass snatches it away.

CASS: I don't want to talk about it.

DORI: ...Did you and Roger break up?

CASS: No, we—

DORI: I didn't do anything, I swear!

CASS: We didn't break up. We can't break up! We need to keep this one. We can't...let this one get away.

Beat. Cass has a slight pain.

DORI: When's his divorce?

CASS: Two weeks, two days.

DORI: And then what.

CASS: ...Vegas.

DORI: Vegas? [*Cass nods, cringingly. Dori gasps, realizing:*] ...Holy...! You're going to get married!

CASS: Nobody said anything about—

DORI: But that's why people go to Vegas! That's what they—

CASS: He just said he wants to take me—

DORI: For how long?

CASS: I don't know! Everything's been going so—

DORI: Are you coming BACK? I mean, you're coming back, aren't you? Or, or am I going to live with you? ...I mean... what's...what am I supposed to do?

CASS: Dori.

DORI: What's going to happen to me?

CASS: ...You know what's going to happen. I keep telling you what will happen.

DORI: ...Nobody's going to want me, Mama.

CASS: [*A nice moment.*] Yes they will. Someday. Someday, you're going to meet a...really...really...screwed up guy. And you'll...get married, maybe. Or you'll just shack up for awhile. And then maybe have a kid. Or two, if you're not careful. And...buy a house maybe. And go into debt. And start fighting. A LOT. And he won't have to be handsome or anything.   He'll probably start getting fat.   Or he'll drink too much.   And you'll turn into a bitch. And your butt will get big.   But you'll love each other, most of the time.   That's the important thing.   You'll have someone to grow old with.   And someone who'll take care of you when you're vomiting.   Unless he dies first.   Or has a midlife crisis.   Or—

DORI: [*Smiling.*]   Mama.

CASS: You'll find somebody, Dori.   You just.   You have to BE what they WANT you to be.

DORI: I try.   I do everything you tell—

CASS: Maybe you try too hard.

DORI: ...Maybe I'll just be a nun.

CASS: I don't think they'd take you.   [*Pause. Dori stands, hurt.*]   ...Tsk! Dori—

DORI: No.   It's okay.

CASS: Dori.

DORI: I know.   ...It's okay.   ...I won't try so hard.   I'll...go back to school.   Or get a job even, if you want.   I'll...I'll be a Methodist again.   And I won't leave a mess.   I'll be what you want me to be.   ...I promise.

> Dori has shouldered the big crucifix and now drags it tragically off to the kitchen.   Beat.

CASS: [*Muttering to herself.*]   Oh, give me a break.

> Beat.   Cass picks up the feather thing and looks at it.   Then, an idea: she and Izzy play with it, ad libbing as necessary.

CASS: ...You want it? You want it, hmm? ...I don't want it. You want it? You want it, don'tcha. ...Can't have it. ...Can't have it. Okay. There you go.

> And so on, the lights narrowing around them, as before. A short refrain plays on the piano— perhaps "You Are My Sunshine," or whatever Cass sang to Izzy. Then:

> LIGHTS TO BLACK.

SCENE TWO

> In darkness: we hear Roger's voice:

ROGER: ...Cass? ...Cassandra? ...Cassandra?

> At rise: Cass is on the gurney, lying on her back and covered by a sheet. Roger stands beside her. Obviously, she's just awakening from anesthesia.

ROGER: ...Earth to Cassandra. ...Helloooo.

CASS: ...Oooooh.

ROGER: Welcome back. How's your throat?

CASS: Uughh.

ROGER: There's usually some discomfort, so I sprayed your oropharynx with lignocaine. You shouldn't eat anything too tough for the rest of the day. Stick to yogurt or applesauce, don't talk too much, and no more laxatives.

CASS: Are we done?

ROGER: Up we go.

> He helps her to her feet.

412

CASS: ...It's so weird.

ROGER: I was right about the ulcer. You owe me ten bucks.

CASS: It's so WEIRD. How long was I—

ROGER: I'm going to start you on some Amoxicillin and some sucralfate to coat the lesion. Do you like oysters?

> He jots down a quick prescription while she teeters.

CASS: Oysters?

ROGER: Smooooth as silk. And they're an aphrodisiac. So is foie gras, but I don't know how to make foie gras. How's Tuesday?

CASS: Umm.

ROGER: Say sixish?

CASS: Sixish?

ROGER: Terrific! Take two of these twice a day, and get plenty of fluids. I'll see you Tuesday.

CASS: But...wait! I...I need to ask you!

> But Roger is gone. Cass stands in a daze, holding the prescription. As before, the lights narrow around her.

CASS: ...Where did I go? ...Could you see me? ...Hello?

> From the darkness, Dori calls:

DORI: [*Off.*] ...Mama.

CASS: Are you—hello?

413

DORI: [*Off.*] Mama?

> Dori enters, holding the kimono, and the lights shift back.

DORI: ...Are you going to put it on?

CASS: Hm?   ...Oh. Oh.

DORI: For someone who hates her job you sure wear this thing a lot.

CASS: ...He uh...he likes it.

DORI: What's he doing in there, boiling his laundry?

CASS: I don't know.   Oh wait: he's...steaming oysters.

> Dori will help Cass into the kimono.

DORI: Ooo—ooo. I've never had oysters.

CASS: Please, Dori.

DORI: But I've—

CASS: Not tonight.   I can't do this tonight.   Just...can't you go to Mass or something?

DORI: It's Tuesday.

CASS: Well, go find my keys and get this filled for me.

> She hands the prescription to Dori.

DORI: I don't have any money.

CASS: Ask your father.

DORI: My father?

CASS: I mean Richard.

DORI: You mean Roger.

CASS: Roger. Roger. Jesus.

DORI: You don't look so good.

CASS: ...I'm just a little foggy. Everything's just...been...so foggy.

> Dori exits to bedrooms. Cass sighs, shakes the cobwebs out, applies lipstick and primps: once more into the breach, dear friends. Then Dori returns, holding Izzy. He is limp, and perhaps wrapped in a towel.

DORI: ...Mama? ...He's really weak. I don't know what's wrong with him.

> Cass removes her kimono and takes Izzy.

CASS: Give him to me. ...Oh no. Oh Izzy. No no no. –Roger?

DORI: He can't stand up.

CASS: Roger!

DORI: I'll go with you.

CASS: No! You—stay here. Keep him occupied. No—just, don't let him leave. But don't DO anything! And don't say anything! –Roger!

> Roger enters.

ROGER: What's up, babe?

CASS: It's Izzy. There's something wrong with him.

415

ROGER: They're almost ready.

CASS: I have to go, Roger.

ROGER: If you don't eat them they get rubbery.

CASS: I'll hurry. I'll be right back. I promise. I'm sorry! Stay here! I'm sorry!

        Cass exits through the kitchen with Izzy. Beat.

DORI: ...He's sick.

ROGER: I know. Diabetes, probably.

DORI: You knew?

ROGER: Polyuria and polydipsia. Laps up water and pisses it out. The smell is keytones in his urine. The weakness in his legs is neuropathy. That's diabetes.

DORI: ...Oh. Is it...?

ROGER: Probably. He's pretty far gone. This is why it's unhealthy to form attachments with animals. This is precisely why. When I was a kid, my mom made us have cats, and it was a disaster.

DORI: Why?

ROGER: All kinds of reasons. Our first cat, her name was Matilda, she had four kittens. My mom gave three of them away and said I could have the runt. I named him Scruffy. He had sleepy eyes and was really skinny, but I loved him. I was five years old but I still remember this. I'd pick him up and hold him up to my face so he could suck on my nose. I used to carry him around in my coat pocket. Once I snuck him into church. So one night I'm sitting on the couch watching TV, and I hear this...this horrible sound, and I look over at the box, and Scruffy's not there.

Matilda had taken him into the closet, and I can hear him screaming.   So I open the door, and there's blood on her face and all over the floor.   She killed him.   Then she licked his body clean and hid him behind my galoshes.

DORI: ...That's—!

ROGER: That's what animals do.   If one of her kittens is sick or hurt or whatever, the mother will kill it, or take it out to the woods and just leave it.

DORI: ...That's so awful.

ROGER: I know.

> Beat.

DORI: ...One summer, when I was at girl scouts, there was this Mama cat, I mean she was like, pregnant? And she crawled up under this car, and when they started the engine, we heard this, this like, like SHREIK and when they opened it up the fan thing had practically ripped her head off.   So they took her out, and her like...her BELLY was moving, her kittens, it was like they were trying to ESCAPE. And nobody knew what to do. So one of the counselors said we should kill them, so he raised up this shovel but all the kids started screaming until he put it down. So instead we all just stood around and...and like watched her until... you know...one by one...they all stopped moving.

ROGER: ...Wow.   That's REALLY sad.

DORI: I KNOW.

> Beat.   Roger takes a piece of fudge from the plate.

ROGER: ...When I was about thirteen, there was this tomcat that lived behind our house. We called him Bob. One day my mom brought home another, and she worried they'd fight, but actually they got along really well.   They

417

would sleep together and eat together and chase each other around and before one would come inside he would go get the other one. Stuff like that.   So one day the Bob gets killed by a dog and the younger one, he drags Bob's body to the back porch and keeps yelling through the screen until my mother finally comes.

DORI: Wow.

ROGER: And when we buried him, the younger one watched us. He slept on his grave every day.

> Beat. Dori begins her tale with no accent, but as the story goes on, she regresses into her giddy British persona:

DORI*:* ...One day, when I was eight, I went out to get my bicycle and found my father hanging from our tree, and I started to scream and scream, and Mummy came out we grabbed his legs and we pulled and we pulled but he wouldn't come down, so she started hitting and punching him as hard as she could, so I started laughing and I starting hitting him too, and then Mummy sent me inside and I laughed so hard my stomach hurt.

ROGER: ...Huh.

> Beat. Roger takes a bite of fudge and looks at her, dubiously. Dori smiles strangely. Finally:

DORI: ...Just kidding!

> Dori takes a piece of fudge and exits to the bedrooms. Roger ponders—and then exits to kitchen.

> Lights change: it is now night. Cass enters with Izzy in her arms. He is limp. She looks stricken, weak.   She sits on the couch, places him on her lap, and strokes his back.   Long pause, until Dori enters in a night shirt.

418

DORI: ...Mama? ...What are you doing?

CASS: Is Roger here?

DORI: What happened?

CASS: Is he HERE.

DORI: He got pissed off and ate all his oysters and drank a whole bottle of wine and fell asleep and woke back up and went home because you wouldn't answer your phone.... Where were you?

CASS: ...I hit something.

DORI: What?

CASS: The car. I wrecked the car.

DORI: Were you hurt? ...Mama? ...Mama, answer me.

CASS: ...I need some...some. Um.

DORI: ...Mountain Dew. Ex-Lax. Fudge. Vicodin.

CASS: No, just some...just some water.

> Dori exits to kitchen. Cass places Izzy on the couch next to her, curled up as if he's asleep, pets him a few times, and stands. And then the dam bursts: her grief floods forth in gasps and hacking moans. Dori returns quickly with some water.

DORI: Mama? Mama! ...Mama?

> Cass is almost wheezing. She catches her breath, turns to Dori, says simply—

CASS: ...He's gone.

—and exits to the kitchen. Beat. Dori goes to Izzy, looks at him, and mutters to herself:

DORI: ...Ohhh no.

Dori crosses herself rather clumsily, perhaps clasps her rosary and takes a shot at earnest prayer. Lights change: Roger enters from the bedroom, carrying a small pill bottle.

ROGER: ...Well, she'll be—

DORI: Ssshhhhh!

Beat. Roger waits for her stop praying. When she does:

ROGER: She'll be pretty sore for a few days. But I don't see anything permanent. ...Apparently she jumped a curb and took out a fence post. She didn't even have her lights on. They cited her for careless operation. You know how much money that is?

DORI: It doesn't matter.

ROGER: Yeah well, I'm the one who's got—

DORI: She was UPSET. Obviously.

ROGER: She was in the next county. Headed in the wrong direction. Why was she on some back road, at night, headed in the—

DORI: I don't know! ...Can she hear you?

ROGER: I brought her some Xanax. She'll be out for a while. [*He puts the pill bottle on the table.*] Her car is pretty shot. Radiator, steering column, bent axle—guess who's paying the deductible.

DORI: ...Thank you, Roger.

ROGER: Yeah well. They're gonna fix her up with a rental.

DORI: [*Clearly upset.*]   ...She was up all night.   I could hear her walking around.   I came in and found her sitting on the side of her bed like a child.

ROGER: Probably just the trauma.

DORI: She can't stop crying.

ROGER: She'll snap out of it.   I mean, you know, life goes on. It's just a cat.

DORI: This is how she is.   She can't cope.   This is what she does.

ROGER: ...She got over your father. [*Dori shrugs, nods.*] ...How'd she do that?

DORI: ...She came home one night with a kitten.

> Cass re-enters with an opaque Tupperware bowl. She will move to Izzy, cradle him, place him in it and seal it.

DORI: ...Mama?

CASS: Oh.   Hi Richard.

ROGER: ...How are you today?

CASS: I'm okay. My legs are stiff. I'm a little tired.

DORI: She's still not sleeping.

ROGER: Looks like you've lost some weight.

CASS: Thank you.

DORI: She's starving herself.

CASS: Did you see the car they gave me? It's bright yellow. It looks like a, I don't know what.

> Cass exits with the bowl back to the kitchen. Dori's gesture to Roger means: see? She's losing it.

ROGER: ...I think she's doing much better.

DORI: [*Increasingly upset.*] See what she's doing? Look. [*She waves him over to the downstage window.*] ...That's his grave. She buried him in a Tupperware bowl and visits him about three times a day, like she's having his funeral over and over again. She even got one of those of do-it-yourself headstone things! It says, "my beloved friend." She sits there and TALKS to him, or she stands here looking out at—

ROGER: You need to calm down. You'll get an upset stomach.

> Beat. Dori tries to calm down. They look out the window.

ROGER: ...What's that?

DORI: A pipe cleaner. She makes shapes with them and puts them on his grave.

> Beat. They watch out the window. Cass will enter with a laptop, sit on the couch, and begin to work on it. Dori and Roger won't register her presence.

DORI: ...She's been Googling him. On my computer. I check. She types in "Izzy" or "Izzy plus cat" and tries to find his picture. Or she visits these websites, the "Pet Loss Network," the "Love and Loss Society." And these...bizarre chatrooms. And this woman, some sort of hippie guru, she runs this—Sadie's Farm—animal refuge thing. They've been e-mailing.

ROGER: ...Maybe she's still in shock from the accident, or.

DORI: You need to go out there.

ROGER: I can't go out there.

DORI: You have to.

ROGER: I'm no good at this kind of thing.

DORI: She won't listen to me. This morning she put on her blue sweater and then looked through her closet trying to find it. And at breakfast, she just stood by the toaster holding a piece of bread, like she didn't know what to do with it. ...It's like she's getting worse. You need to DO something!

ROGER: ...I can't. [*He produces an envelope with a card inside.*] ...I think she may be seeing somebody else.

DORI: What?

ROGER: ...This was on her dresser. It's from someone named David. He's a moron.

DORI: You read her mail?

ROGER: It was open.

DORI: [*Reads.*] "Just this side of heaven is a place called Rainbow Bridge. When an animal dies that has been especially close to someone here, he goes to Rainbow Bridge."

ROGER: It's not something you send to a grown woman.

DORI: "There are meadows and hills for all our special friends so that they can run and play together. They are all

423

happy and content, except they miss someone special, someone they had to leave behind. Finally the day comes when one of them stops and looks into the distance. His bright eyes are intent, his eager body quivers. Suddenly he runs from the group, flying over the green grass, his legs carrying—"

ROGER: See? He's an idiot.

DORI: "—him faster and faster. You have been spotted, and when you and your special friend finally meet, you cling together in joyous reunion, never to be parted again."

ROGER: It's giving ME diabetes.

DORI: "The happy kisses rain upon your face, and you look once more into the trusting eyes of your pet, and then you cross the Rainbow Bridge together."

> Cass sighs, quits what's she's doing on the laptop and leans back into the couch.

ROGER: Do you know who David is?

DORI: Did you look on the back? [*She has done just that, and now hands it to Roger.*] ...It's the veterinarian.

ROGER: You've got to be kidding.

DORI: He sent her a CARD.

ROGER: This is so unprofessional.

DORI: It's the sweetest thing I ever heard.

ROGER: ...Geez. All right. I'll go try.

> Roger exits to the kitchen. Dori turns to Cass, on the couch, and joins her.

DORI: ...You're still up.

424

CASS: I know.

DORI: ...What are you doing?

CASS: ...Nothing.

DORI: Mama?

> Dori takes the laptop and closes it.

CASS: I'm not spying on you.   I don't care what you do.
...I don't know what's wrong with me.

> Dori sits with her, but Cass moves away to the
> window.

DORI: ...We can pray together.

CASS: What good would that do.

DORI: ...I don't know.   Maybe you could talk to Father
Daniel. [*Beat. No answer.*]   ...He was my cat too, you
know.

CASS: ...No he wasn't.

> Beat.

DORI: Well maybe you can get another one.   Or some fish
or something.   Or, or, we could go to Hobby Lobby and
learn how to macramé.   They have all kinds of stuff there.
Like, like, flower arrangements, or origami, or scrap-
booking, we used to do that, remember when we made my
scrapbook?   We used to do lots of stuff like that.   Like
cooking, or, or we could learn a foreign language, or we
could go somewhere, to like, Canada, or....

> Dori's voice fades, as do the lights on her, as
> Cass returns in her mind to the vet's office.
> David is there with Izzy, lying still on the table.

He wears a surgical mask around his neck and holds an electric razor.

CASS: ...Can I hold him?

DAVID: ...Yes.

She takes Izzy in her arms.

CASS: ...His eyes are open.

DAVID: I don't think he can see very much.

CASS: ...What will happen?

DAVID: ...I'm going to shave his leg.   Just hold his head. He won't feel anything.

CASS: Izzy?

DAVID: And then I'll give him the injection.   He'll just...go to sleep.

CASS: ...He won't know.

DAVID: No.

Cass nods.   David starts to shave Izzy's leg, but stops when:

CASS: ...What happens then?

DAVID: ...What do you mean.

CASS: ...I mean...I don't know.

DAVID: ...I can dispose of him for you.   If that's what—

CASS: No. I—

DAVID: There's cremation. A lot of people do that. I can have the ashes delivered to you.

CASS: ...No, I'm. ...I'll take him home.

DAVID: ...Do you want some more time? [*Cass can't think of what to say, shakes her head no.*] ...He won't feel this.

> David pulls the mask up so it covers his mouth and nose. Then he shaves the inside of Izzy's leg.

DAVID: ...You see his veins here. They're collapsed. He's in a...pretty advanced state.

> David picks up the syringe.

CASS: I'm doing the right thing? [*He waits for her to decide again.*] ...I don't want him to suffer.

> He sniffs, and will sniff more throughout the following.

DAVID: ...Is there anything you want to say.

> Cass huffs mightily against the tears, shakes her head no. He readies the needle, but stops when:

CASS: ...I found him when! ...When he was a kitten. I was driving home, it was night time, it was pouring rain, and I saw him, I saw this...kitten sitting there, right in the road, just sitting there. He was soaked and he was all alone. ...And I don't know why, I don't know why, I didn't even like cats, but I got out and I chased him, he ran across the street to this playground, and I kept calling to him, and then suddenly he stopped and he...he was frightened, but he...he...stood up, into my hands...he stood up so I could hold him. And he lay in my lap all the way home. [*Beat.*] ...He held onto me. All the way home.

> Several beats. David sniffs.

DAVID: ...You tell me when you're ready.

> Beat. She nods her assent. He bends to the task.

CASS: Look at me, Izzy. You look at me. ...You look at me.

> Beat. David presses the syringe. Cass whispers softly:

CASS: Look at me, Izzy. ...Look at me.

> Several beats. The cat dies. David sniffs. The moment settles. Then he checks the cat with his stethoscope.

DAVID: ...That's all.

> Cass nods. David sniffs. Then she cradles Izzy closely and wanders away from the vet's office, back to Dori. David removes his mask and watches her—until the lights come down on him.

DORI: ...Mama? Mama? Are you even listening to what I'm saying?

CASS: Hm?

DORI: You didn't hear one word.

CASS: ...I'm sorry. ...I don't know what's wrong with me.

DORI: Why don't you go to bed. ...Mama, why don't you go to bed.

CASS: ...I don't know where he is.

DORI: ...He's dead.

CASS: ...But I don't know where he is.

DORI: ...Go to sleep, Mama.

CASS: I can't.

DORI: You have some Xanax.

CASS: I had a dream. ...I was putting him in his grave... and he was talking to me, he was telling me he was sorry, he thought I was angry at him, that I was punishing him. ...He doesn't understand. [*Beat.*] ...And I put him in his grave, and I'm crying. And I can hear him, in the ground, calling to me. He doesn't know he's dead and I...I.... I don't want to go to sleep.

> Cass wanders away to the bedrooms, with Izzy in her arms. Dori sighs, sees the pill—and swallows it. Beat. She blinks hard, and puts her face in her hands. The lights change.

ROGER: [*Off.*] ...Dori. Dori?

> Dori looks up. Roger re-enters from the kitchen.

ROGER: ...Dori? ...She's gone.

DORI: ...What?

ROGER: Your mother. She's not there. And I think she took the cat.

DORI: [*Dazed.*] ...What are you talking about?

ROGER: She dug him up! She took the rental car. ...She's gone.

> Beat. Dori stands and rushes to the window, places her palms against it and looks out, horrified. A short refrain on the piano, then:

LIGHTS TO BLACK.

ACT TWO

SCENE ONE

> At Rise: David is working in his garden. Presently, Cass enters and approaches, carrying the Tupperware "coffin."

CASS: ...Excuse me. ...Do you remember me? [*Pause. He looks at her blankly.*] ...I brought my cat in to you. Izzy. He was sick. He had—

DAVID: I remember.

CASS: I've decided to go with cremation. [*Pause. He looks at her blankly.*] ...I've decided to have him cremated. Here.

> She tries to hand him the coffin.

DAVID: ...This is my HOUSE.

CASS: You weren't at your office.

DAVID: It's Sunday.

CASS: I couldn't wait until tomorrow. May I please tell you something? [*David looks at her perplexed.*] ...I thought it was unprofessional. ...That card you sent. I appreciated the card but not the poem. It's not something you should send to a grown woman. Is there somewhere we can sit?

DAVID: ...No.

CASS: And when Izzy died. You cried. At a time like that a medical professional has to be stronger. I'm not a doctor

430

but that's just what I think. Do you have any Mountain Dew?

DAVID: No.

CASS: Do you have any carbonated beverages?

DAVID: No.

CASS: Coffee?

DAVID: I can't drink caffeine.

CASS: ...Do you have water.

DAVID: [*No escape.*] ...Yes.

CASS: May I have some?

> David moves across the stage, with Cass following, into the living room of his small house—and the lights follow them. David exits, and Cass puts the coffin down and looks around. She sees a picture and picks it up. David returns empty handed.

CASS: Is this your wife?

DAVID: No.

CASS: ...I'll bet you think I'm a nut. ...I say you must think I'm a nut.

DAVID: That's my...my girlfriend.

CASS: You could be here with your whole family and it wouldn't even occur to me.

DAVID: I don't have a family.

CASS: I'm not a nut.

DAVID: I wasn't crying.

CASS: ...Well, you were.

DAVID: No.

CASS: You were...weeping, you were openly weeping with me, which I appreciate, but it was very upsetting.

DAVID: I'm allergic.

>Beat.

CASS: ...You're.

DAVID: To cats. And most dogs. ...I have an inhaler.

>To prove it, he produces the inhaler.

CASS: ...You're a VETERINARIAN. ...I mean, I know veterinarians can have allergies. But. ...You WEREN'T crying.

DAVID: No.

CASS: ...I feel so stupid. [*Pause. He's no help.*] ...Where is my water?

DAVID: It's coming.

>Beat.

CASS: ...I've been having some difficulty. Your name is David, is that right?

DAVID: Yes.

CASS: May I sit down?

DAVID: ...Yes.

She does. Whether he stands or sits, David keeps his distance.

CASS: I've been having some difficulty. Since Izzy died. David. Every time something moves I think it's him. Every time I hear a squirrel. And then it rained yesterday, and I went to let him in, he hated the rain—that's how I found him, when he was a kitten, he was—

DAVID: Yes. ...You told me.

He takes a short hit off his inhaler.

CASS: ...Yes. So, when it rained that's all I could think of...the rain falling on his grave... and I thought...he could hear it and was afraid...so I went out and covered it with my coat. And I sat by him. In the rain.

DAVID: ...Well it's...it's very difficult.

CASS: It is. Yes.

DAVID: ...I can give you an antidepressant.

CASS: You can do that?

DAVID: No. I can give you one of mine.

CASS: But I don't WANT an anti-depressant. I WANT to be sad. I don't want anything that would make this...less. I mean, life goes on, I know that, that's what...that's what people say.

DAVID: I know.

CASS: But I don't WANT it to. I don't think it should. ...I think it should all stop now. [*David just sits wordlessly. Cass looks again at the picture.*] ...Where was this taken?

We hear a "ding" from offstage.

433

DAVID: Coast Rica.   Excuse me.

> David exits to his kitchen.   Cass looks at the picture.

CASS: ...It's not a very good picture.   I mean, the trees are nice, but you can hardly see her.   ...What's this?

> David has returned with tea for them both.

DAVID: Tea.

CASS: ...Oh. Thank you. ...So you've been to Costa Rica.

DAVID: No.

CASS: Where did you meet her?

DAVID: E-Harmony. She lives in New Zealand.

CASS: Ah.   ...So how often do you get to see her?

DAVID: When she sends pictures. [*Beat. Cass nods.*] ...That one is from Taiwan. That's from Argentina. The ones up there are from Scandinavia.   ...She likes to travel.

> Beat.

CASS: ...I feel so ridiculous. I sit there and pet him, I pretend to, when I'm sitting on my couch. That's where we sat. I sit and pet him, like he's still there and...I thought you were crying. [*Beat. David is having some slight difficulties.*] ...Doesn't tea have caffeine?

DAVID: It's green tea.

CASS: ...Oh. [*Beat.*] ...All right, well. Have you ever heard of a Caroline Waldhauer, or Wildhair, or, uh—

DAVID: No.

434

CASS: She's a spiritualist. She wrote a book. *Our Absent Friends*. It's about when animals die.

DAVID: I haven't read that.

CASS: She lives on a farm. Sadie's Farm. She's like a holy woman.

DAVID: I don't know her.

CASS: ...Well. I was thinking of going to see her. To talk to her. [*Beat. David nods.*] ...David?

DAVID: Yes?

CASS: It must be very hard for you.... I mean...it must get very...difficult. All those animals. All those...pets.

> Beat. David doesn't answer—or can't. Cass takes up the coffin and stands to leave.

CASS: ...Well.

DAVID: Yes. All right. ...Yes.

CASS: Yes what.

DAVID: I'll take care of him.

CASS: I think I've made a mistake.

DAVID: No.

CASS: I don't think I can leave him here.

DAVID: In the morning. I'll take him myself. You can come back on Wednesday. Or...when you're ready. He'll be here.

He places his hand on the coffin and waits. Cass assesses him. He is almost shaking. She smiles slightly and releases the coffin gingerly.

DAVID: ...I'll take...good care of him. I promise.

Cass slowly leaves his area; lights come to black on David.

Elsewhere, lights come up on Caroline, a woman with a young face but long, graying hair. She is feeding some chickens. Nearby is a porch with two rocking chairs, maybe a small table and a bushel of corn. Cass crosses to her.

CAROLINE: [Recollecting.] ...Cassandra.

CASS: Yes.

CAROLINE: ...Cassandra. ...You're the one having dreams.

CASS: Yes.

CAROLINE: Mm. How far did you drive?

CASS: Four hours. I should have called, I know, but, I was...in my car already and I just kept—

CAROLINE: It's all right. They never do. ...People find it strange when they react so strongly to the death of a pet, but I don't know why. They're the most un-complex relationships we will ever have. You would probably say Izzy was your best friend.

CASS: ...Yes.

CAROLINE: I don't mean that figuratively. I don't even mean probably. I mean he really was the truest companion you've ever had.

CASS: ...He was.

CAROLINE: You're grieving, Cassandra.

CASS: I know, but—

CAROLINE: Grief is how we heal.

CASS: I know but...I feel like I'm disappearing.

CAROLINE: You need to let it be exactly what it is. And talk about him, as much as you can. Tell his story to anybody who will listen.

CASS: I know. That's why I'm here.

CAROLINE: ...Huh. All right. Tell me about him.

CASS: Well. He was...mostly white, with blue eyes, and sort of a— [or *whatever color the cat was.*]

CAROLINE: No: tell me about HIM. Just one thing. Your favorite thing.

CASS: ...Oh. Well. He...he used to chase my car. There's a playground down the street, where he liked to hang out, and when I drove past, he would see my car and run after me. I could see him in my rearview, running and running. He'd take a shortcut so when I got home he'd be sitting in my driveway waiting for me.

CAROLINE: Good. So—

CASS: And when I held him, he would cling to my shirt and touch my face and lick my fingers, he loved fingers, he would lick them and like—

CAROLINE: Good.

CASS: —gnaw on them. He followed me everywhere. Out to the mailbox. He'd sit and wait by my shower. He liked

437

pipe cleaners, we played fetch with pipe cleaners. And when I ate I had to feed him too, or he'd yell at me. ...He had bad breath.

Beat.

CAROLINE: ...With the death of every animal comes a gift, Cassandra. You just have to know how to see it. ...Last week I found a young mockingbird that had been mauled. I knew at once there was no saving it, so I sat down and kept it company during its passage. I spoke aloud to it, helping it on its way, so it would know it wasn't alone. It shuddered in my palm, and for a moment it spread open its wings and fanned its tail. It stretched forth its beak as if were about to cry out, but then, with an elegance and deliberation I'll never forget, it folded its wings to its body and lay down its head. And suddenly there was an inexplicable lightness to it. A lightness I've felt it a hundred times.

CASS: ...The soul.

CAROLINE: The prawna, the chi, there's a word for it in every language. It's the light that flows through all living things, and when we die, whatever it is becomes the air. [*Pause. Cass nods.*] ...Cassandra, it's never our loved ones we grieve for. Their suffering is over. It's our own lives we mourn. ...Isn't that true.

CASS: ...Yes.

CAROLINE: I can't stop your suffering. You have to do that yourself. But there are some things I can show you. If you're willing to look for them, and see them.

CASS: ...I don't have much money, but I can—

CAROLINE: Are you afraid of work?

CASS: No.

CAROLINE: All right. You'll start in the morning.

438

CASS: ...Well, I wasn't expecting to—

CAROLINE: And when you go, you can make a tax-deductible contribution in any amount you choose.

CASS: I didn't bring any clothes or—

CAROLINE: They never do. Your first task is to count the ducks.

CASS: Um.

CAROLINE: Short necks. Wood ducks. Beautiful colors. Then meet me on the porch.

> Caroline heads toward the porch and exits.
> Cass turns to find the ducks—and counts
> them. She looks around the farm and marvels
> at it. Then she moves across stage to the
> porch. Caroline returns with two glasses of
> wine. She'll drink hers quickly.

CASS: ...There's seven.

CAROLINE: Good. When there are six you need to tell me. Your room is upstairs, first door on the right. There's some overalls in the closet. Here.

CASS: What's this?

CAROLINE: Pomegranate wine. I always begin with a toast. Namaste! "I honor the place where you and I are the same." [*They toast and will sit at some point during the following:*] In the morning I'll introduce you to Sasha and Pasha, the horses. Pascha loves everybody but Sascha's a little skittery so you'll want to praise her.

CASS: For what.

CAROLINE: Anything you can think of. That fern there, there's a family of chickadees nesting, so try to go around. But watch your step. These chickens lay wherever they want. I cook one meal in the morning, one in the evening, usually a vegetable quiche or soufflé. You'll be responsible for clean up. And now I'm going to give you your second task.

CASS: Okay.

CAROLINE: Do you know who this farm is named for?

CASS: Sadie. Your dog. A Golden Retriever.

CAROLINE: She and I were together for sixteen years—longer than all of my husbands combined. And I've never shared such a sense of...of knowing with anyone. In fact, when I got pregnant, she started to lactate, and when she contracted cancer, I could feel myself growing weak with her. For sixteen years, Cassandra, I could...I could look into the very eyes of love, I could hold love in my hands and speak to it. And love would smile back at me and wag its tail. But it wasn't until I finally put her to rest that I began to truly understand love. I began for the first time to grasp the Mystery. And as Izzy was passing, Cassandra, you did too.

CASS: ...I did?

CAROLINE: ...In that moment...that one moment of ecstasy...you felt your hearts converging. Didn't you.

CASS: ...Yes.

CAROLINE: And just for that moment, you could see beyond the veil. You could hear his voice. In the language of compassion the two of you shared, you could hear him whispering.... What was he saying, Cassandra? As he was departing. What did he want you to know?

CASS: ...I...I don't—

CAROLINE: He was thanking you. Wasn't he. For his life. For yours. For everything.

CASS: [*Tentative.*] ...Yes.

CAROLINE: He was telling you it was all right. That everything was all right. That you can be grateful too.

CASS: ...But...how do I KNOW that? How...how do I know he's not angry? In my dream, he doesn't know he's dead. How do I tell him, how do I—

CAROLINE: You're not hearing him. He wants you to hear him, but you're filled with your own anxiety. Beginning tonight, I want you to be still, and open yourself and...and listen. [*Beat. Caroline squeezes Cass's arm, perhaps brushes the hair from her eyes.*] ...More wine wouldn't hurt.

> Caroline takes both glasses and exits. Pause. Cass rises and comes to the edge of the porch, closes her eyes, and listens.
>
> Beat. The lights change. She opens her eyes. Now it is the next morning. Caroline enters with two cups of coffee.

CAROLINE: Good morning!

CASS: I hope I didn't wake you.

CAROLINE: I heard you get up. You didn't sleep very well.

CASS: No. I don't know why.

CAROLINE: Of course you do. Coffee?

CASS: Thank you.

CAROLINE: How many ducks this morning?

CASS: Seven.

CAROLINE: Good.

CASS: What are we watching for?

CAROLINE: Sophie.   One morning you'll look out and you won't see her, so we'll have to go find her.

CASS: Which one is Sophie?

CAROLINE: You'll see. I'm going to make breakfast. You want to shuck some corn? It's very simple. You just grab it here—and tear. Can you do that?

CASS: I think so.

CAROLINE: A couple from town comes by at noon and buys most of it, I like to have it ready.

CASS: Okay.

CAROLINE: Any word from Izzy?

CASS: ...I don't know.

CAROLINE: Sometimes it takes a while.   If you want, try calling to him. Out loud. Tell him you're still in pain. He'll hear you. He might even show up.

CASS: Show up?

CAROLINE: Sure. Until I was healed Sadie used to come visit me.   The first time, I was sitting in the back, and she actually came around the corner and just...sat down in front of me. I saw her, as clear as day.   It happened three more times.   Until I told her I was okay.

CASS: ...Mm.

CAROLINE: ...I'm not a charlatan.

442

CASS: Oh, I—

CAROLINE: I hold a Doctorate in Spiritual Healing from the Universal Life Church and another in Prayerful Science from the University of Global Faith. At present I am a teaching Reiki master and study under a fully accredited East Indian Roshi. [*Cass doesn't know what to say.*] ...I am also a licensed beautician, a welder and a Jedi. [*Beat. Cass doesn't get it. Caroline presses on:*] ...The point is, I know she was there. We sat and looked at one another, and when she stood and walked back around the corner I knew what she was telling me. ...She was saying: nothing ever dies. Not really. [*This news moves tangibly through Cass like a wave.*] ...Behind this life is another one, Cassandra. I want you to think about that, where life goes when it leaves us...and watches us...and waits. [*Cass nods, smiling. Caroline kisses her on the head.*] ...I expect a full report at breakfast.

> Caroline exits. Cass sits and shucks an ear of corn. She thinks. Lights come up elsewhere on a confessional booth. A priest, Father Daniel, sits waiting. Cass stands with an ear of corn and considers going to him.

CASS: ...Father Daniel?

FATHER DANIEL: Yes, my child.

CASS: ...My name is Cassandra.

FATHER DANIEL: You don't have to tell me that. Just when your last confession was.

> She approaches and sits.

CASS: Oh. I'm a Methodist.

FATHER DANIEL: Well. This must be a whopper.

CASS: I have some questions. I thought you might be able to help me. Unless this violates some rule or something.

FATHER DANIEL: Have you asked your pastor?

CASS: ...I'm a terrible person, father.

FATHER DANIEL: Ah now. Never too late. I'm happy to help if I can.

CASS: Well. My...um. My daughter. Had a cat. That died. And she...my daughter...wants to know if animals go to heaven. If there's an afterlife. For cats.

FATHER DANIEL: Well that's an excellent question. What have you told her?

CASS: I said...yes. If heaven is perfect. Then. Yes. That...God will let her see him.

FATHER DANIEL: And did that make her happy?

CASS: Yes. It did.

FATHER DANIEL: Well, then you should probably leave it at that.

CASS: ...What do you mean?

FATHER DANIEL: Well, as I recall, you Protestants don't believe that animals have a soul. Which is what you're talking about.

CASS: But...is that true? That...that animals—

FATHER DANIEL: Of course it's not true. We Catholics know that all living things have a soul. The only difference between us and the animals is our capacity for reason. We can choose to act in such a way that our souls are rewarded with heaven. But animals, they don't have that particular kind of intelligence. The fact that they are free of that burden makes THIS world their heaven.

CASS: ...THIS is their heaven.

FATHER DANIEL: Yes. And I think the same is also true of plants.

CASS: ...So, okay, when they die, the animals, if they don't, if they can't—

FATHER DANIEL: The Catechism tells us that when animals die, their souls go out of existence.

CASS: ...Which means what.

FATHER DANIEL: Well. Whereas you and I, our souls, will proceed to our just reward, our animal friends will...simply be no more.

CASS: So Izzy...the cat...he won't remember.

FATHER DANIEL: ...There will BE no him. He will be...gone. [*Pause. Cass is horrified.*] ...God gave us our pets to comfort us in this world. In the next world we will not be concerned with pets, or...jewelry or TV shows. The blessed will have better things to do than to play with cats.

CASS: ...So what's the point?

FATHER DANIEL: The point of what?

CASS: Of having a soul? If, if Catholic cats have a soul, but they cease to exist, and Methodist cats don't have a soul, what's the—

FATHER DANIEL: Oh, yes, well, that—

CASS: And animals DO have reason. They understand words and they, they give affection and withhold affection, they make choices—

FATHER DANIEL: I think animals give us their affection because we care for them. I think we should consider that. They seem attached to us because we, we feed them and pay them attention.

CASS: ...But that makes them no different from men.

FATHER DANIEL: ...Well you've got me there.

CASS: Have you ever had a colonoscopy, Father?

FATHER DANIEL: ...Have we changed the subject? ...Cassandra? [*Beat: no answer.*] ...Cassandra, are you there?

CASS: ...Maybe this is hell.

FATHER DANIEL: ...Come again?

CASS: This world. For us. Maybe this is our punishment. Because everything is so awful here. Nothing is the way it should be. And there isn't anyone to love. Not really. Just for a short time, maybe. And then it's gone. And that's even worse.

FATHER DANIEL: ...God loves you, Cassandra. Always. As I'm sure your daughter does too.

CASS: ...I don't have the slightest idea who God is. ...And I don't even like her.

FATHER DANIEL: Now I know you don't mean that.

CASS: Yes I do, I do, she ruins everything. On her last birthday, she said, I felt so bad. She said: thanks for not giving up on me Mama. And I thought: oh my darling, I give up on you every, every day.

FATHER DANIEL: ...We have a family counseling service for our members. I can give you a pamphlet.

CAROLINE: [*Calling, distantly, from off.*] Cassandra?

CASS: ...I'm sorry, Father.

FATHER DANIEL: And if you'd like to know who God is, you could join us for Mass sometime. Some of our adults have formed a study group, all on their own—

> Cass moves away, back to the porch.

CAROLINE: [*Off.*] Cassandra?

FATHER DANIEL: —and I'm sure they wouldn't mind having you along. ...Cassandra?

CASS: ...I'm sorry.

CAROLINE: [*Off.*] Cassandra?

FATHER DANIEL: ... Cassandra?

> But Cass has already wandered away, back to the porch, carrying her ear of corn. Lights to black on Father Daniel.

> Caroline enters the porch holding something wrapped in a blue towel. She places it on the table.

CAROLINE: There's a CD player in the den. Can you get it for me?

CASS: What's that?

CAROLINE: This is Sophie.

> Cass exits. Caroline unwraps what's in the towel: a duck that appears to be asleep. Cass enters with a CD player.

447

CASS: What's wrong with her?

CAROLINE: She's dying.

CASS: Of what.

CAROLINE: A broken heart. Her husband, her mate, he was by struck by a car. His name was Chuck.

CASS: How do you know?

CAROLINE: Well, I don't know, I just called him Chuck, I thought it sounded right. Chuck the Duck.

CASS: I mean, how do you know she's dying?

CAROLINE: Oh. Ducks mate for life, you know, and females take it very seriously. When a male dies the female just...curls up and goes away. She's already stopped eating.

CASS: But...you're not going to, I mean, can't you help her or—

CAROLINE: I am helping her, Cassandra. Do you see this towel? For a dying animal the best color is blue or gray, and cotton is always better than rayon.

CASS: But—

CAROLINE: This is what she wants. Animals know how to die. I've been trying to tell you this. They know intuitively that infinite peace that awaits on the other side. If we pay attention, she can help us to learn the way ourselves.

CASS: ...Oh.

> Caroline turns on the CD player. We hear soft chanting.

CAROLINE: ...These are Gregorian chants. They're very soothing. Classical is good too, especially Albinoni or Samuel Barber, but birds are particularly sensitive to the human voice. There are sutras, too, that my roshi taught me. There's the Prajnaparamita or the Mandukya, the Taittiriya, the Chandogya and of course the Svetasvatara. For a time like this though, the Avalokitsvara is best.

Caroline hands Cass a sheet of paper.

CASS: ...You want me to read this.

CAROLINE: Softly. Melodically. So she can breathe it in.

CASS: Um... "Gate'...gate...paragate'...parasamagate'... bodi...svaha...gate'..."

CAROLINE: [Overlapping, translating.] "Gone, gone, all the way over, everyone is gone to enlightenment." Good. And with it the Phowa, an ancient Buddhist ritual of transition, whereby we visualize Sophie's chi taking wing into the light of eternity. So: [Her gesture means: starts chanting again. Cass does. Caroline closes her eyes and gently strokes the air just above the duck.] ...I want you see her...to watch her...to behold her going deeper into the Mystery, joining all the energies from which we are birthed. [Beat. Cass chants; Caroline luxuriates.] ... Can you feel her? Can you see her?

CASS: ...Yes.

CAROLINE: Don't be afraid, Sophie! Go to him! We love you and want you to be free. Joy to you, Sophie! Joy to us all! [Caroline breathes deeply, rhythmically, and beams. Cass watches her. Caroline is most earnest about this.] Be free, my sweet girl. Come visit us when you want, but leave us now and go into love.... Go into love.... Go into love.... [Etc., as necessary. Caroline slows down, then places her hands on Sophie. Beat.]

CASS: ...Is she...?

CAROLINE: ...Nope. Sometimes it takes awhile. Looks like we'll need more wine.

> Caroline exits. Cass inspects Sophie, maybe poking at her a bit. Caroline enters with two glasses of wine. They sit.

CAROLINE: ...Izzy show up yet?

CASS: ...I don't know, Caroline. I'm. I'm afraid.

CAROLINE: Good. Of what.

CASS: ...I...I think about him, I, I see him, I try to see him, in my mind.... But it's getting harder. I'm afraid...that I'm forgetting him. Little by little. That he's going away. And I don't want him to. Even if it means feeling this way, forever, that's okay. I don't want him to go away.

CAROLINE: Healing doesn't have to mean forgetting.

CASS: Yes it does. That's how it feels. To keep living is to forget. To keep forgetting. ...And I don't want that to be true. ...Maybe I should go home.

CAROLINE: You can if you want.

CASS: I don't want to go home. This has been the best week of my life.

CAROLINE: Decide tomorrow.

CASS: I'm starting to sleep again. My phone ran out. My stomach doesn't hurt—I'll bet I've put on five pounds.

CAROLINE: Sascha and Pascha have taken a real liking to you. So have the goats.

CASS: ...I'll decide tomorrow.

> Beat. The lights change: time passes. They
> lean into one another.

CASS: ...I'm so drunk.

CAROLINE: Isn't it fantastic?

CASS: I can't believe how kind you've been. I wish I'd
always known you. I don't know how you—

CAROLINE: I can't listen to this.

CASS: I don't mean to embarrass you.

CAROLINE: No.... The Japanese have a saying: "a good
person is not aware of her goodness." I try every day of my
life to be that person. But of course as long as you're
TRYING....

CASS: Ohhh.

CAROLINE: You can't say these things to me or you'll
throw my zen out of whack.

CASS: But don't you ever...run out? Of. Of.

CAROLINE: Yes. Every day. [*Beat. Caroline thinks about
that. She rises and goes to Sophie, gently stroking her.*]
...And no. Never. We must never run out. There must
always be more. There is so much suffering, Cassandra.
So much sorrow. It's the price we pay for love. To be
happy is to let go of dreams of a happy life and...simply
hold open your hands to everything the world puts into
them. And be thankful. ...Because there is only life.
That's all that matters. ...Only life.

> She has taken Cass' hand and with it has
> begun stroking Sophie. Cass now understands
> that Sophie is dead.

CASS: ...Oh.

> Several Beats. Then Caroline covers Sophie in the towel, picks her up and starts off.

CAROLINE: ...I'll be back in a while.

CASS: Where are you going?

CAROLINE: ...To tell the others.

> Caroline exits the porch. Cass comes to edge of the porch and watches her go. She is obviously drunk—and in the grip of The Mystery. Perhaps she calls to Izzy silently—mouthing his name and holding open her arms.
>
> The light changes: time passes. It is evening: we hear crickets. Caroline enters with a saucepan and spoon.

CASS: ...Ready?

CAROLINE: Almost. The rolls aren't finished. Try this. Tell me if I put in too much curry.

> She spoon-feeds Cass.

CASS: ...Well it's delicious.

CAROLINE: Isn't it? It's a Malaysian satay.

> Cass tries some more.

CASS: ...Mmm. Mmm. This is meat.

CAROLINE: Special occasion.

CASS: It's incredible. Chicken?

CAROLINE: No.

CASS: Turkey?

CAROLINE: No. [*Cass suddenly realizes and stops chewing.*] ...I also put in some ginger and a little orange peel. Can you taste it?

CASS: ...Is this?

CAROLINE: Sophie.   Of course! [*Caroline takes a bite and speaks with her mouth full.*] It's called mortuary feasting. Our culture is very uncomfortable with the idea of death. As you know, or you wouldn't be here.   But there are other cultures—Venezuela, ancient Crete—they ate the bodies of their dead is a way of cementing their kinship.   There's a tribe in the Amazon who actually wait for the bodies to decay. It shows the intensity of their grief.

CASS: ...I guess I'm just surprised.

CAROLINE: Good! Sophie would be pleased! Jesus, at the last supper: this is my body, take and eat. What do you think he meant?

CASS: I never figured that out.

CAROLINE: See? Time well spent! I'm sorry to see you go.

Cass produces a check.

CASS: ...I've written you a check.   I know it's not enough. [*Caroline scoffs—but takes the check and perhaps sneaks a peek at it.*]

CASS: ...I mean really.   For all your kindness.

CAROLINE: Kindness isn't kindness if you have to pay. And besides, I haven't helped you.

CASS: You have, though.

CAROLINE: No. I didn't think I could, actually. When you lied to me, that first morning. I knew you wouldn't let me. [*Beat.*] ...When you told me, about Izzy. That you knew he was grateful. You didn't really hear him at all.

CASS: ...Yes I did.

CAROLINE: When I asked—

CASS: No, I know.... His eyes, I could see in his eyes, he was frightened. He...knew that...something was happening and he told me...he was telling me no. ...He was frightened.

CAROLINE: ...Oh Cassandra.

CASS: I saved him once. He thought I was going to save him again.... But I killed him. [*Beat.*] ...All of this you do, I understand it, I admire it, I admire you, I really do, but I want to know—I want HIM to know—I want to say to him...that I love him. That's all. That's all I want. ...Can you do that?

CAROLINE: ...No. ...But I know someone. [*Cass looks at her hopefully.*] ...It's a long drive.

CASS: Where.

CAROLINE: He's very unusual. I don't know him very well, and I don't know if I trust him.

CASS: Who is he?

CAROLINE: His name is Elias. He calls himself a Communicator. I'd have to call and get permission.

CASS: Could you?

CAROLINE: There are things you need to know first.

CASS: What?

Elsewhere: lights up on Elias. He is an older
blind man and sits perhaps in a wheelchair.
Cass will move toward him, and the lights will
follow her there.

CAROLINE: He can be difficult. He's blind. He's probably
autistic, too, but that's his gift. He sees images, in his
head. He can't speak to animals, it doesn't work like that.
But he...he thinks in images, like they do. And he'll
demand money.

CASS: How much.

CAROLINE: It changes. And he only takes cash.

CASS: How do I get there.

CAROLINE: I'll draw you a map.

CASS: You'll call ahead for me.

CAROLINE: Are you sure about this? ...Cassandra?

CASS: Yes. Please!

CAROLINE: Are you sure?

The lights go to black on Caroline. Cass is now
with Elias. Beat.

CASS: ...Hello. ...Are you—?

ELIAS: You're the woman sent by the other woman.

CASS: Yes.

ELIAS: ...She's a very strange woman.

CASS: Well. I don't know.

ELIAS: She is. ...You've lost a friend.

CASS: I did, yes. ...Yes. [*Beat. No response. Elias smiles cryptically.*] ...Yes, and I was hoping, I was wondering if you...she told me that you could—

ELIAS: [*Abrupt, almost derisive.*] You didn't have to come here.

CASS: ...Well, I, I wanted to.

ELIAS: But you didn't HAVE to come here, you didn't HAVE to.

CASS: ...I won't stay long.

ELIAS: No. You didn't HAVE to come here.

CASS: I'm willing to pay. If that's what you mean.

ELIAS: Lawyers charge twenty dollars for an hour.

CASS: I think they charge much more than that.

ELIAS: Doctors charge more than that.

CASS: Tell me what you want.

> Beat. Then she goes through her wallet.

CASS: ...I went to the bank...I've got...two hundred and twenty five dollars. It's all I have left.

> She holds it out. He doesn't take it. Then she remembers he's blind and puts it in his hand. He feels it—as if counting it.

CASS: ...His name was Izzy. He was my cat. [*Elias smiles, chuckles, and closes his eyes.*] ...What. ...what is it. [*No answer.*] ...He was gray and white with blue eyes.

Elias shakes his head, snorts derisively: she
doesn't get something.

CASS: ...What.

ELIAS: There was a boy who hit his head. He lay in the
hospital for days. When he woke up he smelled everything.
He could smell food in rooms on the floor above his. He
could smell blood on floors that had already been cleaned.
And he could hear things. He could hear people whispering
in rooms down the hall. Why.

CASS: Why what.

ELIAS: Why! Why!

CASS: I don't know, because—

ELIAS: Because he hit his head! ...Hitting his head awoke
in him the abilities he had always had. Hitting his head
made him forget that he could NOT smell everything and he
could NOT hear everything. For two weeks he could smell
everything and hear everything. And then his head got
better and it went away, and he was crippled again.

CASS: ...Do you want me to hit my head? I don't
understand, I can't do what—

Elias suddenly stiffens—or something gets his
attention. His tone is suddenly softer:

ELIAS: ...He's here. With you. He followed you here.
[*Cass looks around.*] He sees...he sees your...foot. Your
heel. Ankle. He is at your ankle. [*A wave rushes over
Cass. She looks about her ankles.*] ...He goes where you
go. Always.

CASS: I know! He goes where I go!

ELIAS: He sees your hair.

457

CASS: ...Oh, he! Yes! I used to...he would ride on my shoulder. I used to carry him on my shoulder.

ELIAS: This is the sensation of love. This is what he feels when he feels love. He sees...I don't know what it is.

CASS: What.

ELIAS: It's long, and, and...white, it's—

CASS: Long and—

ELIAS: He plays with it, he carries it, I don't—it's soft, he's—

CASS: Pipe cleaner! It's a pipe cleaner! My daughter made some project with pipe cleaners and they drove him out of his mind. If you'd throw them he'd—

ELIAS: Yes.

CASS: —he'd bring them back to you and paw at your leg until you—oh God! Can he—can he hear me?

ELIAS: Tell me what you see.

CASS: ...I—

ELIAS: Tell me what you see!

She remembers.

CASS: ...When he wants in he...sits and waits on the window sill. He just sits there, and when he sees me, he calls to me. He'll walk back and forth on the window sill and call to me.

ELIAS: ...Yes.

CASS: ...We dance together. I hold him and we dance, and he licks my cheek. He kisses me and puts his paw on my

458

face. [*Elias is smiling in utter ecstasy. Cass wells up, touches her cheek.*] ...I can't put him down. He won't let me put him down. ...He touches my face!

ELIAS: With his hand, yes.

CASS: Yes. He clings to me and won't let me go! ...Can he hear me?

ELIAS: Always. Always.

CASS: He's at my feet, isn't he.

ELIAS: Always.

CASS: He's looking at me.

ELIAS: Always.

CASS: ...Oh my God. Thank you.... Thank you.

> Overcome, she rises and walks slowly, careful of where she steps, aware of the presence near her. Elias' manner changes again:

ELIAS: ...But he is afraid. ...He's afraid to be alone. Where he is...he knows that he's...away from you. He is afraid you will forget.

CASS: Oh...no.

ELIAS: He wants you to stay.

CASS: I will. I can! I...can I come back?

ELIAS: You don't HAVE to come back.

CASS: I understand that. I can't DO what you do. I WANT to come back.

ELIAS: You don't have to.

CASS: I need to. I need you to help me. ...I need you to help me.

ELIAS: ...Five hundred dollars.

> Beat.

CASS: ...I. I don't.

ELIAS: You don't HAVE to come here.

CASS: ...I can do some work for you, I could clean your house or—

ELIAS: Five hundred dollars.

CASS: ...I can't...I don't have that—

ELIAS: He is running. On a road, he is running on a road, there is a car.

CASS: I can't pay that much.

ELIAS: He follows your car.

CASS: Stop.

ELIAS: A yellow car, he knows that it's you, he follows you. To a house.

CASS: ...My.

ELIAS: To a house, it's your house. Yes. Always. He waits for you there. Always.

CASS: ...How do you know it's yellow? [*Several beats.*] ...I don't even have a yellow car. The car I came in is yellow. But.

ELIAS: ...He followed you here. In the yellow car. He follows you always. [*Pause. Cass realizes—with a gasp.*] ...No. He rode with you. He rode in your lap! On your shoulder! He is here now.

> Beat. Cass is overwhelmed with anger, almost speaks. Composes herself. Then:

CASS: [*Softly.*] ...Shame on you.

ELIAS: ...I—

CASS: Shame on you!   ...Shame on you both.

> The lights on Elias fade and, as she moves away, narrow around her. She stands with her arms empty, hanging at her side. The piano plays a few bars. She strokes her shoulder, as if Izzy were there, and tries to cry. Cannot. Tries again. Cannot. She looks at her empty hands.

LIGHTS TO BLACK.

SCENE TWO

> In darkness: We hear Cass' voice:

CASS: ...Dori?   ...Dori?

> At rise: we are back at Cass' home. Dori, dressed in the kimono, is lying unconscious on the couch. Cass enters, carrying a small box.

CASS: ...Dori.   ...Wake up.   ...Dori?

> Beat. Cass puts the box aside and sees a pill bottle on the table. She reads the label, and shakes the bottle. Then she tries again to wake Dori:

CASS: ...Dori. ...Dori! ...DORI!

> Dori opens her eyes and looks at Cass. Then she throws her arm around Cass and hugs her.

CASS: ...It's okay. It's okay. ...Dori? ...You're hurting my neck. ...Dori. You're hurting my neck. [*Dori loosens her grip.*] ...How many did you take.

DORI: [*Weakly.*] Where were you?

CASS: How many did you take.

DORI: I thought you were gone.

> Cass holds the bottle in Dori's face.

CASS: Dori. Listen. How many of these did you take?

DORI: I don't know. Two. No. Yes.

CASS: Just two.

DORI: Or. I think so.

CASS: Jesus. Stand up. Come on.

DORI: Where did you go?

CASS: Can you stand up?

DORI: I tried to call you.

CASS: Stay there. I'll be right back.

DORI: Where are you going?

CASS: I'll be right back!

> Cass exits to kitchen. Dori drowsily sits back down and rubs her nose and face.

462

DORI: ...What day is it. ...Mama. ...MAMA?

>   Cass returns with a Mountain Dew.

CASS: I'm right here. Here. Come on. ...Drink.

>   Cass joins Dori on the couch and gives her the
>   drink. Dori takes a big gulp. Then another.
>   In between gulps:

DORI: ...'s good.

CASS: I know. ...More. ...More. [*Dori chugs it, then
signals for a break. She smiles blearily.*] ...Have you had
anything to eat?

DORI: Yes. ...Today?

CASS: You're thin.

DORI: I'm losing weight.

CASS: You don't need to lose weight.

DORI: Yes I do.

CASS: Here. Finish this, then take a shower.

>   Cass pours more Mountain Dew down Dori's
>   throat until Dori signals for another break.

CASS: ...Better?

DORI: I already took a shower.

CASS: Take another one. You smell like...you smell like
Windex.

DORI: I cleaned the house.

CASS: With Windex?

DORI: It smells good now.

      Cass sighs. Dori drinks.

CASS: ...You want another one?

      Dori shakes her head no. She looks like a baby
      with a bottle.

DORI: ...Where were you?

CASS: I just had to go.

DORI: Were you mad at me?

CASS: No.

DORI: Why didn't you tell me?

CASS: I didn't know.

      Dori hugs Cass again.

DORI: I thought you were never coming home.

CASS: ...It's okay, Dori. Come on.

      Dori realizes she's wearing the kimono.

DORI: ...Oh! I'm sorry. I was—here—it got cold and—

CASS: No, it's all right. I don't care. I've probably been
fired by now anyway.

DORI: You were. They called. So did Roger. He's been
calling every day. You missed his divorce.

CASS: I know.

DORI: He's pissed.

CASS: I know.

Dori sees the small box.

DORI: ...Who's that for?

CASS: ...Oh. Me.

DORI: From him?

CASS: No.

DORI: ...Somebody new?

CASS: [*Wistfully.*] ...No.

DORI: What is it?

CASS: Go take a shower. Then we'll eat something and I'll show you.

DORI: Don't forget.

CASS: ...I won't.

Dori exits. Pause. Cass surveys her household, then looks at the box and picks it up. David enters. He holds a small jar.

DAVID ...Well.

Cass looks up at him. The lights change and she crosses to him with the box: we're now in his house.

DAVID: ...I was beginning to wonder. ...I thought something had happened to you.

465

CASS: ...I thought so too. [*She smiles, puts down the box and picks up the picture.*] ...I see you have a new picture.

DAVID: Oh. Yes. She went to Cambodia.

CASS: ...You can hardly see her at all.

DAVID: She wanted to get the...the whole temple, or—

CASS: Oh well yes. It's a great temple.

DAVID: In the spring she's going to the Galapagos.

CASS: Are you going to join her?

DAVID: I don't travel. [*Beat.*] ...Would you like some tea?

CASS: No, I've put you out enough. Is that...?

DAVID: ...Yes.

He holds the jar out, but she doesn't take it.

CASS: ...It's so small. [*No answer. She won't take it.*] ...I don't have any money.

DAVID: Um...that's—-I uh, have something else for you. In that box there. You should sit down. [*Cass sits and picks up the box.*] ...Go ahead.

Cass opens the box and withdraws a life-size fake cat, curled up asleep. (They're called Perfect Petz™.) It looks a bit like Izzy.

CASS: ...Oh.

DAVID: It looks like him, doesn't it?

CASS: ...Yes it does.

DAVID: And if you push this button, on the bottom, look.

466

CASS: ...He's breathing.

DAVID: He's asleep. ...You can, uh, sit with him. And, and, uh, pet him. Or I thought: leave him on the couch. So. When you come in. He looks very real. Doesn't he?

> Cass considers it for a while, puts it on her lap and strokes it.

CASS: ...I don't know what to say.

> Beat. She seems gone for a few seconds...then puts the fake cat in the box, puts the box on the couch, and stands.

CASS: ...This is a very lovely thing you've done, David.

> Now she takes the jar—and with it his hand.

CASS: ...Just when I needed someone to do something lovely.

> David smiles shyly, averts his eyes. They hold hands like that for a long, awkward moment, until he withdraws his diplomatically.

DAVID: ...I have a girlfriend.

CASS: ....Good for you.

> She sighs with some finality, clutches the jar and collects the box.

CASS: ...Well. ...Goodbye, then. David.

> From the darkness, and in the distance, we hear a phone ringing. David smiles, and the lights fade to black on him and change: we're now back in Cass' living room. Dori enters in

the kimono, with a blue towel on her head, and carrying a phone.

DORI: ...Mama?

Cass puts the box on the couch and turns to her.

DORI: ...It's him.

CASS: ...Who. Oh. ...Tell him I'll call him back.

DORI: [*Into the phone.*] She'll call you back. ...Okay. ...No. ...No ...Okay. —He says he really needs to talk to you.

CASS: Take a message.

DORI: [*Back and forth.*] I can take—. —He says he doesn't want to leave a damned message you stupid—what? ...Okay. —He would like to please speak with you please.

Cass sighs and takes the phone. Elsewhere, special comes up on Roger, on the phone.

CASS: ...Hello, Roger.

ROGER: Who is he, Cass.

CASS: Roger.

ROGER: I think I have a right to know.

CASS: It's not like that.

ROGER: Then where were you.

CASS: I just.... I was...beginning to wonder.

ROGER: ...What does that mean. You were "beginning to wonder."

CASS: Can I ask you a question?

ROGER: What does that mean?

CASS: Why are we together?

ROGER: ...What does THAT mean?

CASS: Why. Why did you even ask me out.

ROGER: ...Well. ...Because. Obviously. I thought...you were a woman of real substance.

CASS: ...Colonoscopy joke.

ROGER: No! No! I don't know! We have a good time together, don't we. ...Cass? [*Cass sighs.*] ...I take care of you, don't I?

CASS: Roger.

ROGER: Just tell me there's no one else. [*Beat. Cass looks at the jar.*] Tell me there's no one else, and I'll forget everything. We'll start all over. Just tell me.

CASS: ...There is no one.

ROGER: That wasn't so hard. See? ...So can I come over tonight? ...Cass?

CASS: ...Roger.

ROGER: Tomorrow then. You tell me. I know you're probably short on cash right now.

CASS: ...Well see.

ROGER: ...Please, Cassandra. [*Several Beats.*] ...Please. ...Please.

CASS: ...We'll see.

> Cass hangs up, and lights go to black on Roger.
> Beat. Cass holds her stomach and winces
> slightly.

DORI: ...Want to talk about it?

CASS: ...No.

> Cass comes downstage and looks out the
> window, clutching the jar. She looks first on
> the window sill and holds her hand to the pane.

DORI: ...I was going to fill it up.

CASS: Hmm?

DORI: The...the hole. I was going to fill it up. But.

CASS: [*Now looking out at the yard.*] ...We'll get to it.

> Beat. Dori offers the plate.

DORI: Peanut brittle? [*Cass shakes her head no.*] ...I
could make some more truffles. Or, or that mousse stuff.
With the layers. That you like. You want some?

CASS: ...Okay.

> Dori starts off, and Cass watches her go, then
> stops her with:

CASS: ...You're a good person, Dori.

DORI: ...I am? [*Cass nods.*] ...I thought you'd given up on
me.

> Cass shakes her head no. Dori smiles exits to
> kitchen. Cass stands alone, looking out the
> window, clutching the jar.

470

Now she moves across stage—perhaps following a light that leads her there and narrows around and behind her, on the little box on the couch. We hear the sound of children laughing. She is on a playground.

She looks up. The sun is bright. She holds the jar. Finally she twists it open and looks inside. A short refrain plays on the piano. She holds one hand out and slowly pours the ashes into it...then lightly tosses them into the air. Again. Then she pours out what remains...and blows it gently from her open hands. She whispers:

CASS: ...Goodbye.

Beat. Then: a note or two on the piano. The lights on Cass fade to black, and she's gone. Beat.

Another note or two on the piano. The lights narrow on the box; time passes. Beat.

Another note or two on the piano. The lights narrow on the box; time passes. Beat.

One last refrain on the piano. The lights on the box fade to black.

END.